Kites

KITES

Ron Moulton

ILLUSTRATED BY
PAT LLOYD

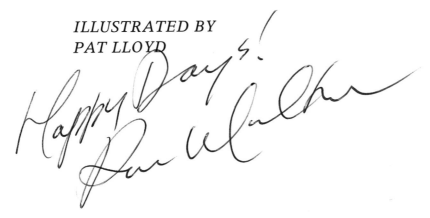

Pelham Books
LONDON

First published in Great Britain by Pelham Books Ltd
52 Bedford Square, London WC1B 3EF
1978

ISBN 0 7207 0829 X

Set by Monophoto in eleven on twelve point Apollo
and printed in Great Britain by
BAS Printers Limited, Over Wallop, Hampshire
Bound by Dorstel Press, Harlow

Contents

Acknowledgements

Books are by people, for people, and this one is no exception. Many friends have unwittingly played their part in enabling me to assemble it.

The kite manufacturers deserve special thanks for their help and encouragement. I am grateful to many creative designers for their contributions of special features – Ron Prendergraft, Vince Redfern, Dave Checkley, Maria and Wieslaw Schier, Bill Bigge, and in Japan, Larry Hoffman and T. Hiroi who produced the height estimation table from his famous book *Kites – Designs in the Sky*.

Particular thanks are due to Professor Clive Hart, whose book *Kites – An Historical Survey* is a constant and reliable source of reference, and to Robert Ingraham for his quarterly *Kite Tales* (now produced by Valerie Govig), which is invaluable for topical news. Also to the inspiring demonstrations by Tom Van Sant who first showed us how to produce beautiful new kite shapes using glass fibre and rip-stop nylon. These enthusiasts must be congratulated for their high standards of accuracy and their ability to communicate statistics.

I am grateful to the Controller of Her Majesty's Stationery Office for permission to reproduce various British patent drawings in Chapter 9.

The explanation of kite aerodynamics has eluded many authors. It is easy to confuse one's readers with scientific terms, and yet difficult to express the theory in simple language. I am indebted to Martyn Pressnell for his advice on Chapter 2, which sets out to break through the mystique of kite flight.

For my illustrations, I thank Sue Knight who traced some of the construction sketches, and Pat Lloyd whose line drawings do much to convey the many different shapes of kites. A fellow kite flyer, Pat has been so close to this book that he is virtually co-author.

In all the flight tests I have had one faithful assistant, launcher, tree climber and unraveller of tangled lines – Jonathan Moulton, whose range of clothing from T-shirt to heavy anorak, as you can see from the photographs, shows that it has been an all-weather operation.

The tedious chore of preparing the typescript has been cheerfully undertaken by Evelyn Barrett. Her drive and enthusiasm for kites have enabled me to complete what became a major effort of research, photography, sketching and writing. Evelyn's initiative and interpretation of my scrawl have made this book possible.

R. G. Moulton
Bushey, Herts

Introduction

A delightful feeling of freedom overtakes every kite flyer as the wind lifts the canopy high against the blue of the sky. Once soaring aloft, with its line straining in variable gusts, the colourful shape and trailing tail are in poetic motion. The taut sail is both a plaything and an art form.

Some people look upon kite flyers as lightheaded intellectuals seemingly unaware of the harsh realities of the world – they call them nut-cases and crackpots. Kiters have been depicted in literature as escapists, or as people of such fanatical dedication that they try to involve everyone around them in their subject. The kite itself is illustrated as a symbol of outdoor life and of childhood.

This book sets out to show that there is much more to the subject than just a shallow activity of passing interest. In an age when all our energy sources are becoming more precious, there is a resurgence of enthusiasm for the kite. Wind power is free. Make good use of it, and, in so doing, enjoy kites and their many variations.

Above: *Traditional Chinese Lantern kite.*

Right: *Woman kite, another elaborate design from China.*

ONE

Origins and History

While it is not the purpose of this book to cover in detail the whole story of kites through the ages, it is interesting to reflect on the way that kites have evolved and the purposes to which they have been put.

THE FAR EAST

The kite was probably first put to practical use about 200 BC, when the Chinese General Han Hsin is said to have used one to ascertain the length of a tunnel he needed to dig from his lines to the walls of a Palace which he was besieging. Even if you regard this as just a legend, the very early use of kites in China is clearly substantiated by the many other instances of sending 'red lanterns' aloft and despatching messages from kite lines. Subsequently, the kite was used in the East for amusement and at ceremonial festivals. Kite flying gradually spread through Korea, Japan and Malaysia to India and across the South

Pacific to the Americas. The kite was to become part of the traditional heritage of Asia and the Far East.

The development of the trade route around the Cape of Good Hope brought Eastern kites to Europe, though they were not the decorative and complicated Oriental types that we immediately associate with China and Japan. The European kite was derived from the simple two-stick fighting kite. At first, this kite consisted of a curved bow lateral stick at the top of the spine to make a round-headed (peg-top) or peardrop shape. Later the two-stick kite was used with a straight lateral. A tail was used, essential for stability in European conditions, and the original concept of the Asiatic fighting kite disappeared with a demand for something that would be easier to fly. Fortunately for all kite enthusiasts, progress did not stop with the adoption of the simple pear shape. And, equally fortunately, the Eastern traditions were maintained over the centuries. Apart from changes of materials, the shapes and character of the Chinese, Japanese, Malaysian and Indian kites of the present day closely resemble those of their forebears.

THE SOUTH PACIFIC

Before we become involved in the better-known kite variations, let us look at the native South Pacific kites, which are remarkable in a number of ways.

Made from plaited grasses, leaves and tree bark, Polynesian kites were used for the practical purpose of trailing fishing hooks, and at ceremonial events of great social importance. Some New Zealand Maori kites are said to have been man-lifting and there are many legends attached to their shapes. Most have a bird outline and trailing tails which carry symbolic ti-tree leaves, feathers or dog hair. Regarded as sacred, the South Pacific kites form an important part of Polynesian tradition and illustrate close links in the development of

widespread communities. A typical legend is one from Hervey Island, where, after a kite fight between the brothers Tone and Rango, the elder brother Rango became the victor and thus also the Patron of the Archipelagos, giving his name to the type of kite with a projecting spine, or backbone, with eight leaves stitched to four upright canes. Rango is said to be the god of peace, war . . . and kites.

The Franks Collection in the Museum of Mankind, London, contains some fine kites from the islands of Melanesia. No one has yet attempted to produce commercial copies of them and it seems unlikely that these heavy kites would perform well outside their native Pacific environment where the winds are very strong and constant.

EUROPE, USA, AUSTRALIA AND CANADA

After the arrival of the Malay diamond-shaped fighter, and its early transition to the peg-top shape in Europe, the first record of the serious use of kites (apart from legislation to minimise kite-flying nuisances in France in 1736) came in the mid-eighteenth century, with simultaneous experiments in Scotland, France, Italy and North America to conduct electricity from the atmosphere. The first of these attempts was made by a Scot, Alexander Wilson, who in 1749 sent thermometers aloft with fused releases to drop at intervals. The American statesman, Benjamin Franklin, achieved greater fame. In 1752, after six years of study, Franklin succeeded in conducting lightning along the damp hemp kite twine from a spike aerial on his diamond-shaped kite. Ridiculed for some time, and contested by De Romas who claimed earlier discovery without practical demonstration, Franklin had invented the lightning conductor. Later experiments with wire kite-lines in Europe resulted in explosive discharges – a warning not to fly kites in a thundery atmosphere.

At the beginning of the nineteenth century, Sir George Caley used the peg-top kite as a

Painting on wood depicting an eighteenth-century kite design. The original hangs in the Aero Club de France.

glider. His model of 1804 and subsequent man-carrying glider for which he became known as the 'Father of the Aeroplane' were to anticipate discoveries of a century later. Caley was not the only aerodynamicist to learn from kites. Lilienthal, Pilcher, Chanute and the Wright brothers all used kites first as a study, using their findings later in the making of man-carrying sail-wing gliders, as emulated today by the hang glider.

Weather kites began to be used 'in train'. D. Colladon used three peg-tops on a common line to conduct electricity at Geneva in 1827 – their spars were 39 ins (1 m) long – and the search for knowledge of the atmosphere began to bear fruit. The same year also saw the publication of a remarkable work by George Pocock entitled *The Aeropleustic Art of Navigation in the Air by the Use of Kites or Buoyant Sails*. Pocock had harnessed a pony chaise to a pair of kites and discovered that, according to wind strength, it was possible to move up to half a ton on the carriage. Special 'charvolants' were made for these first horseless carriages, and the largest held sixteen lads who no doubt enjoyed a thrilling ride. Until the arrival of telegraph wires and railway bridges, it was claimed that the Pocock kite carriages could race mail-coaches from Bristol to London and back. The basic kite design used was the peg-top but with modifications for a four-line control to capture an angled wind. Remember that this was the heyday of sail; a mastless aerial rig would not have been

An historic Drachen *from Germany; a wall display in the British RAF museum.*

so unusual a spectacle at the time. A pilot kite went aloft first, then the main kite, and then, if needed, another. Any number could be used, but for carriage work two were usually enough. To stop, a line was slackened, the main kite collapsed, and a hoe-like brake stopped the carriage. Pocock's other claims to fame were to send his daughter Martha aloft in an armchair to a height of 300 ft (90 m); and to become the grandfather of the renowned W. G. Grace, who travelled to some of his cricket matches by kite carriage.

In 1828 (two years after he obtained patent 5420 in partnership with Colonel James Viney, RA) Pocock demonstrated the char-volant at Ascot racecourse to King George IV. Immediately afterwards, he raced against horse-drawn coaches on the road between Staines and Hounslow, handsomely beating them all. At the Liverpool Regatta on 18 July 1828, one Alfred Pocock and nine others traversed the Mersey against strong tides and winds with a kite-drawn two-masted boat, to register 'great surprise among the nautical parties who witnessed it' (*The Engineer*). Viney and Pocock proposed that the kite carriage should have a 'dandy-cart to carry a pony in the event of the wind failing or being of an unfavourable direction', but the plan does not seem to have been carried out. Traction by kites continued to attract interest up to the turn of the century, but by then internal combustion and steam had been harnessed to provide more reliable means of propulsion.

Long after Pocock's carriage first raced, the kite was put to another use when the celebrated Samuel Franklin Cody conducted man-carrying kite trials (Fig. 1). With Mrs Cody as an experimental passenger, a special boat towed by box kites successfully crossed the English Channel from France to England. But we jump ahead, for in the last ten years of the nineteenth century, the kite was developed rapidly and an entirely different range of shapes appeared for special purposes. They deserve particular mention.

In 1891, a photographer by the name of William Eddy, from Bayonne, New Jersey, created a bowed form of the diamond-shaped Malay kite by tensioning the lateral spar (Fig. 2). This, in effect, applied a 'dihedral' to the design. (On aircraft this is the upward and outward sweep of the wings – an essential for stability. Applying it to a kite has a similar effect.) Eddy's kite was also much simpler than the peg-top, and adapted itself to an elementary bridle of two lines. Moreover, the kite was stable enough not to need a tail, and it could be flown in tandem. Up to eight Eddy kites were flown in train, and the combined lift was enough to overstrain the line, with amusing results. Once a whole train broke away to trail across Staten Island to New York Bay, with the owner in chase by train and ferryboat.

The bowed Eddy kite is still a popular shape. Although it needs a tail in British conditions of changing wind forces and gusts at lower altitudes, an Eddy made from non-porous plastic will perform in the lightest of breezes, while a cloth Eddy will perform in gale-force conditions. Eddy himself was an experimenter. He took aerial photographs of battles in Cuba during the American–Spanish War and sent up flags and lanterns for publicity.

Similar in shape, 'Parakites' were the creation of a jeweller from Yonkers, New York, who rejoiced in the name of Gilbert Totten Woglom. In 1896, G. T. Woglom published a book which described how, on 4 May 1895, he trailed a 10-ft (3-m) American 'Old Glory' flag at 1,000 ft (300 m) above the military and civil ceremonies during the dedication of the Washington Memorial Arch in New York City (Fig. 3). Woglom set up a train of Parakites from the Judson Memorial Tower to carry the heavy flag aloft and was widely praised for his clever gesture. Newspaper reports quoted the number of kites variously as three, four, six and eight, but all agreed that Woglom stole the day with his

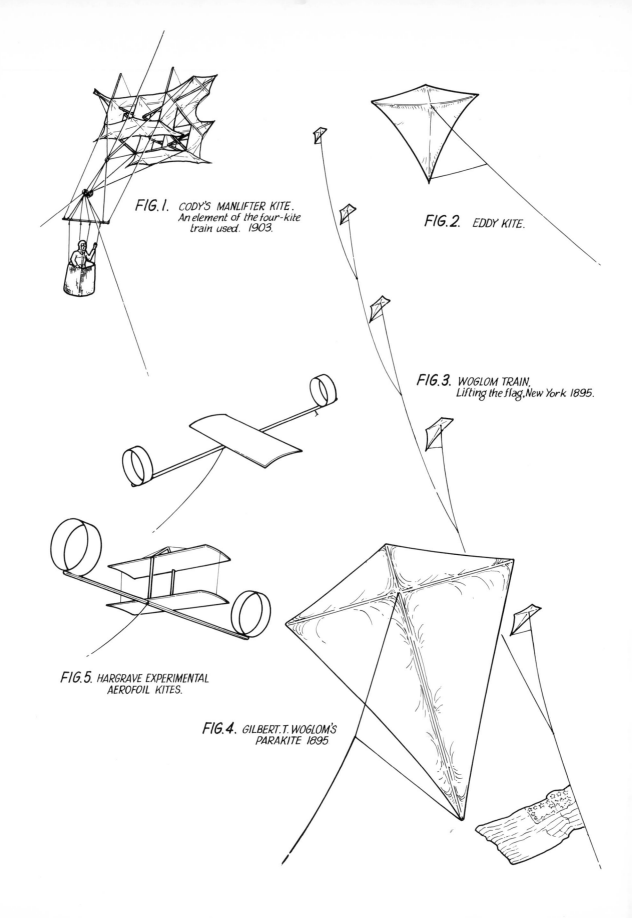

FIG. 1. CODY'S MANLIFTER KITE.
An element of the four-kite
train used. 1903.

FIG. 2. EDDY KITE.

FIG. 3. WOGLOM TRAIN,
Lifting the flag, New York 1895.

FIG. 5. HARGRAVE EXPERIMENTAL
AEROFOIL KITES.

FIG. 4. GILBERT. T. WOGLOM'S
PARAKITE 1895

spectacle; and none more so than Woglom himself in his book *Parakites* which, even eighty years after publication, and although written in quaint terminology, remains a classic reference to the Japanese, Malay, Chinese and Eddy types. It is worth recording that Woglom was the first to publish any reference to the aerofoil shape of the bowed two-stick kite. He called it the '"Twin concaves" – each as the inner side of that third of an egg shell which might be sawed off lengthwise from an egg'. Woglom was drawing attention to the sail curvature of the lower section of the kite which, as we shall see, is an important factor in its performance (Fig. 4). Woglom's train of kites used separate lines, each connected to the lower line at a point sufficiently well extended from the bridle to avoid fouling the kite below. The method has advantages in that each kite on the train is then free to oscillate, or head in any direction without directly affecting the others. The alternative means of linking lines, directly through each bridle from one kite top to the next and so on, is best limited to the rigid, centre-stick, modern Rogallo design.

So in many ways, as kite-train flyer, flag lifter and author of the first general book on kites in the English language, Gilbert Totten Woglom deserves all the thanks that kite flyers of the present day can heap upon him.

Woglom was not, however, the first to produce technical reports. Scientific studies were available to academic bodies and among the most influential papers were those of Lawrence Hargrave. A trained engineer, Hargrave left England for Australia in 1866 and, in his search for the achievement of manned flight, began to experiment with kites during 1893 (Fig. 5). Following the principle established by F. H. Welham in a paper delivered to the Aeronautical Society in 1866, Hargrave created the biplane box kite after first inventing his monoplanes (which are still impressive for their simplicity). All Hargrave's kites had the characteristic of fore and aft planes, supported by a framework. They preceded the wing, tail and longeron fuselage concept of the aeroplane by a whole decade, and appeared in every possible configuration (Fig. 6).

The most influential, however, was the box kite (Fig. 7). Hargrave called it, quite correctly, the 'cellular kite', and he fully recognised that his biplanes adopted a cambered aerofoil in flight. This shape was to be widely adopted by many other pioneers, not only for kites but also in early full-size French aeroplanes, though not, as commonly supposed, by the Wright brothers. Two aeroplanes even became famous when named Box Kites, although in fact they had only a remote association with the Hargrave concept. The Grahame-White Box Kite aeroplane did not even have a biplane tail, although it used two rudders, and the Bristol's Wright-style foreplane elevator made it nothing like a Hargrave cellular kite. Nevertheless the name persists, and regular flights are still made by a Bristol Box Kite replica from the Shuttleworth Collection aerodrome at Old Warden, Bedfordshire. It was built to appear in a film called *Those Magnificent Men in Their Flying Machines*.

Lawrence Hargrave's papers were published in the *Journal of the Royal Society of New South Wales*, and the information in them was quickly noted in America and Europe. On a lecture tour in England during 1899, he loaned some kites to the gliding pioneer P. S. Pilcher who was influenced by their success, but more important was their effect on Captain B. F. S. Baden-Powell and Samuel Franklin Cody.

Hargrave's box kites went on sale in toyshops and Cody bought one for his son Vivian. He made larger versions, added extension 'wings' with wire bracing, and within a year was to take out a patent (23566) for Sky-kites which would ascend in a train to lead a man-carrying kite with a wicker basket for an aerial observer. Some of the main kites reached spans of 36 ft (11 m) and required substantial anchorage as well as very careful rigging.

Cody's system was simpler than that used by Baden-Powell, who linked four large hexagon kites with two lines anchored wide apart to form an inverted v. The observer's basket was then slung from each of the v-shaped cables and hoisted aloft, not always with results amenable to the occupant! The system was known appropriately as the Levitor.

In America, the US Weather Bureau was given money to conduct experiments with kites, and Hargrave's cellular construction was adapted by Professor C. F. Marvin to what became known as the Weather Bureau Hargrave–Marvin Box Kite (Figs 8 and 9). These were designed in three sizes for varying wind strengths, and the moderate wind kite had a 6 ft 8 ins (2 m) span, was 6 ft 6 ins (2 m) long and 2 ft 8$\frac{1}{2}$ ins (82 cm) deep. It had a total lifting surface area of 66 sq ft (6·13 m²), weighed 8$\frac{1}{2}$ lb (4 kg) and was covered with Lonsdale cambric with sails 2 ft 1$\frac{1}{2}$ ins (65 cm) wide and 6 ft 5 ins (2 m) long. A head kite lifted the meteorograph, while secondary kites, attached to the main line with cords 124 ft (38 m) long, lifted the whole assembly many thousands of feet for observation. From 1897 these kites were flown at seventeen stations in the USA, once reaching a record height of 23,835 ft (7265 m).

Much later, during World War II, kites of similar design were deployed to carry defensive barrage cables from ships that were liable to attack by dive bombers.

Further north, in Nova Scotia and Newfoundland, two scientists were making separate kite experiments which were to have a profound influence. When Guglielmo Marconi lifted his 600-ft (183-m) receiving aerial on 12 December 1901 at St John's to make the historic radio link with a transmitter at Poldhu in Cornwall, he used a winged box kite. Significantly, the same type of kite that was used by Marconi for his experiments is still

sold. It is now known as the Brookite Master, and its design has not changed in almost eighty years.

Alexander Graham Bell's researches were directed at developing a flying machine. Inventor of the telephone, President of the National Geographic Society, and contemporary of Hargrave, he left Scotland to live in Canada and subsequently became a citizen of the United States. Bell admired Hargrave's work with box kites, and appreciated the one essential feature of the design – the open space between fore and aft planes. Bell found that the larger the space, the better the stability of the pitch. He also praised the value of the vertical end plates which made up the boxes, but thought the structure required for rigidity was detracting from the efficiency of the box kite and objected to the drag-producing internal bracing. So Bell made triangular box cells (Fig. 10) which eliminated the internal bracing; he came to the conclusion that:

> So far as I can judge from observation in the field, kites constructed on the same general model as the Hargrave Box Kite, but with triangular cells instead of quadrangular, seem to fly as well as the ordinary Hargrave form and at as high an angle. Such kites are therefore superior for they fly substantially as well, while at the same time they are stronger in construction, lighter in weight, and offer less head resistance to the wind.

Three-quarters of a century later, any present-day kite flyer will bear out what Bell said in his masterly account of 1903 (*National Geographic Magazine*, Vol. XIV, No. 6, June 1903). The box kite needs strong winds to overcome its weight penalty.

Bell did not rest with the triangular box kite; he made it in coupled triplicates (Fig. 11), then built up the units to a fifteen-cell compound and developed the tetrahedral frame of assembled triangles. Made to vast proportions and used in lateral-wing shape, box or compound triangle configuration

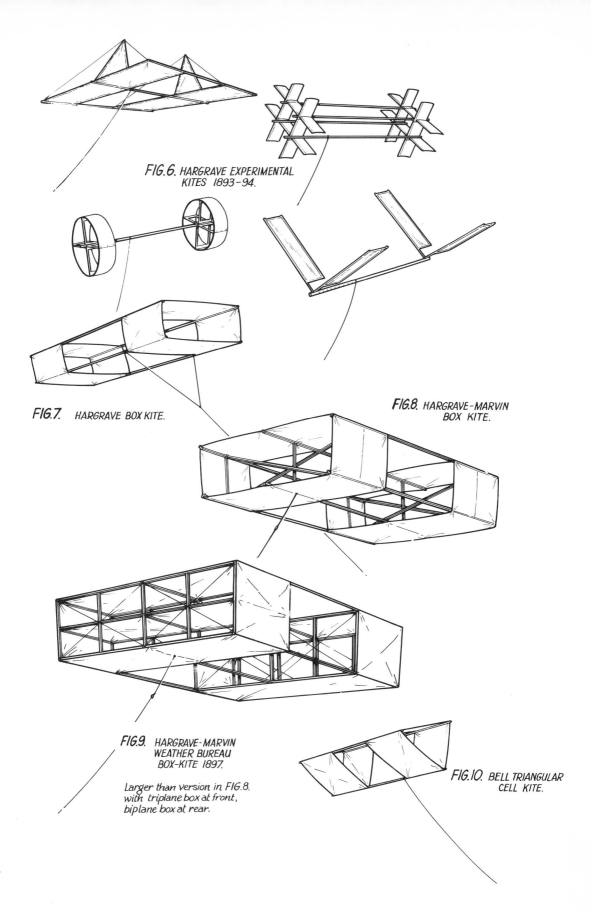

FIG.6. HARGRAVE EXPERIMENTAL KITES 1893-94.

FIG.7. HARGRAVE BOX KITE.

FIG.8. HARGRAVE-MARVIN BOX KITE.

FIG.9. HARGRAVE-MARVIN WEATHER BUREAU BOX-KITE 1897.

Larger than version in FIG.8. with triplane box at front, biplane box at rear.

FIG.10. BELL TRIANGULAR CELL KITE.

(Fig. 12), Bell's tetrahedral kites made a spectacular sight and were close to achieving the appearance and performance of an aeroplane (Fig. 13). One 'floating' kite, which had two lateral tetrahedrons spaced apart on three fore and aft triangular bodies, lifted two men off the ground before its thick manila rope parted. The Floater pitched violently (as would any glider if its towline broke) and then settled down to land on an even keel, undamaged after its rough experience. The date was a year before the Wright brothers' flight further down the east coast of the USA. Bell's kite had shown that in free flight it was quite stable; but he did not take his experiments any further toward achieving manned flight. Much of his Nova Scotia laboratory work is preserved at the Alexander Graham Bell National Historic Park Museum, Baddeck, Nova Scotia, where the originals are splendidly displayed.

Meanwhile, in France, another book appeared – *Les Cerfs-Volants Observatoires* by J. Lecornu. The author had created his own variant of the Hargrave box kite by piling three cells one above the other in ladder form. When properly braced with a rigid vertical member on either side, and a forward-reaching bridle, the Lecornu ladder (Fig. 14) had great lifting power, and was like a rigid first cousin to the modern parafoil. Lecornu's book revealed details of other pioneers, including Madiot and Saconney who had adapted the Hargrave box with side wings and created man-lifting trains (Fig. 15). Hargrave's influence was truly worldwide.

Like Bell, Louis Blériot (who was later to be the first person to fly the English Channel) preferred the triangular-section box. He added triangular side wings to the upper plane of the triangular-section main body, and this shape was made in quantity as the Military Kite. Blériot formed the central box frames and their panels with rigid bracing and extended the length so that instead of fore and aft boxes some had three filled-in panels, one forward, one central, and one aft. The shape proved to be extremely stable over a broad wind-speed range and it was adopted by Silas J. Conyne in the USA (Fig. 16).

The Conyne kite had a difference in that the central body – or box frame – was made up of three longerons and fabric so that the triangular box had flexible sides. This gave the advantage that once the single lateral spar was detached the whole kite could be rolled up. This feature had been well established in the Brookites on sale then (and now) in Britain, and shows what little change has been made to the basic winged box kite in the twentieth century. Larger versions of the Blériot require two lateral sticks to extend the side sails of the flat kite portion, and some have extensive bracing in the box sides to keep the panels extended. This is an important point, for the airflow through the box is considerable, and the panels should not be allowed to flap – or luff.

This account of the early days of kiting has of necessity glossed over the achievements of many other pioneers who worked in parallel with those mentioned. It is not the intention of this book to provide a complete historical account, but to explain how shapes and types were derived. Now we enter the twentieth century, in which organised competitions were planned to promote progress.

CONTESTS

It seems incredible now that as early as 25 June 1903, the Aeronautical Society of Great Britain should be holding its thirty-eighth session – for the Wright brothers had yet to make their first powered flight. The Society's interest was centred upon balloons and airships, and at this meeting, for the first time, on kites. An international contest was organised for the highest flight above 3,000 ft (900 m) attained by a single kite, and the award was a silver medal.

More than a thousand people assembled on that Thursday at Findon, including repre-

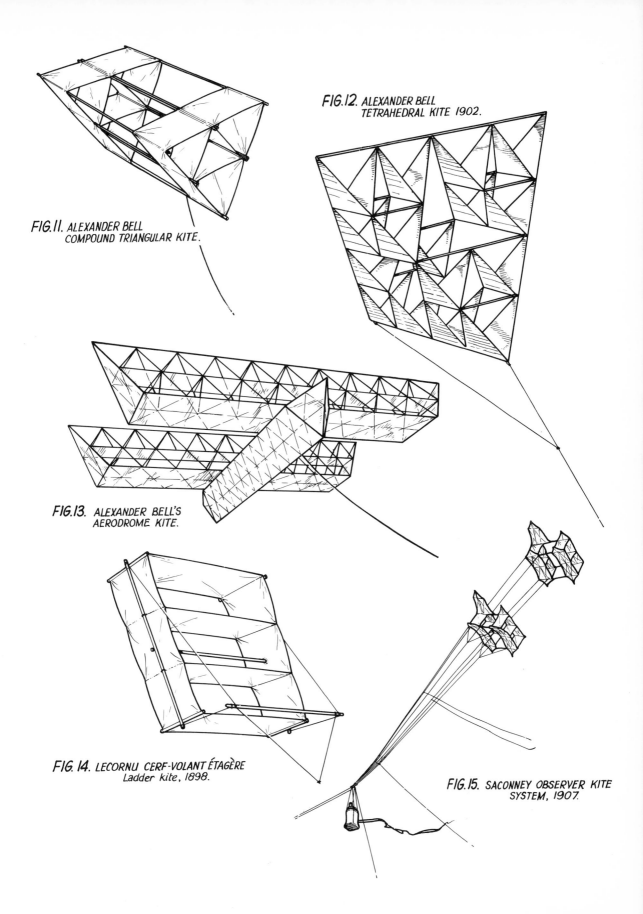

FIG.11. ALEXANDER BELL
COMPOUND TRIANGULAR KITE.

FIG.12. ALEXANDER BELL
TETRAHEDRAL KITE 1902.

FIG.13. ALEXANDER BELL'S
AERODROME KITE.

FIG.14. LECORNU CERF-VOLANT ÉTAGÈRE
Ladder kite, 1898.

FIG.15. SACONNEY OBSERVER KITE
SYSTEM, 1907.

sentatives of the Russian, German and Austro-Hungarian governments. Among six eminent judges was Sir Hiram Maxim and the eight competitors included the President of the Society, Major Baden-Powell of the Scots Guards. S. F. Cody was favoured to win with his bat-winged box (Fig. 17), and he was backed by a second entry flown by his elder son, Leon. The wind, however, was too light. No one reached the 3,000-ft (900-m) target and the contest was won by Charles Brogden's six-winged bird kite which registered a greatest height of 1,816 ft (548 m) (Fig. 18). This kite was huge, with a span of 18 ft 8 ins (5·5 m) and a length of 17 ft (5·18 m). One centre pole supported three laterals and these formed leading edges for the six wings. In other words, it was an enormous Eddy type with four cut-outs to break the mainsail into six parts. Cody expressed confidence that his kite would eventually lead to a powered flying machine, and on that he was indeed prophetic. S. H. R. Salmon was another competitor who favoured multiple cells. He flew a rhomboidal kite at this contest, and at a 1907 contest used an eighteen-winged, 10-ft (3-m) span monster (Fig. 19) which flew in the lightest of breezes and took a meteorograph to 1,600 ft (480 m).

Another early contest was that organised by the Italians to celebrate the inauguration of the Simplon Tunnel. It was an international event and was held at the Milan Exhibition of 1906. Split into two sections, it was first a contest for altitude above 1,000 m (3,280 ft) with a 2-kg (4·4-lb) payload, and second an event for passenger-carrying kites that, in the words of the regulations, 'realised most completely the idea of the competitor'.

BRITISH ORGANISATIONS

Meanwhile, the Kite Flying Association of Great Britain had been formed under the presidency of Major Baden-Powell, and exhibitions began to be planned at Olympia in conjunction with other sports and pastimes.

W. H. Akehurst was the organising secretary and it was largely due to his hard work that the KFA developed, with a long list of famous patrons and councillors, into the Kite and Model Aeroplane Association in February 1909. Typical of the K and MAA activities were lectures, by personalities such as Marconi on 'Wireless Telegraphy and Kites', while at Wimbledon Common regular events were arranged for 'the most practical and useful method of employing a Kite or Kites to Life-Saving, Photography, Signalling, etc.', and open events where angle of line, stability, construction and portability were given points.

Kite contests usually stipulated a statutory length of line – 900 ft (275 m) – and opened with a bugle call. If a kite came down before the bugle sounded the close of the contest, it was disqualified.

Programmes for these annual meetings carried fascinating advertisements. Brookite illustrated, with the Marconi Wireless Telegraph Company's endorsement, kites that are still sold today, and James J. Hicks of Hatton Garden offered patent self-registering altimeters 'as used by Mr Cody' and the W. H. Dines meteorograph for registering the pressure, temperature, humidity and wind velocity of the upper air.

In the course of time, not to mention the outbreak of war in 1914, the KFA and K and MAA activities ceased. Organised kite flying faded away and although the columns of *Flight* and *The Model Engineer* sustained exchanges of ideas, it was not until 1975 that any move was made to re-establish a British Kite Flying Association.

A rally organised by the author at Old Warden on 12 October 1975 started a revival of the KFA, with a newsletter service to co-ordinate national activities. In 1977, a European Kitefliers Association was created to foster international activities, and together, the BKFA and the EKA illustrate the strength of British kiting.

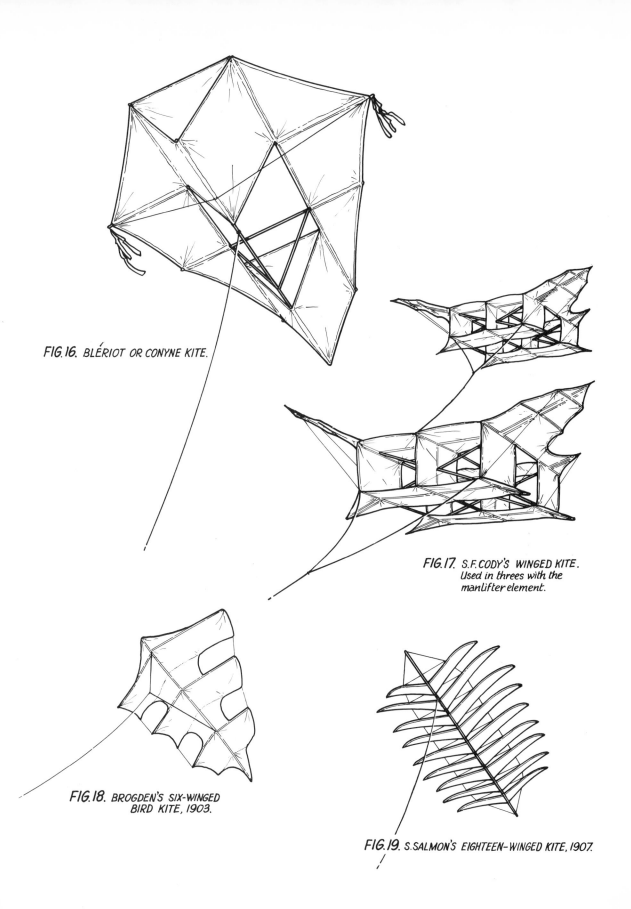

FIG. 16. BLÉRIOT OR CONYNE KITE.

FIG. 17. S.F. CODY'S WINGED KITE.
Used in threes with the
manlifter element.

FIG. 18. BROGDEN'S SIX-WINGED
BIRD KITE, 1903.

FIG. 19. S. SALMON'S EIGHTEEN-WINGED KITE, 1907.

AMERICAN ORGANISATIONS

In America the AKA (American Kitefliers Association) provides a quality magazine for its members, and co-ordinates news of festivals, new products and books. In the pages of *Kite Tales* we can learn of new materials or old pioneer designs, where to find specialist kite shops, or what happened at the Washington rally. It is the only USA publication offering exclusive news on kites alone, and many enthusiasts outside the USA become members of the AKA in order to keep up with developments. Badges and car stickers can be purchased to declare allegiance to the pastime, and since its launching in October 1964, *Kite Tales'* readership has grown continuously. For years it was dependent on the work of Robert M. Ingraham, who stimulated the AKA through his personal efforts. In 1977, it was taken over by Valerie Govig, a similarly dedicated enthusiast.

Will Yolen, raconteur exceptional in the kite world, and author of several books on kites, is also founder and president of the IKA or International Kitefliers Association. The world headquarters is at 321E 48th Street, New York, NY 10017, USA. Another organisation in New York is the Go Fly A Kite Association based in the world-famous specialist shop at 1434 3rd Avenue, New York, NY 10028, USA. The west coast equivalent is Dave Checkley's Kite Factory at 678 W. Prospect, Seattle, Washington 98110, USA.

Inside the 'Go Fly a Kite' shop in 3rd Avenue, New York. The colourful display includes kites from all over the world.

ORGANISATIONS IN OTHER COUNTRIES

Many nations have regular kite festivals. Japan is, of course, a traditional centre for the highly decorated O-dako huge kite, which is flown at Hammamatsu with great ceremony. Poland has many enthusiasts of the *swieto latawca*, as the kite is known in Polish. Czechoslovakia has a keen following for *draky*, Germany for its *drachen*, and so on in Guatemala, Brazil, Chile, etc.

In Japan the JKA was started by author and lecturer Professor Tsutomu Hiroi, who made a great impression with his demonstrations in France and Britain in 1976. The JKA is based at 4-32-7 Kitakarasuyama Seragaya-ku, Tokyo 157. In India the KFA of India is at 3126 Lal Darwaza Bazaar, Sita Ram, Delhi 6, India.

TWO

Kite Design

'KITE, **n**; a device consisting of a light frame of wood and paper constructed to fly in the air by means of a string.' That is one dictionary definition which is a generally acceptable description of what the kite is about. But is it really correct? Wood, paper and string are not necessarily used, but a tether line is essential to restrain the kite relative to the ground while it is subjected to wind forces which may then be sufficient to keep it aloft. Some light is thrown on this by considering the aerodynamics of the situation.

AERODYNAMIC THEORY

Daniel Bernoulli, a Swiss mathematician (1700–82), formulated a law expressing the constant of energy in a moving fluid. The total energy comprises kinetic energy, caused by the velocity of the fluid, and potential energy, associated with its dynamic and static pressure. Although an exchange of forms of energy can take place, according to the law the total remains constant. Air, being a fluid, is subject to the law. When applied to the flow of air around aerofoils and kites, Bernoulli's Law comes to this: the greater the speed of the air, the less will be the pressure on the surface where the moving fluid applies; conversely, the less the speed of the air, the greater will be the pressure at that point.

For a simple practical demonstration of Bernoulli's Law take a strip of postcard and bend it slightly to the shape of a wing section,

Sampson cloth Eagle showing aerofoil contours when viewed from rear.

with a gentle curve, rather like the section of an eggshell. Pull the card over the edge of a table and a permanent curve will form. Make a lip at the leading edge so that it will hang on a pencil and swing freely when you blow over the convex (upper) surface of the card. The strip will move upwards in the stream of air, demonstrating that a lifting force is generated which can raise it up to a level position as long as there is a steady airflow (Fig. 20).

The reason for this has to do with the camber, or curvature, of the aerofoil section of the strip of postcard, which causes the air to be accelerated over the top of the wing and decelerated below it. As Bernoulli's Law states, the pressure is thus reduced on the upper surface, and increased on the lower surface, with the result that the aerofoil obtains lift.

In the case of a kite, which might not have an aerofoil section and is more like a flat plate set at an angle to the airflow, the effect is more complicated because the airflow may become detached from the surface of the kite in a rather turbulent manner. But the principle still applies to all kites, and particularly to those which adopt a cambered form (e.g. parasails, Rogallo and the Lecornu ladder). The curved section of these kites (sometimes referred to as canopy kites) helps to direct the airflow and delay its separation from the top surface even at the very steep angles at which kites operate. Additionally kites of this type used a proofed rather than a porous surface, which improves the lift coefficient.

Most kites can be regarded as flat planes. Like the canopy or curved plane kites, they deflect the airstream downwards as it approaches the undersurface. The analogy that the air bounces off the kite is not strictly correct, but gives a notion of how a force is exerted on the surface. Airflow over the upper surface breaking away from the plane in a turbulent flow produces some lift, but not nearly as effectively as when this can be avoided. If the flow could be made visible in a

Musha rectangular rigid-framed kite with eye pattern, using streamers to stabilise its flight.

smoke pattern it would consist of vortices separating from the edges of the kite (Fig. 21), known in aerodynamic parlance as a stalled condition. Some aerofoils operate at angles of up to 15° or 18° before they stall (Fig. 22). This occurs with loss of the low-pressure lift on the upper surface, leaving inadequate positive pressure on the lower surface to sustain heavily loaded aircraft at low forward speeds. The kite's angle usually *starts* at 18° or more, and is almost invariably stalled to some extent, only sustaining the kite because of its relatively low loading (Fig. 23).

In addition to the essential lifting forces, kites are subjected to considerable drag forces acting in the direction of the wind. When the flow is detached and highly turbulent (as is usually the case) the drag force is of the same order as the lifting force.

The actual relationship between the lift and drag forces can be gauged by observing the angle of the tether line to the ground. When this is about 45° the drag force is 70 per cent of the line tension and the lift on the kite exceeds the drag by the weight of the kite itself. If line angle is less, the drag is higher and the lift less (Fig. 24). Conversely, if the angle of the line to the ground is higher than 45°, the lift is greater and the drag less. The effect of any adjustment made to the kite with a view to increasing the lift or reducing drag can be gauged at once by the increased angle of the line when flown in the same wind strength.

In strong winds the kite lift and drag forces become large compared with the weight of the kite and they are about equal to each other when the line is at 45° to the ground. Kite drag is also augmented by the drag of the tether line itself.

The aerodynamic forces acting on a kite (Fig. 25) are proportional to its surface area and to the square of the wind speed. The forces on a large kite can become very large and a kite of 100 sq ft ($9 m^2$) area flying in a 30 mph (48 km/h) wind could lift a man. In terms of much smaller kites flown as a leisure sport or pastime, the process is scaled down to lift forces of 5–10 lb (2–4 kg) at normal wind speeds.

Many arguments have arisen over the application of Bernoulli's Law to kite flight, and over the effect on performance of the porosity of the surface, and numerous theories on the aerodynamics of the kite have been presented.

The question might be asked, 'Why use a flat plate or canopy kite at stalled and therefore inefficient angles, when a cambered aerofoil surface and aeroplane configuration should be much more efficient?' The simple answer seems to be that such elaboration is unnecessary, because, with their low loading, kites are able to fly in relatively slow airflow conditions. Though various aeroplane configurations are operated over a wide range of air speeds, all require a forward speed which is usually greater than the wind speed owing to their greater loading. Even a model glider on a tow line generally needs to be pulled forward into wind to achieve sufficient air speed to climb to the top of the line before release into free flight.

Clearly, model gliders, with their light loadings of about 4 oz per sq ft (1221 g/m^2), will not sustain themselves on a tethered line unless wind speeds equal their normal gliding air speed, and in any case they are not designed with enough inherent stability to maintain station at the end of a tethered line.

So we can see that the kite is somewhat unusual in aerodynamics. It flies when it should not and it will lift many times its own weight, without even moving forward relative to the ground! The explanations offered are of course a simplification, glossing over the intricacies of the distribution of pressure on the kite surface, or the detailed nature of the flow past the body with the frictional forces which are derived.

A TEST

To help understand these aerodynamic effects, try a simple test when out in the car and there is no other traffic about. Open the window when the car is travelling at moderate speed, and you will at once be aware that the airflow is noisy. This is created by the pressure fluctuations as the air deflected off the windscreen meets the flow along the sides and becomes highly turbulent in a thick boundary layer developing into vortices. Now extend a hand at a flat angle, edge-on to the airflow. Lift the leading edge of your hand gradually. You will feel the pressure on the palm, and as the

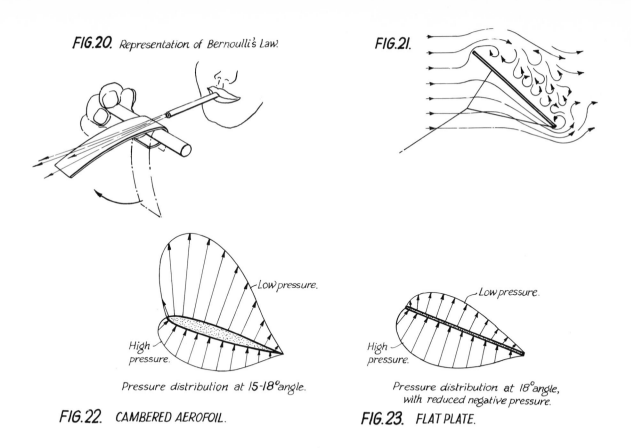

FIG.20. Representation of Bernoulli's Law.

FIG.21.

FIG.22. CAMBERED AEROFOIL.

Low pressure.

High pressure.

Pressure distribution at 15-18° angle.

FIG.23. FLAT PLATE.

Low pressure.

High pressure.

Pressure distribution at 18° angle, with reduced negative pressure.

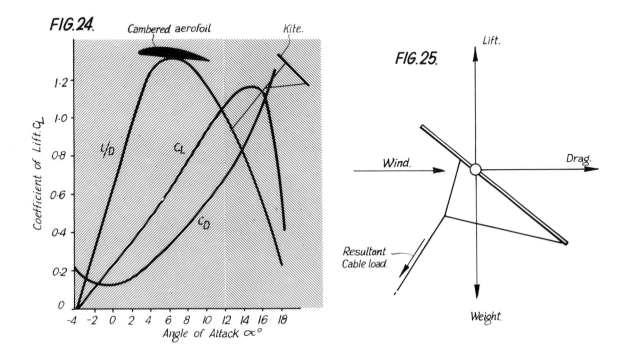

FIG.24.

Cambered aerofoil

Kite.

Coefficient of Lift. c_L

1·2

1·0

0·8

0·6

0·4

0·2

0

L/D

c_L

c_D

-4 -2 0 2 4 6 8 10 12 14 16 18

Angle of Attack $\propto°$

FIG.25.

Lift.

Wind.

Drag.

Resultant Cable load.

Weight.

angle increases, the hairs on the back of your hand will be picked up by the turbulence in the low pressure region. Increase the angle to over 20° and the hand wants to lift high, move it to right angles and the pressure increases to discomfort. Somewhere in the middle, at our kiting angle of 20–35°, the hand is relatively comfortable as the airflow presented by the forward speed of the car supports it. The hand is 'stalled'; it has no aerofoil camber to improve its lift and relies on the pressure of the oncoming airflow on the palm, and the reduced pressure on the back of the hand, balanced by the weight of the hand, and the drag pulling the arm backwards.

STABILITY

The position at which the line is attached to a kite has a considerable effect on the stability of the kite, in both the longitudinal pitching sense and the lateral yawing sense. If the line is attached too far aft, when the kite is launched it will swing off uncontrollably to one side. This is known as a lateral divergence. If, on the other hand, the line is attached too far forward, a zig-zag flight can result where the kite is directionally unstable and this may increase to the point of being uncontrollable. An alternative effect of having the line too far forward is that the kite will not assume sufficient flying incidence (angle of attack, or nose raised into wind), particularly in lighter winds. The line position is the principal adjustment or trimming aid on a kite and you must be prepared to experiment with this to get it right. The kite's bridle is helpful to the longitudinal stability, effectively lowering the point at which the line is attached. Even so, a kite may not have adequate inherent stability. This brings us to the second adjustable feature – the tail. This stabilises the kite, but because it is long and flexible it is subject to eddies in the wind and its effect is never constant. This causes a continuous variation in stability so that the kite 'dances and prances' on the end of

Indian fighter kite in flight over New York's Central Park – flown by the author.

its line and adds considerably to the pleasure of watching it.

Some kites, such as the traditional Malay or Indian fighter, deliberately have a system of very low stability with a simple two-line bridle on a diamond shape, so that any centre-of-pressure movement can be taken advantage of by the flyer who will use variation of line tension to increase or diminish the effect, as desired (Fig. 26).

PRESSURE DISTRIBUTION

The pressure distribution over the surface of a

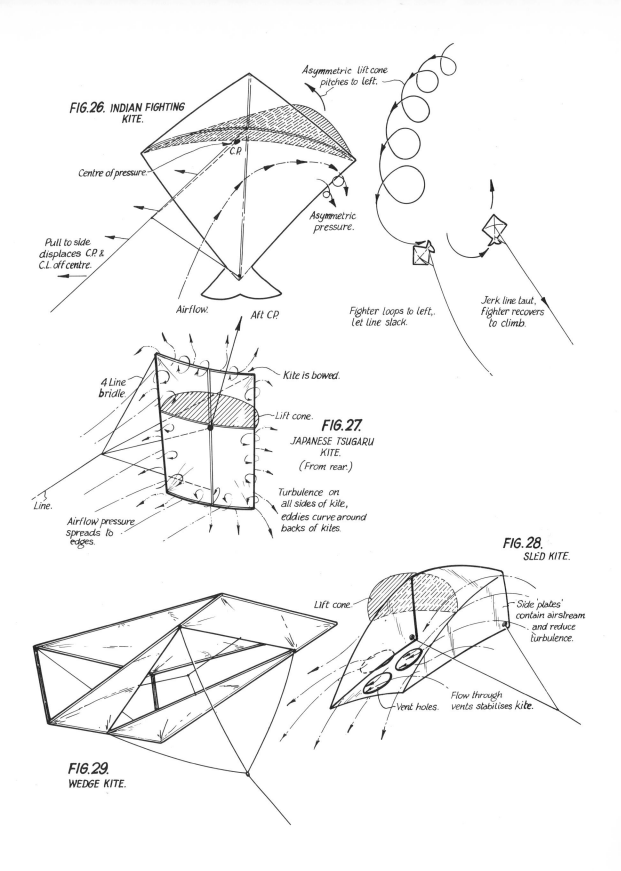

FIG.26. INDIAN FIGHTING KITE.

Asymmetric lift cone pitches to left.

Centre of pressure.

C.P.

Pull to side displaces C.P. & C.L. off centre.

Asymmetric pressure.

Airflow.

Aft C.P.

Fighter loops to left, let line slack.

Jerk line taut, fighter recovers to climb.

4 Line bridle.

Kite is bowed.

Lift cone.

FIG.27. JAPANESE TSUGARU KITE. (From rear.)

Line.

Airflow pressure spreads to edges.

Turbulence on all sides of kite, eddies curve around backs of kites.

FIG.28. SLED KITE.

Lift cone.

Side plates' contain airstream and reduce turbulence.

Vent holes.

Flow through vents stabilises kite.

FIG.29. WEDGE KITE.

kite varies considerably, depending on the kite's general shape, which brings up another aspect of the airflow.

If it were possible to measure the pressure at different points over a normal kite's surface, we would find that it is greatest near the centre and falls off towards the extremities. A typical situation is illustrated by the rectangular Japanese kite, where we see that the lift cone, or pressure distribution, falls off towards all edges as extreme vortices develop and roll around the edges (Fig. 27). Tsutomu Hiroi bows and trims with delicate adjustment of up to five bridle points. The Sled kite (Fig. 28) uses its flexible side plates as part of the bridle, at the same time tending to contain and dampen the turbulence within the 'sack', but its lift cone remains deepest at the centre of span, tapering to the edges.

The vents in a Sled or the centre hole in a Blériot or wedge, allow the airstream to flow through with rather less turbulence. The aft part of the kite becomes a stabilising factor which obviates the need for a tail (Fig. 29).

If the kite is disturbed and moves sideways, the lift cone becomes asymmetric, and this must tend to restore the attitude of the kite if it is to be stable. Low stability, and hence sensitivity, is specially associated with kites which have a high centre of pressure. Try to fly some Eddy kites, for example, without a tail and they will immediately pitch to one side. As the kite turns, the tail continues to trail downwind, its drag producing the necessary opposite turning effect to straighten the kite (Fig. 30).

Control-line kites with two lines use deliberate variation of line length to change the angle presented by the kite (Fig. 31). Different line tensions apply in the two lines with the result that a strong turning couple is exerted on the kite. A further phenomenon, rather like that of a sail on a dinghy, occurs when a control-line kite is brought into a sideways heading and is permitted to come round the circuit even as far as heading into wind. As the

Top Flite Eddy kite, its spars bowed, billowing out as wind pressure is applied.

kite rolls over from the downwind position and moves through 90°, the lift vector is canted sideways and forwards, with the result that the kite very often increases speed on a sideways swoop.

So far we have not included the box kite, but it should be clear that it incorporates many of the requirements for stability: the lifting surfaces have endplates to control turbulence; the upper surface vortices are stabilised by the effect of the box; and the separation of the fore and aft panels provides stability to cope with any oscillation in pitch or yaw (Fig. 32). Owing to its relative complexity of construction, it has heavier area loading and needs stronger winds for successful flight. The box is the most stable of all kites – and for that reason it is also the least exciting.

DIHEDRAL AND CAMBER

Dihedral is the upward and outward sweep of

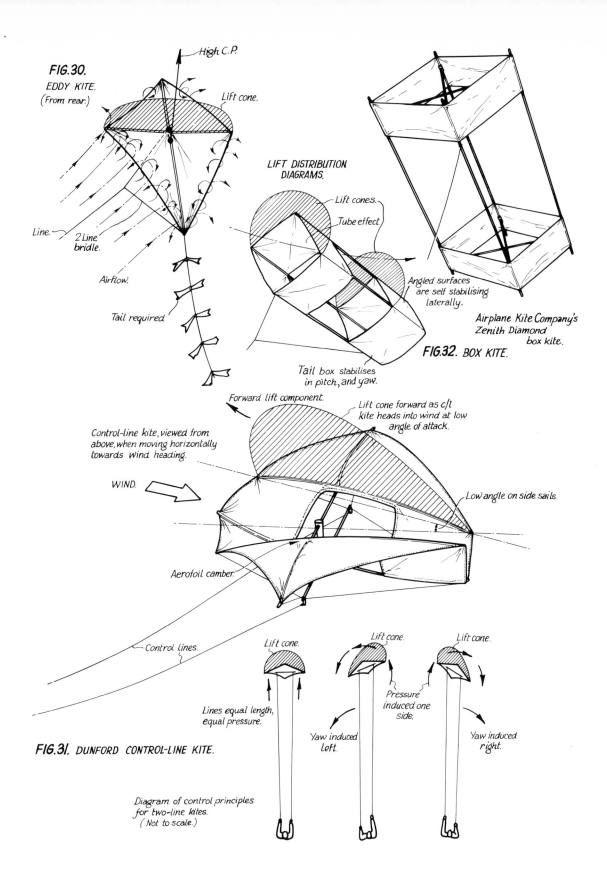

FIG.30.
EDDY KITE.
(From rear.)

High C.P.

Lift cone.

Line

2 Line bridle.

Airflow.

Tail required

LIFT DISTRIBUTION DIAGRAMS.

Lift cones.

Tube effect.

Angled surfaces are self stabilising laterally.

Airplane Kite Company's
Zenith Diamond
box kite.

FIG.32. BOX KITE.

Tail box stabilises in pitch, and yaw.

Forward lift component.

Lift cone forward as c/l kite heads into wind at low angle of attack.

Control-line kite, viewed from above, when moving horizontally towards wind heading.

WIND.

Low angle on side sails.

Aerofoil camber.

Control lines.

Lift cone.

Lines equal length, equal pressure.

Lift cone.

Pressure induced one side.

Yaw induced left.

Lift cone.

Yaw induced right.

FIG.31. DUNFORD CONTROL-LINE KITE.

Diagram of control principles for two-line kites.
(Not to scale.)

the wings (or lateral spar). It was introduced in the Eddy kite, and has been 'rediscovered' a thousand times since. All you have to do is apply a bow string between the tips and tie the string so that its tension 'bows' the lateral spar into a curve (Fig. 33), with the convex face towards the kite line. This has an important effect with regard to lateral stability.

If the kite is disturbed by being rolled over a little, the down-going side presents a greater area to the wind than the up-going side. The centre of pressure moves towards the down-going side with the result that a restoring rolling movement is produced.

A very similar effect may be introduced in the longitudinal direction by the introduction of negative camber (spar raised to front and rear), having much the same effect on longitudinal stability as the bridle. Because positive camber (spar lowered to front and rear) helps to produce lift it is preferable to retain it, although few kites (Brookite and Dunford 'Snipe' are two examples) make use of it.

Most modern commercial kites incorporate both dihedral and camber. Some kites are constructed so that the camber and dihedral are obtained by the bowing of the structure, owing to the tension of the covering or its string outline. These effects can produce pleasantly curvaceous surfaces which undoubtedly improve the aerodynamic performance and may help to smooth the higher pressure flow on the undersurface. This is particularly evident in non-porous plastic-

Wepa Eagle kite in full flight. Note the very wide spacing of bridle attachment points.

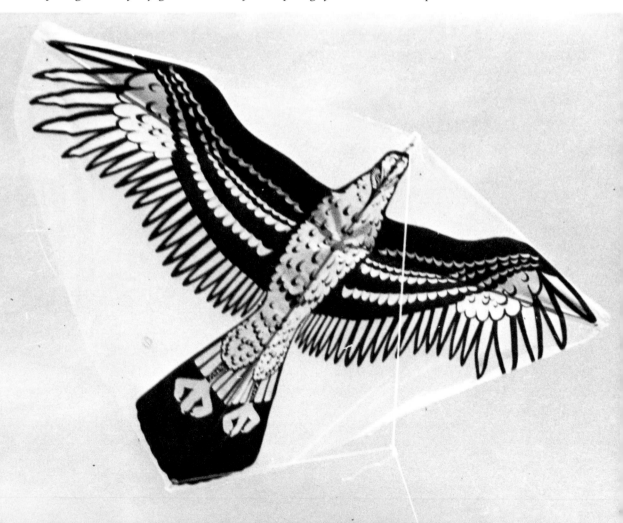

film-covered kites, such as the film-covered Rogallos and parafoils.

One brand of kite which utilises bow in both the longitudinal and lateral planes is the Blackhawk series by the Airplane Kite Company of Roswell, New Mexico. These use a cord round the outline, tightly tied to bow the two spars. There are cut-outs in the kite surface so that the remaining 'solid' area resembles the silhouette of a hawk, vampire bat, eagle etc., and these cut-outs, combined with the curvature, produce a kite design of extremely good stability which does not require a tail (Fig. 34).

Curvature in the form of the kite canopy can certainly be an improvement to whatever shape it adopts.

FLEXIBLE SHAPES

In the case of the Sled, or flexible half-bag kite, it has been shown that if the two longerons are curved outwards, the tension they apply to the flexible canopy ensures that the kite does not collapse when air pressure reduces on the underside.

Even the age-old Malay or Indian fighter has a curved lateral spar, and though this is flat as far as the diamond-shaped kite surface is concerned when static, it permits a controlled bow-curve under airflow pressure.

Some kite flyers have tried to compare the performance of various shapes with the sails of a yacht. Under certain conditions, with the wind abeam or from behind, there are similar-

Blackhawk in flight; the cut-out shape is braced by an outline cord.

ities, but that is all. The so-called Marconi Rig Kite (Fig. 35), attributed to a W. M. Angus in the 1940s, revived a sail-like arrangement first used by Reinhold Platz for his hang gliders in the 1920s. Platz was an aircraft designer for Fokker aeroplanes (but for whose designs Anthony Fokker gleaned the credit). Reinhold Platz initially made glider models, then a full-size, man-carrying slope soarer in which the pilot sat amidships controlling the angles of two horizontal planes rather like jib sails. The main source of lift was a back-to-front delta below the level of the jib sails (Fig. 36). By changing the pitch of these up or down, together or in opposite directions, Platz observed the effect of elevators or ailerons respectively, which are used today on all conventional aircraft.

What has come to be called the Marconi copies this idea in a kite. But it is very difficult to fly, and depends critically on an accurate centre-of-gravity position just forward of the mainsail leading edge. It makes a better glider than a kite, being suited to flying horizontally with high lift and low drag rather than beyond the stall in the region of lower lift and much higher drag, as a stalled kite. If you want to have fun with this rig, try it first in a paper model, cut from one piece of A4 with the fore-sails bent to an aerofoil and curved above the mainsail. It works well as a ground-effect (very low altitude, floor-hugging) machine – but this is not kiting!

KEELS

Another variation on the two-stick Eddy is the Keel kite (Fig. 37). This adds a second, vertical component to the main canopy, and 'fills in' the area of the bridle. Thus it does two useful jobs: it controls the airflow on to the under-side of the kite by bisecting it, and thus prevents turbulence where it is undesirable. It works very much like an aircraft wing fence, and it becomes a bridle in itself. This is a feature of the cloth Brookite, and has been so

Scalecraft Footballer sled kite with three vents; a long bridle is essential.

for almost the whole of this century despite many claims by others to originality. It still carries the traditional title of Cutter (Fig. 38).

OTHER SHAPES

Though there are many other variations of configuration, all that remains in this survey of the design and shape of kites is perhaps the oldest of all, the semi-flexible shaped kite. This ranges from the South American pap-agaios bird shapes to Chinese butterflies or profile aeroplanes – even clipper ships. In each, the main spar is the leading edge of the kite and what follows can be allowed to flap or 'luff' at will. Mostly they are for light wind forces of up to 15 knots (30 km/h), and are flown on shorter (150–250 ft/45–75 m) lines, because, after all, they are decorative and need

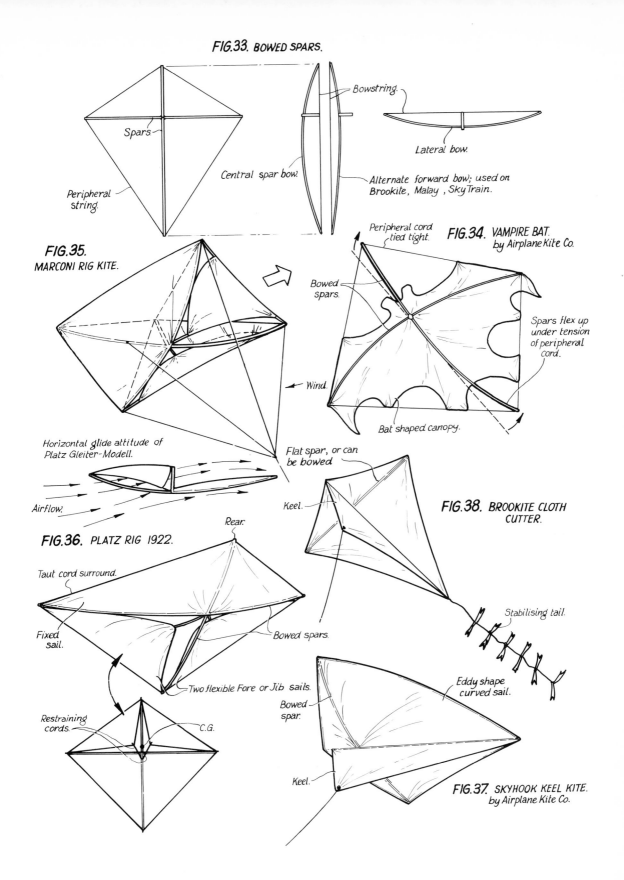

FIG.33. BOWED SPARS.

Bowstring.

Spars.

Lateral bow.

Peripheral string.

Central spar bow.

Alternate forward bow; used on Brookite, Malay, Sky Train.

FIG.35.
MARCONI RIG KITE.

Peripheral cord tied tight.

FIG.34. VAMPIRE BAT.
by Airplane Kite Co.

Bowed spars.

Spars flex up under tension of peripheral cord.

← Wind.

Bat shaped canopy.

Horizontal glide attitude of Platz Gleiter-Modell.

Airflow.

Flat spar, or can be bowed

Keel.

FIG.38. BROOKITE CLOTH CUTTER.

Rear.

FIG.36. PLATZ RIG 1922.

Taut cord surround.

Fixed sail.

Bowed spars.

Two flexible Fore or Jib sails.

Stabilising tail.

Eddy shape curved sail.

Bowed spar.

Restraining cords.

C.G.

Bowed spar.

Keel.

FIG.37. SKYHOOK KEEL KITE.
by Airplane Kite Co.

to be within reasonable range of vision to be appreciated. My favourite kite is one of these – a pure silk butterfly from China, exquisitely hand painted and made in finest cane with delicate bone joints that enable the whole assembly to pack away in a slipper case! It flies realistically, the wings flapping in the turbulent airflow, and has rotating 'eyes' in the antennae which add to the fun. My second favourite is the Squadron Kites' Sopwith Camel, which will stay up in the slightest breeze. This, like most other non-rigid, 'flapping' surface kites, depends on long-span, narrow-chord wings (high aspect ratio) where the effect of the stalled conditions and fluttering trailing edges demands good lateral stability.

SUMMARY

To sum up this discussion of design and shapes, there are six basic forms for the kite, each incorporating a family of differing shapes and many, of course, lending themselves to secondary uses as will be described in Chapter 4.

Rigid (solid-framed): Chinese/Japanese Shojo or Oniyocho figure painted; South Pacific grass fishing kites; bucket kites; Maori ceremonial kites.

Semi-rigid (cord-braced frame or tensioned cloth): Malayan/Indian fighters; Eddy; Peg top; Brazilian bird kites; Centipede; Bowed Blackhawk; Conyne; Cody; Brookite Master; Bermuda 3-stick; Guatemala ceremonial; Japanese Tsugaru or Sanjo, rectangular and hexagonal; wedge.

Flexible (stiffeners only): Allison Sled; Vented Scott; Zammo; Condor Magpie; Malayan Snake; Jalbert Parafoils; Scalecraft Ghost.

Semi-flexible (leading edge spars only): Chinese ornamental birds, insects; Squadron Kites aeroplanes, ships; Delta wings; Marconi rig; Synestructics' Air Scoops.

Cellular (composite cells): Hargrave boxes; Bell tetrahedrals; Brookite box.

Aerodynamic (cambered surface): Rogallo; Dunford control-line kite; Peter Powell Stunter; Glite; Cambridge; Frisbee Skite; Hargrave lifting surface; Rotakite; Gunther Deltaplan; Flexifoil.

THREE

Go Fly Your Kite

Of hundreds of thousands of commercial kites sold annually, remarkably few achieve a satisfactory performance at first handling. There are many reasons for this dismal result, but they fall under two headings: (a) flight attempted at an unsuitable site; (b) flyer does not understand basic kiting techniques. A crowded beach, nestling under cliffs or adjacent to tall buildings on a promenade, is no place to start kiting. Nor is a park, surrounded by tall trees or high-rise tenements (Fig. 39); or the corner of a farmer's field, just inside the five-bar gate in the lee of a row of trees. Get right out into the open.

Catch the wind where it is steady and strong, free of turbulence and clear-cut in its direction (Fig. 40). That is half the battle. The other half depends entirely on the flyer. Don't be hasty, give the kite a chance, and allow it to climb into clear air.

WIND

The energy for kite flight comes entirely from the wind. While there are some lightweight kites that will rise in calm air when the flyer applies tension on the line by pulling or running, there is always a limit to how far you can, or even want to, convert personal effort into this sort of flight.

Wind comes to us in varying directions by virtue of the 'Coriolis effect' as a result of changes in atmospheric pressure, which are now (thanks to those TV forecasters) familiar to everyone. Britain's maritime climate gives a broad selection throughout the year, ranging from periods of complete calm to the tempests of March and the chestnut scatterers of October. Throughout Europe, the end of June is generally poor for kiting, with winds of low velocity, while August gives a whole month of opportunity to take even the heaviest kite into the air. The vast American continent has such a range of weather patterns that it is impossible to generalise.

As long as there is reasonable wind strength, the kite should fly. Wind speed usually increases with altitude, and temperature decreases. These factors help a kite to support the weight and drag of the line as it is allowed to rise. Nature helps you, but you have to give her a chance, and the first step towards successful kite flight is selecting a site that is free of obstructions, and this means free of power lines too.

It may be all very well to walk round the block to a convenient patch of waste land, but if it is in the lee of buildings or trees, you are wasting your time. For a start, you will need at least 50 ft (15 m) of line paid out to achieve a reasonable first launch, and that alone defines the minimum area needed. If it were possible to launch a new kite in a small space we would all be flying from our back yards!

Of course, there are exceptions. The flat-roofed houses and terraces of some hillside housing estates enable the flyer to get above the immediate level of obstructions. But this assumes that there is a steady, gust-free prevailing wind. You need to live in Hong Kong to obtain such circumstances. So let's get back to the basics.

First, the suitable site. We already understand that it has to be free of obstruction and 'open'. This means *exposed* to wind, preferably on rising ground or on beach dunes where there are no buildings to break up the otherwise 'cleanest' of sea breezes (Fig. 41).

You do not have to be anti-social, nor will you have to travel very far. Every town has a suitable site, and all the kite flyer has to do is to take a little trouble in finding the free space.

It may be of interest to the reader to learn that Francis M. Rogallo, inventor of the kite shape which bears his name and who is synonymous with hang gliding, chose his retirement home at Kitty Hawk, North Carolina. It was on this long, narrow beach, standing off the US mainland and thus exposed to the Atlantic easterlies, that the Wright brothers made their kite, glider and first powered aircraft flights in 1903. Francis Rogallo certainly selected the finest of all sites for his kiting.

Trees offer an immediate assessment of wind strength over the critical initial launching height from ground level up to 75 ft (22·5 m). But, as we have already warned, they must not be close upwind. In any case you'll be looking at the lee side of the tree if it's on

Wepa Eagle (Dutch) flying with an onshore breeze against cliff behind. Note the sail form.

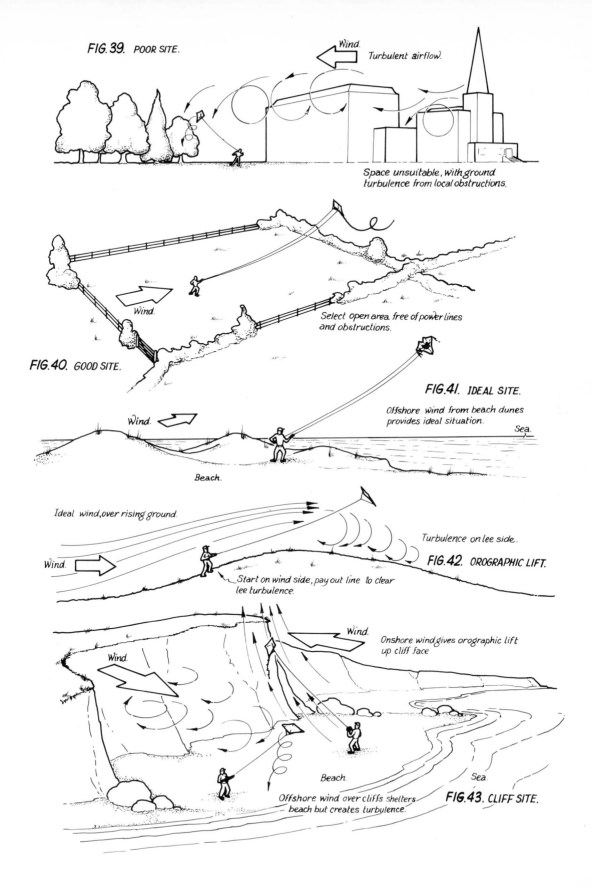

FIG. 39. POOR SITE.

Wind. Turbulent airflow.

Space unsuitable, with ground turbulence from local obstructions.

FIG.40. GOOD SITE.

Wind.

FIG.41. IDEAL SITE.

Select open area free of power lines and obstructions.

Offshore wind from beach dunes provides ideal situation.

Wind.

Sea.

Beach.

Ideal wind, over rising ground.

Turbulence on lee side.

Wind.

FIG.42. OROGRAPHIC LIFT.

Start on wind side, pay out line to clear lee turbulence.

Wind.

Onshore wind gives orographic lift up cliff face

Wind.

Beach.

Sea.

Offshore wind over cliffs shelters beach but creates turbulence.

FIG.43. CLIFF SITE.

the windward side of you. Study trees (which should be at least 250 ft (75 m) away) which are in the direct flight path downwind. Watch the top branches. If they are swaying steadily, then everything is fine. If they are almost stationary, with movement showing intermittently, then the wind is too light for sure success. On the other hand, if the top branches look as though they are hanging on for dear life, it is obviously over-strong for pleasant flying. When the leaves are turning and showing their undersides all over the tree, you have ideal conditions for the first launch. The actual wind speeds we seek are 10–15 mph (16–24 km/h) at ground level. Kites are flown in winds up to 30 mph (48 km/h) or in as little as 3–5 mph (5–8 km/h), but these speeds, higher or lower than desirable, call for expertise and experience.

If, on an open slope, there is a natural speeding up of the airflow as the ground rises (Fig. 42), the wind is deflected and gives what is known as orographic lift. This is the upward wave of air that gliders, model and full-size, employ for 'slope-soaring' and which permits safe hang-glider activity with Rogallo-shaped sail wings. The strongest orographic lift is obtained at cliff sites with an onshore wind (Fig. 43).

Another excellent indication of wind speed is chimney smoke. Though less easy to see, thanks to the laws on air pollution, and mostly applicable to winter months as far as domestic fires are concerned, a chimney smokestream is ideal in view of its height and freedom from turbulence.

Meteorological forecasts give wind speeds to be expected and these are given for a height of 33 ft (10 m) above ground. Actual speed will vary not only with altitudes (up to 20 mph (32 km/h) faster at 200 ft (60 m), but over half this difference at 33 ft (10 m)), but also with local terrain (Fig. 44).

Having established that there is wind, and

WIND STRENGTH

Beaufort scale	Wind speed (mph*)	Description	Visible effect
0	Under 1	Calm	Smoke rises
1	2	Light air	Smoke drifts
2	5	Light breeze	Leaves rustle
3	10	Gentle breeze	Leaves move
4	15	Moderate breeze	Branches move
5	21	Fresh breeze	Small trees sway
6	28	Strong breeze	Large branches move
7	35	Moderate gale	Trees move
8	42	Fresh gale	Twigs break
9	50	Strong gale	Branches break
10	59	Whole gale	Trees fall
11	69	Storm	Violent blasts
12	75 +	Hurricane	Structures shake

* 1 mile = 1·6 kilometres

Brookite Box Kite – checking bridle attachment angles before flight.

located an open area which is suitable, the next stage is to understand kiting techniques.

ASSEMBLING THE KITE

Whichever kite you have selected, it must be collapsible. One of the pleasures of kiting is that you can so easily carry a kite in a roll little bigger than an umbrella. This also means that it has to be reassembled on site in the correct manner.

Study the assembly carefully before leaving home. Ignore the dictum 'when all else fails, consult the instructions'. Ensure that the bridle points are firmly tied and ready for use at the field. Double-check that you have all the parts, and a few extras such as Sellotape, cord, even a tube of quick-setting glue, Plasticine, and, of course, the tow line.

SAFETY

At the site you have one more very important matter to remember – to observe a commonsense safety code.

Damp kite lines can conduct electricity, so always avoid flying in stormy weather, or close to power lines. Check that you are sufficiently upwind to clear housing, roads, railways, even motorways, if the kite collapses when all the line is paid out. See that the area immediately downwind is clear of people. This is especially important when flying a two-line controlled kite for the first time.

THE LAW

You may also wonder why, when you buy a commercial kite in Britain, the length of line is usually limited to 200 ft (60 m). There is a good reason. Article 67(a) of the Air Navigation Order reads: '[within the United Kingdom] a captive balloon or kite shall not be flown at a height of more than 60 metres [200 ft] above the ground level or within 60 metres [200 ft] of any vessel, vehicle or structure.' Section (d) of the same Article reads: 'a kite shall not be flown within 5 kilometres [3 miles] of an aerodrome'. Article 93(b) states under the heading of 'Small Aircraft' that the provisions of the Order do not apply to any kite weighing not more than 2 kg [4·4 lb], other than Article 67(a) and Article 44. In other words, the small kite is generally exempt from the requirements of the Air Navigation Order except for Articles 67 and 44 which are directly restrictive. If the kite weighs more than 2 kg (4·4 lb) it has to comply with the rules of the air as observed by airline pilots. In fact, even if the kite weighs only a matter of ounces, it would be both foolish and hazardous to contravene the height limit within range of an aerodrome, or near to regular airlanes.

In the early 1950s a chilling incident took place over Hyde Park, London, when one of the Croydon-based De Havilland Dragon

Rapide sightseeing flights collided with a kite line at over a thousand feet. The kite was drawn into the aircraft rigging before the line snapped. Luckily, the line remained clear of the airscrews and the aircraft returned safely. More recently, a London police helicopter reported a kite at a higher level than itself over Hampstead. A radio-car traced the kite flyer, and the twist to the tale is that both the police-car driver and the helicopter pilot bought a kite from the operator!

I have yet to learn of any prosecutions, but there have been warnings. So the kite flyer is not in any way exempted by having a kite of less than 2 kg (4·4 lb). Article 44 of the Air Navigation Order states that: 'A person shall not wilfully or negligently cause or permit an aircraft (kite) to endanger any person or property', which is an open clause, calculated to close loopholes.

It is plain commonsense to respect the height limit, and in my experience, pointless to fly higher if you really want to see what is happening to the kite.

Aside from the laws of the air, there may be a local by-law affecting kite flying on public grounds, which include beaches. It is extremely rare, but local authorities have managed to obtain Home Office approval for restrictive by-laws concerning model aircraft flying, and the same attitudes sometimes apply to kites. Park notice boards are notoriously difficult to read, so in case of doubt apply to the local authorities for a copy of the by-laws applicable to parks and recreation grounds in your district. Remember – if these by-laws make no mention of kites, no restriction applies. If a local authority in Britain bans an activity which is well established on a site, it has to make an alternative site available for continuance of that activity elsewhere.

LINE

It is extremely difficult to lay down specific recommendations for line, because so many variables arise in the size and weight of the kite, and the wind strength in which it will fly best. Generally the rule is: the lighter the kite, the lighter the line. Don't expect a small plastic kite to soar if linked to a length of common string or, conversely, for it to remain tethered on a cotton line. Commonsense should prevail. For small kites a 10-lb (4·5-kg) monofilament fishing line is adequate, but beware of line burns! Use braided nylon line or flax line of up to 100-lb (45-kg) strain for larger kites, especially if joining two or more control lines together. A nearby source for line is the ironmonger's, where several grades of braided cord are sold for Venetian blinds or picture cords. The most economic means of purchase is to buy a 'cop' from one of the kite specialist shops. It is most important to seal the knot in any nylon line. The heat of a match is enough to fuse the strands and prevent the knot slipping. Nylon has the advantage of remaining constant in damp weather, it dries quickly, and is durable though stretchy. Some manufacturers do not advise it, both for the last reason and because it can cut or burn if allowed to pass through the fingers rapidly. The moral is: always wear gloves.

LAUNCHING

Aware of the need for safety, and, with the aid of a helper, the kite properly assembled, we are now ready for the first launch. Pay out about 50 ft (15 m) of line and clip or tie the end to the bridle point.

It is best to have a strong – 50-lb (22·5-kg) or 100-lb (45-kg) strain – fishing line swivel and snap clip on the end of the line, and a brass (not plastic) ring on the bridle. The hook-up is then a matter of seconds. An alternative is to make a loop on the end of the line and, still using a brass ring on the bridle, use the well-established link of 'loop through the ring, ring through the loop' to make a quick detachable knot. Whichever method you adopt, be sure the hook-up is strong.

If the kite needs a tail, lay it out in front of your helper. Then lift the kite so that it is sloping forward a few degrees into wind and ensure that the bridle is free of tangles and as designed.

The line must be within a few degrees of the checked wind direction. Precise alignment is not needed, because once airborne the kite will quickly sort itself out. You may be surprised that what seems to be the downwind direction for the launch does not agree with the line of flight when airborne. This is a function of the wind gradient. The most classic case of directional change was observed in the USA when two famous kite flyers found themselves with crossed lines and the kites flying at exactly opposite angles! Widely quoted, this experience stretches the imagination, but it is a fact that in coastal areas opposing winds meet in a vertical sheer. This is a hazard that has affected airports such as Newark, New Jersey, and Prestwick in Scotland.

But to return to our launch. You, the flyer, have the line reel; the helper is holding the kite. When you can feel a steady breeze on your back, pull the line steadily and call for the helper to release.

There are all sorts of releases. Kites need a smooth, upward and forward swing of the arms. *Not* a throw, or a drop – simply a gentle cast-off.

The flyer will be rewarded with either an upward arcing sweep of the kite to about a 60°

Brookite Master Kite poised for self launch, with the bridle held high.

line angle, or a frustrating pitch over to one side or the other as soon as the kite gains air speed. Try again. And again. Persistence is required to establish whether this diving and crashing is due to low-level turbulence or a bad bridle arrangement (Fig. 45).

If the pitch-over persists, put a small 'tuck' into the front leg of the bridle to shorten it. The effect of this will be to bring the bridle centre forward and decrease the angle of the kite (Fig. 46). Try again. And again. Is it still pitching without any sign of improvement? A lot depends on the shape of the kite, but generally such an adjustment works by taking the centre of pressure forward, which helps to get the kite up quickly and into the undisturbed free air (Fig. 47).

If the hitch in the front bridle does not work, release it and try another hitch in the rear leg of the bridle. In the case of light wind, this hitch is often required to increase the angle of flight, but you are unlikely to be testing unless there is a reasonable wind.

If the bridle-hitch idea fails, the kite must have faults in its symmetry. Check if it is evenly balanced laterally. Add Plasticine to one side if the other is obviously heavier. If it is a two-stick Malayan kite, bow the lateral with cord from tip to tip, so that it has dihedral (tips lifted). If the instability persists, add a tail, which in an emergency can be a handkerchief or a length of cord (Fig. 48). The effect of this is to shift the centre of drag lower and move the centre of gravity aft. By so doing you develop a kite that is steady but as unexciting as a flying barn door. It is better by far to have a kite that twitches when low, for it will respond beautifully to control when in full flight.

FLIGHT

Now that we're airborne, the kite is pulling on 50 ft (15 m) and anxious to go higher. If it isn't, possibly the wind is too light, or the line too heavy for the kite surface area. Cloth kites

Brookite Cutter Kite. Cloth traditional kite, in production for over sixty years, in full flight over flat ground.

need stronger winds than those with sheet plastic surfaces. Box kites need lots and lots of wind. Paper kites need light line – even carpet thread. Big kites need a 'tug of war' technique to see-saw them up into the levels where the wind is stronger.

Manipulation of the line is everything, and a Malaysian, Indian or any other nationality of kite flyer working on the reel is a marvellous sight. Before we get to their exotic heights, we will try to keep our own kite in the air, and on a simple spool of line.

Hold the main reel, spool or whatever, in

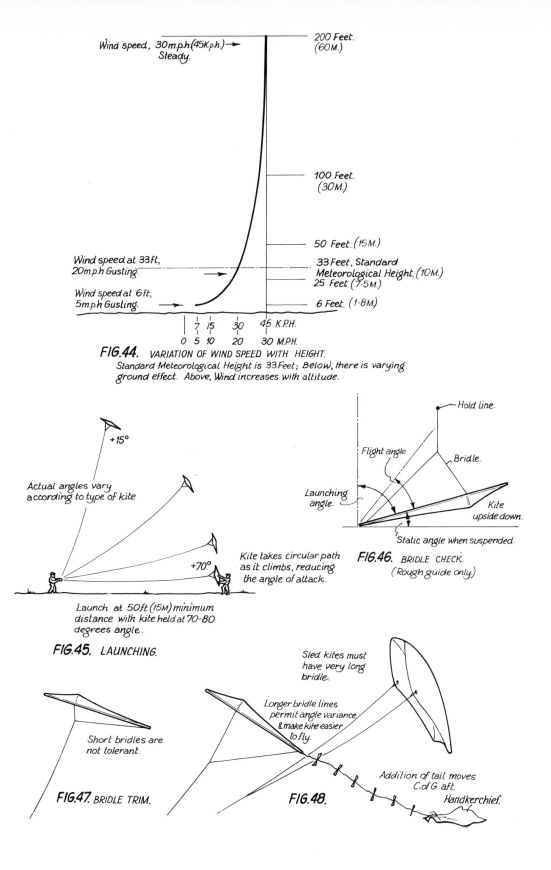

Wind speed, 30 m.p.h (45 K.p.h.) →
Steady.

200 Feet.
(60M.)

100 Feet.
(30M.)

50 Feet. (15M.)

Wind speed at 33 ft,
20 m.p.h Gusting.

33 Feet, Standard
Meteorological Height. (10M.)
25 Feet. (7.5M.)

Wind speed at 6 ft,
5 m.p.h Gusting.

6 Feet. (1.8M.)

| | 7 | 15 | 30 | 45 K.P.H. |
| 0 | 5 10 | 20 | 30 M.P.H |

FIG.44. VARIATION OF WIND SPEED WITH HEIGHT.
Standard Meteorological Height is 33 Feet; Below, there is varying
ground effect. Above, Wind increases with altitude.

+15°

Actual angles vary
according to type of kite

+70°

Kite takes circular path
as it climbs, reducing
the angle of attack.

Launch at 50 ft (15M) minimum
distance with kite held at 70-80
degrees angle.

FIG.45. LAUNCHING.

Hold line.

Flight angle.

Bridle.

Launching
angle.

Kite
upside down.

Static angle when suspended.

FIG.46. BRIDLE CHECK.
(Rough guide only.)

Short bridles are
not tolerant.

FIG.47. BRIDLE TRIM.

Sled kites must
have very long
bridle.

Longer bridle lines
permit angle variance
& make kite easier
to fly.

Addition of tail moves
C. of G. aft.

Handkerchief.

FIG.48.

DOs	DON'Ts
Fly safely; avoid people.	Fly near high-tension wires.
Wear gloves – nylon burns.	Leave discarded line on the field.
Use a reel and line clip.	Fly too high.
Choose a clear area.	Cross lines with other kites.
Liaise with your helper.	Drop heavy messenger devices.
Make friends with other kiters.	Give up trying when all seems lost.

FAULTS	CURES
Kite will not rise.	Not enough wind, or on wrong site.
Kite pitches over sideways without rising.	Shorten rear bridle, add tail.
Kite twitches, is unstable when in the air.	Curve bow in boom(s).
Kite loops on line when in flight.	Lengthen bridle lines, add tail.
Kite pulls to one side.	Check balance, add weight to light tip.
Kite pitches over and dives forward.	Lengthen front bridle and bring bridle/line attachment forward.

one hand and take up the line in the other. Let the line out steadily, paying out with the free hand as the tension is maintained. The object is to gain altitude and then, when all but a few feet are left on the spool, you can start to relax and have fun.

Let's assume the kite is pulling very steadily, bobbing and weaving but generally holding position. This is just right for trying a trick. Let go of about 10 ft (3 m) of line. A manoeuvrable kite will dip to the right or left, and circle. When it is pointing up, or to one side, take up the slack quickly. The kite ought to recover swiftly and, especially if it's a diamond (Asiatic) type, it will move off in the direction it points to, until it reaches a zenith. Let go more slack, and tweak it again to move elsewhere. Fascinating! But not easy. It takes practice and a degree of patience to master the technique. Expert flyers pay the line out over a finger with the lightest touch. The reel is tumbled like a horizontal cocktail shaker, and line paid out or taken up by an action that resembles someone shaking a tombola drum. A pull to the right or left, and the kite follows with amazing dexterity.

The majority of kites sold in Britain are not suitable for such sky dancing, the exceptions being the control-line kites of which more can be read in Chapter 5. But the first kite we are most likely to be flying in this exercise is one of the decorated plastic diamond shape, with either Rogallo section or two-stick Eddy construction.

It will still respond to the paying-out manoeuvre, and will recover easily when the line is pulled tight again. But it is unlikely to hold a sideways heading. Getting the best performance out of the plastic-film kite is largely a matter of ensuring that it is going to hold its shape (i.e. not fold up), getting it to accept fun devices such as messengers, other kites in train, long streamer tails, etc., and transferring the line onto a quickly wound reel or handle for convenience.

Cloth kites have an entirely different 'feel'

about them which some flyers refer to as 'majestic'. In general they are much heavier, have porous covering and need a larger surface area. They last considerably longer than other kites and, once aloft, are rock-steady through the higher wind speeds. Most of the fun comes in holding their altitude. Experts in London's Kensington Gardens despise anything not made with cloth covering. They demonstrate their ability by operating from a regular spot near the famous Round Pond and never moving from there. All the control through launching to touchdown is effected by large (about 9-in./23-cm diameter) reels which are gripped by one arm while the other hand winds in or out. To run would be

sacrilegious, and to have a kite fall into the pond or trees is a disgrace! With cloth, the kite adopts a shape and form, as well as variety in colour, that few plastics have even tried to match. The only fly in the ointment is that the heavier loading of the cloth kite inevitably means that one has to get it up quickly into the stronger wind levels.

Longer line paid out before launch (about 75–100 ft/20–30 m), and if you haven't a Kensington Gardens style reel, a quick run into the wind to tow the kite aloft, is the best way to ensure good performance. When it comes to carrying weights, messengers, cameras etc., the cloth kite has few peers – as we shall see in the next chapter.

FOUR

Fun with Kites

A kite that is rock-steady, flies as high as one wishes and remains passive even in gusty wind conditions is unlikely to satisfy unless (a) you made it yourself – in which case regard it as a remarkable success; or (b) your kiting is of the short-term variety – a few moments while walking the dog, so that reliability is your main requirement.

Most kite flyers like to feel that they have a measure of control over their kites, and seek ways in which they can exploit their load-carrying or manoeuvrable characteristics.

FISHING

We have already mentioned the Polynesian technique of fishing by kite line. What may not be generally realised is that kite fishing is a regular and accepted practice, using modern designs.

E. R. (Bob) Lewis of Florida patented his Pompanette fishing kite (US 3314630) and sells a square-shaped Lewis fishing kite in three types for light, medium or heavy winds. With the kite you can purchase a collapsible rod, mahogany reel and 60-lb (27-kg) strain Dacron line. As the kite has to withstand dunking in sea water the collapsible frame is made from glassfibre and the fabric is porous. Lewis says that there is no better way to present live bait than with a kite. The method he uses is to extend the kite line out from a boat or shoreline position, and attach the fishing line

from a separate fishing rod to a point on the kite line where it will not affect stability. The square kite flies 'on edge' as a diamond and is stable in typical sea breezes. But it does not fly high. The extra weight of the fishing line attached to the kite line up to 50 ft (15 m) or so from the kite keeps the lines low.

The fishing line attachment is automatically disengaged when a fish takes the bait or when the angler strikes. A simple, wooden clothes peg with a wire spring can be used for experiment. Clip the peg to the kite line and pass the fishing line through an eyelet which in turn is passed between the spring clip jaws of the clothes peg. On striking, a caught fish will jerk both fishing line and the running eyelet from the peg jaws, and the fisherman can play the fish on the separated line.

Anglers will readily appreciate the advantages of being able to place bait in a good area, especially one which is well outside normal casting range. It depends on one's kind of fishing, but the possibilities seem limitless – why not use this method for lakeside fishing? The Eddystone lighthouse keeper uses similar techniques to 'catch' his mail!

Variations on the techniques, apart from the playing out or pulling in either or both lines in the Lewis system for positioning, are considerable (Fig. 49).

Japanese fishermen are said to be able to combine the purpose of both fishing line and kite line into one (though exactly how I do not

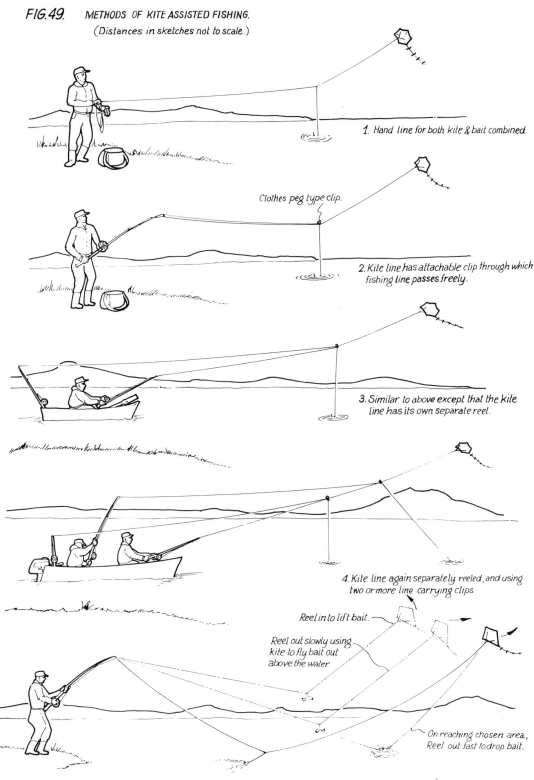

FIG. 49. METHODS OF KITE ASSISTED FISHING.
(Distances in sketches not to scale.)

1. Hand line for both kite & bait combined.

Clothes peg type clip.

2. Kite line has attachable clip through which fishing line passes freely.

3. Similar to above except that the kite line has its own separate reel.

4. Kite line again separately reeled, and using two or more line carrying clips.

Reel in to lift bait.

Reel out slowly using kite to fly bait out above the water.

On reaching chosen area, Reel out fast to drop bait.

By adjustment of reeling speed to kite/wind speed, the kite can be used to draw the bait through the water.

know) and obviously there is potential in the use of a control-line kite such as the Dunford, which will be discussed in more detail later.

The fishing kite of southern California is long-established though little-used today. George Farnsworth of the Tuna Club was the originator. He was one of many big-game fishermen who found that the tuna was hard to strike on a conventional rod and line with lure or bait. In 1909 he invented a kite to help catch the bluefin tuna and the device was so successful that he made all his associates swear on oath they they would not divulge his secret technique. Eventually, when his performance as a tuna prize fisherman grew to tremendous proportions, he gave the game away by returning to Avalon Harbour with one of his kites trailing.

Even then, many people refused to accept that a kite could aid fishing, and when others tried to copy with paper kites, they were unsuccessful.

Farnsworth's fishing kite was a 'barn-door' shape. That is to say a 28 × 36 in. (71 × 91 cm) rectangle with the corners cut off the upper edge and a 4-in. (10-cm) wide cloth tail fitted to a bridle at the base. The tail was made up of one to four sections, each 72 ins (2 m) long, the length varying according to wind strength. The kite line carried a breakaway line which trailed from a point 50–100 ft (15–30 m) from the bridle; the other end of the breakaway held the fishing line. When a strike was made, this line detached or was snapped. When using flying fish as the bait, the tactic was to play the kite and the fishing line so that the lure skipped from wave to wave, jumping up to 12 ft (3·5 m) in the air. Leaping tuna could hardly resist the temptation. Such kites were called Tunaplanes and, as all kite flyers will appreciate, their success was dependent on the skills of two line operators plus the boat helmsman. So it is not surprising that Farnsworth's well-developed technique did

This photograph, engineered by H. J. Taplin in the 1930s, was taken from a kite at approximately 400 ft (120 m).

A train of six Glites linked by parallel bridles and connected to control lines for formation aerobatics.

not come easily to others.

If we are to adapt later experience to advantage, the parafoil appears to be the perfect carrier for a fishing line. It has enormous load-carrying capacity and could support more than one fishing line easily.

PHOTOGRAPHY

The parafoil also has particularly useful applications in aerial photography. There is nothing new in the idea; George E. Henshaw sent up a plate camera 500 ft (150 m) above New York in 1895. He used a separate shutter trip line and had to employ heavy (and breakable) glass plates. So did Gilbert Woglom, who also photographed New York. With the invention of film, and much lighter equipment, aerial photography by kite became a popular pastime in the early 1920s. One pioneer of the process was H. J. Taplin who surveyed the north Kent coast towns of Birchington and Herne Bay. Colonel Taplin was a most inventive man, and apart from his

airborne camera he created many impressive ideas, from an automatic pilot for aircraft to a range of small diesel engines for models. His camera was made of wood, and a timer operated the shutter.

Modern cameras have automatic wind-on features, and it is possible to control them remotely, by radio. The only cautions that have to be exercised are to ensure (a) that the load is securely retained, (b) that the shutter speed is fast enough to cope with motion, (c) that the photography does not represent an intrusion into other people's privacy, and (d) if remotely controlled by radio, that the appropriate transmitting licence is held.

KITE TRAINS

Flying kites in tandem is great fun. There are two basic methods of hooking up the train, and the choice depends largely on the type of bridle used.

All keel kites, or those with three-leg bridles, are best connected using the method employed by Gilbert Woglom way back in

53

1895 in New York. Treat each kite as if it were on a separate line and tie each line to the next, about 20 ft (6 m) from the kite below. If the kite is a twin bridle, or even a single point line kite such as the North Pacific Glite, it is better to tie each line to the bridle centre point of the kite below. In other words, link the kites bridle-to-bridle through the chain. An advantage of this is that the train angle becomes steeper and lines do not interfere with each other.

Using the Glite, it is possible to get half a dozen different printed patterns and to have a line-up of very impressive Rogallo-shaped flyers.

At the time of writing, Brookite are the only manufacturers to produce a special kite train. Theirs is a triple Malay kite system with porous cloth covering, and for stability the kites have positive bow in each of the spars. The shape is the traditional two-stick Malay or Eddy, but the centre-line curve is downward. These kites have a distinctly different look, and because they are very stable and well tested by the largest established firm in the business they are to be recommended.

Kite trains were always used by meteorologists, even as far back as 1750, and were also used for man-carrying experiments by Cody and his contemporaries at the beginning of the twentieth century. You must take care in positioning the spacing. If too close, there will be oscillation because wind flow is blanketed. If too far apart, remember the wind-speed variation with height and that the higher kites will have stronger winds to contend with. The pull on the line is not the total of that expected from the combined individual kites; but it is still considerable. The line-breaking strain for the lower kites in a lengthy multiple train must be capable of withstanding several times the pull of a single kite.

Joining Eddy kites with parallel lines from the bridle points at spar crossing and rear, point-to-point, is the method advised if spacing of about 10 ft (3 m) apart is wanted. This follows the style of the Chinese Cen-tipede, where close spacing is controlled by a continuous quadruple bridle, and the formation aerobatic kites by Peter Powell, and Tom Chapman of Mettoy as described in Chapter 5. The longest recorded Centipede is 300 ft (92 m), by T. Hiroi. Centipedes 750 ft (225 m) long are said to have been flown in China.

The length of the kite train is restricted only by the time taken to tie on the linking lines. A leading exponent is Bill Bigge of the Maryland (USA) Kite Society. He has made several attempts at breaking world records for the number of kites on one line. In October 1974 he sent up 261, which was over 50 better than the number achieved by G. Kudo of Japan, but a long way short of Bill's aim to put up 1,000. His kites are small and are kept in a container with pre-tied line for uninterrupted launching. They are a beautiful sight when airborne, though one is tempted to ask if so many miniatures have the same appeal as a mixed train.

Using a steady 'pilot' kite it is possible to have a whole mixture of shapes in a train. Given good wind, a large box kite can lead a selection of others, each on an individual line which is linked to the line of the kite below. A separation of 100 ft (30 m) is advised, and twisted nylon line should be avoided as it has a habit of twirling itself into horrible knots because of the inevitable rotation of the lines. If anything in kite flying is calculated to annoy, it is the tangling of multiple lines. Apart from the obvious precaution of keeping lines apart, it pays to be careful in selecting the line material. Braided nylon burns when it is allowed to slip through bare fingers, and knots should be heat-sealed to prevent slippage. A touch with a soldering iron on the knot will secure the join by welding the nylon as it melts.

MINI-KITES

It is possible to make a kite so small and light

Bill Bigge with an indoor miniature kite at Lakehurst Airship Base, New Jersey.

At the opposite end of the scale are the maxi-kites, of which surely the biggest was the 1,440-sq ft (134-m²) monster flown by the Otako group of Yokaichi City. Hardly for indoors!

MUSICAL KITES

Wind music is a tradition of the East. For centuries the Chinese have employed vibrating reeds and wind-driven cups which beat bamboo sticks and drums in their kites, but the technique has not been adopted widely. There is scope for development here, but you would first need to study the types of paper material used as membranes on the tin kazoo instruments which children buy. Air pressure over the reed has to be high but the problem is not insurmountable. You could also use the tinkling chimes sold by Eastern emporiums for pendant decorations in the house. If the dangling pieces of fine glass and metal could be prevented from tangling, this kind of music would be fascinating.

MESSENGERS

If you have a line up to the sky, why not make use of it? 'Messenger' is a collective term for devices which can run up the line, release objects at a predetermined height and then slide back down the line to be reloaded. The term originates from the purpose of sending a message aloft, to be dropped off at a distance.

Another idea is the fixed carrier which is suspended close to the kite and has a delayed-action release by means of a clockwork timer. These releases are sold in small numbers and use timers made for cameras (Autoknips) or model aeroplanes (Graupner, KSB or Tatone). They have one advantage in that the precise moment of release can be determined by setting the delayed-release dial; but weighed against this is the need to send the whole unit aloft with the kite, and once only per flight.

Commercial messengers are surprisingly

that it will fly indoors! A miniature Eddy, covered with condenser tissue, can be lifted by a fan and will lift from corner to corner of an ordinary room. The fan in a convector heater is sufficient – preferably without the heat bar switched on. Balsa wood spars should be 4 ins (10 cm) and 5 ins (12 cm) long. Bill Bigge makes even smaller Eddy kites, covers them with microfilm and tows them around his head as he sits still! Microfilm is model aeroplane 'dope' which has been poured onto the surface of water and scooped off on a frame. It is the lightest form of skin covering you can make.

In Japan, the mini-kite is more a work of art. Measuring only 4 × 2 ins (10 × 5 cm), they are scaled-down Suruga or Edo types, each with the traditional painted image of a Kabuki actor's head in brilliant colour. Yet they fly, it is said, on human hair lines, and over the thermal convection of a charcoal brazier.

rare. In fact, only one recommendable device exists in Europe, the Paul Gunther Ferry. It operates on the same principle as the home-constructed types in the sketches, but it can easily be adapted to carry a model glider or to drop parachutes. The manufacturers appear to have intended the Ferry just to go up and down the line.

The principle is that the messenger hooks over the line. It is infinitely advantageous if it can be detached from the line: but of course it has to be held to the line in such a way that it will not fall off. It is also better in action if it

has two pulleys for easy running on the line (Fig. 50). To move it up, it has a sail which will be set to collect wind pressure. Hanging vertically from the messenger, it is at right angles to the line. Some parachute droppers use the parachute itself as a sail (Fig. 51). Along the body of the messenger there will be a moving rod, one end of which engages a release catch, the other end being bent as a striker which projects ahead of the messenger. On the line, near the kite, there has to be a stop. This can be a piece of tubing with a cork in it to plug the centre and so lock on the line,

Gunther Ferry, arranged to sail up line with wings extended.

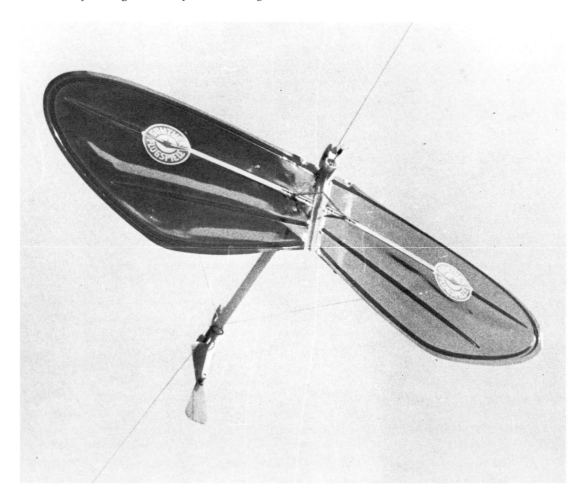

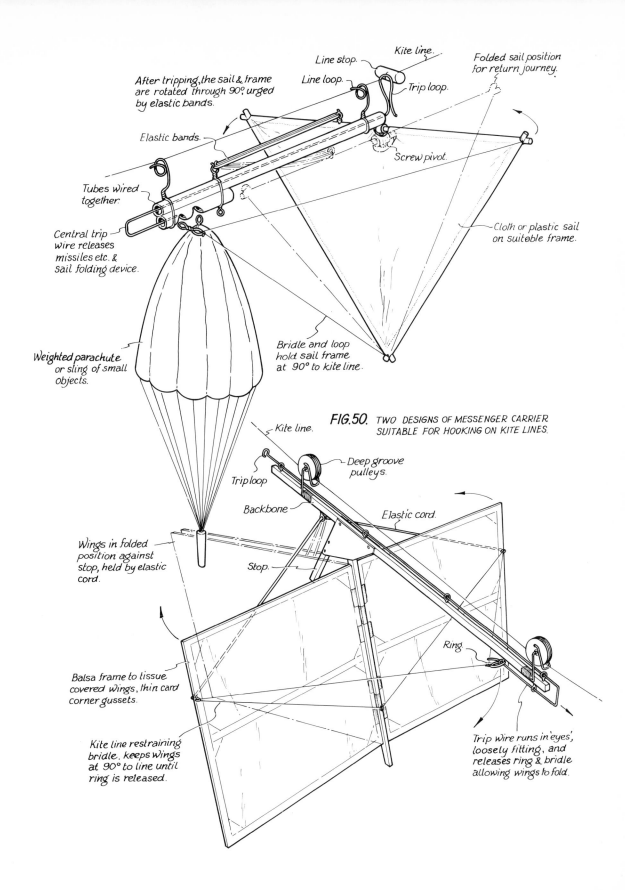

Line stop.

Kite line.

Line loop.

Trip loop.

Folded sail position for return journey.

After tripping, the sail & frame are rotated through 90°, urged by elastic bands.

Elastic bands.

Screw pivot.

Tubes wired together.

Cloth or plastic sail on suitable frame.

Central trip wire releases missiles etc. & Sail folding device.

Weighted parachute or sling of small objects.

Bridle and loop hold sail frame at 90° to kite line.

FIG.50. TWO DESIGNS OF MESSENGER CARRIER SUITABLE FOR HOOKING ON KITE LINES.

Kite line.

Deep groove pulleys.

Trip loop

Backbone

Elastic cord.

Wings in folded position against stop, held by elastic cord.

Stop.

Ring.

Balsa frame to tissue covered wings, thin card corner gussets.

Kite line restraining bridle, keeps wings at 90° to line until ring is released.

Trip wire runs in 'eyes', loosely fitting, and releases ring & bridle allowing wings to fold.

or it can be a short stick (dowel) tied on to the line. When the striker hits this stop, the body of the messenger carries on and the release is effected.

There are many ways of making the sails collapse. In the Ferry, they are tensioned to fold back by a rubber band. In others the sail flips back into line with the kite line, but, whatever happens, it must fold up or reduce its area to such an extent that the messenger can drop back to the flyer, against the wind pressure, with gravity.

One messenger design actually incorporates a mousetrap! This early messenger is illustrated (Fig. 51) because it is one of the most positive in action.

There is only one snag to the messenger and that is the simple fact that if there is enough wind for the kite, and thus for the messenger, the drift of whatever is dropped will be at that same wind speed over the ground. The messenger recovery team must be prepared to walk! Parachutes and gliders have a knack of soaring in the thermal currents when released at 200 ft (60 m) – model glider towlines are 164 ft (50 m) long – and this all adds to the fun.

BANNERS

The sight of the Old Glory flying high over New York in 1895 must have started the craze for banner flying which has never faded. There's a certain pleasure to be gleaned from seeing the national flag streaming at height. And when, at distance, there is no visible means of support, the flag-flying ceremony becomes quite mysterious. Banners have to be so arranged that they do not wind up and become a tangled mess. Flags can be attached to the line so that they trail in the normal way. Long banners are often best braced with a strip of bamboo or dowel across each end, and then attached by a long bridle to the base of the kite if using a flexible sled shape or parafoil. Flags also trail well behind a box kite, but the bridled banner is not suited to hang on to the

Malay or Eddy. A very simple and fun-creating idea is to get party streamers, and tie a loop in crêpe paper round the line when the kite is well up. The streamer gradually works its way up the line. Send up a series of different colours, and you will have a very long tassel aloft.

NIGHT FLYING

Given reasonably good conditions, and subject to safety requirements, flying a kite at night can be a lot of fun, especially if the kite is highlighted by a small flasher bulb powered by a Pencell battery. Beware the alarmists who will claim they have sighted a UFO, or those of nervous disposition who will claim visitations from above. The night kite can also be used for one of its original purposes – that of lifting a receiver aerial. For short-wave radio enthusiasts this gives an opportunity to pick up distant transmissions.

Reflective Mylar or Melinex dragon kites can make very strange shapes in a moonlit sky. The mirror effect of the plastic is often more apparent under these conditions than in daylight. Just the thing for a warm but breezy summer evening! I hesitate, however, to suggest the Chinese habit of sending fireworks up at night time. Aerial firecrackers could be disconcerting.

FIGHTING

The diamond-shape fighting kite is flown all over the Far East. It is a remarkably alert type, capable of being controlled to move left, right, up or down, and is extraordinarily simple to make. Small, usually 12–18 ins (30–45 cm) square, it is flown on a light line up to about 300 ft (90 m) on the reel and never needs a tail or the Eddy bow spar (Fig. 52). It is flat, flies fast and furious, and is, for most Westerners, a difficult kite to fly. The bridle is a two-point type, usually fixed at the cross point of the spars and at one hand's span towards the rear.

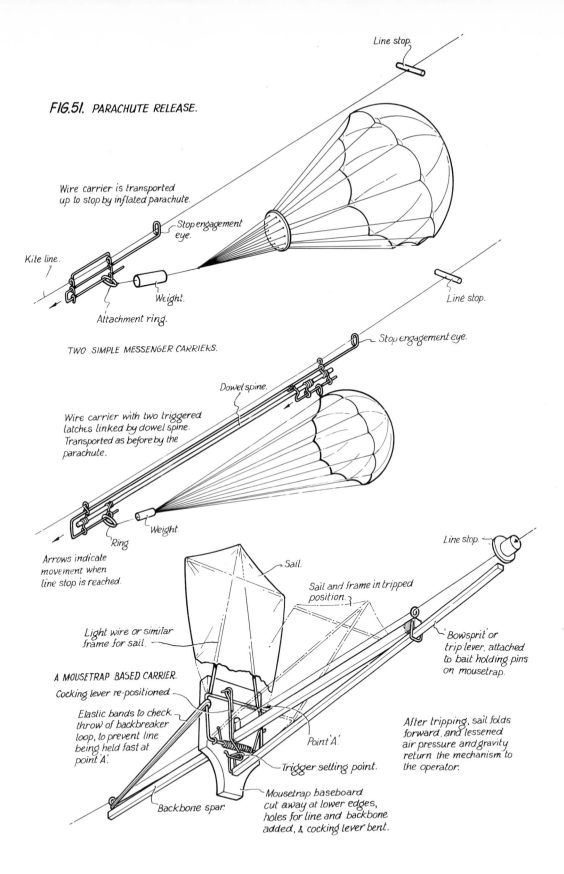

FIG.51. PARACHUTE RELEASE.

Line stop.

Wire carrier is transported up to stop by inflated parachute.

Stop engagement eye.

Kite line.

Weight.

Attachment ring.

Line stop.

TWO SIMPLE MESSENGER CARRIERS.

Stop engagement eye.

Dowel spine.

Wire carrier with two triggered latches linked by dowel spine. Transported as before by the parachute.

Weight.

Ring

Arrows indicate movement when line stop is reached.

Sail.

Sail and frame in tripped position.

Line stop.

Light wire or similar frame for sail.

A MOUSETRAP BASED CARRIER.

Cocking lever re-positioned.

Elastic bands to check throw of backbreaker loop, to prevent line being held fast at point 'A'.

Point 'A'.

Trigger setting point.

'Bowsprit' or trip lever, attached to bait holding pins on mousetrap.

After tripping, sail folds forward, and lessened air pressure and gravity return the mechanism to the operator.

Backbone spar.

Mousetrap baseboard cut away at lower edges, holes for line and backbone added, & cocking lever bent.

These kites are flown from roof tops, and in all countries – Japan, China, Malaysia, Indonesia and India. They are generally known as 'fighters', for good reason.

The Indian term for these kites is *goodie*, and they are best known at Rampur, Gujerat and Ahmedabad where the annual ceremony of Utran is the scene for spectacular kite fighting. The line is made of *manja*, a cotton thread used for sewing. This is stretched and treated with a paste mixture of dye (red is favourite), finely ground glass and porcelain. When dry, the line becomes an abrasive string which will cut through other lines. It is then ready for the game of *Vakata*.

Fighting kites are flown using rollers (reels), and control is established by quick rotation, paying out or rolling in the line while drawing it from side to side or up and down. A good kite will traverse quickly in one dart and answer to the slightest touch of the line.

The object of the exercise is obviously to destroy the opposition by cutting through its line. Thus the advantage goes to whoever flies highest, for if one is on top, then a dive across the other's line, followed by paying out so that the upper line bears down on the lower, will produce a cut. The upper kite can always recover upwards. There is no protocol to observe in the cutting, and a third party may well join the fray to take advantage.

Kite fighting can be very exciting when lots of kites are involved simultaneously, as in Hong Kong at the end of the summer season. It demands particular skills which have yet to become adopted in Europe, even though the first reports on making and flying fighters were published in *Model Engineer* over seventy years ago. One elementary reason for the absence of the fighter from the West is that it is a very lightweight kite, made for the steady, balmy winds of hot climates. Flying a fighter is not unlike catching a butterfly. Some of the time you get near enough to capturing it, and this makes up for the time spent when the pursued is in control of the pursuer!

Tibetan fighting kite (underside).

Indian fighting kites are imported into Britain and are among the cheapest you can buy, but the outlets are restricted to specialist shops. Hammoco Designs market an unusual twin kite pack in Europe which makes up into a pair of fighting kite shapes of strong enough structure to withstand gusty breezes and occasional contact with land. Otherwise the fighter is disappointingly ignored in the West, except for the Indian exponents led by the Bahadurs in New York and San Francisco, USA.

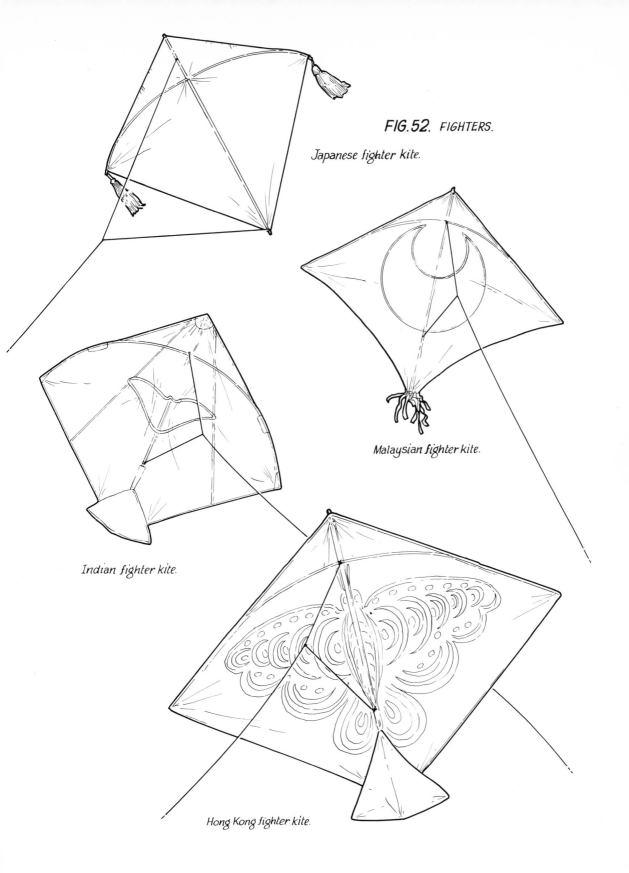

FIG. 52. FIGHTERS.

Japanese fighter kite.

Malaysian fighter kite.

Indian fighter kite.

Hong Kong fighter kite.

MARATHONS

Everyone likes a record, and it is logical that duration of flight should become a kiting target. Efforts to establish long records have centred on Bermuda where the hexagonal kite is the traditional shape. A team from Rhode Island managed 37 hours 17 minutes in 1972, but the outstanding claimant is Vincent Tuzo who kept his battered hexagon up on 600 ft (180 m) of line for 49 hours 40 minutes during Easter 1972. Tuzo is the leading kite exponent in Bermuda, and among his achievements is surfing over the waves on a giant inflated inner tube pulled by a kite. He makes and sells kites to his own design, and, apart from their symmetrical hexagonal or octagonal shape, they have unusually long (110 ft/37 m) tails made of light towelling strips.

ALTITUDE

Although a restriction on altitude applies in Britain, a lot of fun can still be gained from height-judging events. The actual altitude of the kite depends largely upon its efficiency. If it flies at a shallow angle and will lift the weight of the line, the kite can reach almost the full 200 ft (60 m) using that amount of line. Most kites, operating at 20°–30°, lift the line to 45°–60° angles where the actual height is considerably *less* than 200 ft, on 200 ft of line. The altitude can be calculated by sighting the angle, with known line length. Assuming a taut line, height is line length multiplied by the sine of line angle.

The best and easiest means of determining which kite is the more efficient is to fly in pairs on a 'knock-out' basis, until the highest flyer for standard length line is determined by an eliminating tournament.

CONTESTS

When the American Kitefliers Association determined rules for a championship held at Honolulu in Hawaii, they recommended a basic six-part event with the following categories for judging:

1. *Most Beautiful Kite in Flight:* to be judged on four determinations: the most colourful (including the accessories); originality of design; kite construction; and its flight performance.

2. *Highest Flying Kite:* all flown on maximum of 600 ft (180 m) of line in a period not to exceed two minutes with elevation determined by the highest establishment of flight angle on the predetermined line length.

3. *Longest Distance Flyer:* The kite flown the furthest distance from the designated area flying-line marker at the end of two minutes' flying time from actual launching.

4. *Smallest Kite in Flight:* Minimum string length held at 25 ft (8 m). Kite must fly above the head of contestant and must have a frame of some type. Size of the kite not to include vertical stabilisers, tails, etc. The frame need not necessarily be of wood sticks but must constitute 'framing' in the definition of a dictionary.

5. *Largest Kite in Flight:* Minimum length of flying line is 400 ft (120 m). Kite must be airborne and flying at the full 400 ft within whatever time is designated by the committee or judges, or both. Size of the kite will be determined by the area of the total lifting surface, with the exception of vertical stabilisers, tails, etc.

6. *Free-style Kite Flying:* Description of this event is the controlled manoeuvrability of the kite, uniqueness of flying technique and originality of design; the flying time to be designated by the committee or judges, or both.

These are the basic events in the Hawaiian contest. It doesn't mean that more cannot be added or some removed from the listing. The principal aim of such a contest is to encourage craftwork activity. For this reason, all kites entered must be constructed by the entrant. In the case of contests for youngsters, it is

SIMPLE HEIGHT ESTIMATION
(Assuming taut line of known length)

To use, measure line angle. Read down column under appropriate angle to level of known line length. Height is in metres.*

Line angle°		10°	20°	30°	40°	45°	50°	60°	70°	80°	90°
100 m	H	17·36	34·2	50	64·28	70·71	76·6	86·6	93·97	98·48	100
	V	98·48	93·97	86·6	76·6		64·28	50	34·2	17·36	
200 m	H	34·72	68·4	100	128·56	141·42	153·2	173·2	187·94	196·96	200
	V	196·96	187·94	173·2	153·2		128·56	100	68·4	34·72	
300 m	H	52·08	102·6	150	192·84	212·13	229·8	259·8	281·91	295·44	300
	V	295·44	281·91	259·8	229·8		192·84	150	102·6	52·08	
400 m	H	69·44	136·8	200	257·12	282·84	306·4	346·4	375·88	393·92	400
	V	393·92	375·88	346·4	306·4		257·12	200	136·8	69·44	
500 m	H	86·8	171	250	321·4	353·55	383	433	469·85	492·4	500
	V	492·40	469·85	433	383		321·4	250	171	86·8	
600 m	H	104·16	205·2	300	385·68	424·26	459·6	519·6	563·82	590·88	600
	V	590·88	563·82	519·6	459·6		385·68	300	205·2	104·16	
700 m	H	121·52	239·4	350	449·96	494·97	536·2	606·2	657·79	689·36	700
	V	689·36	657·79	606·2	536·2		449·96	350	239·4	121·52	
800 m	H	138·88	273·6	400	514·24	565·68	612·8	692·8	751·76	787·84	800
	V	787·84	751·76	692·8	612·8		514·24	400	273·6	138·88	
900 m	H	156·24	307·8	450	578·52	636·39	689·4	779·4	845·73	886·32	900
	V	886·32	845·73	779·4	689·4		578·52	450	307·8	156·24	
1000 m	H	173·6	342	500	642·8	707·1	766	866	939·7	984·8	1000
	V	984·8	939·7	866	766		642·8	500	342	173·6	
1500 m	H	260·4	513	750	964·2	1060·65	1149	1299	1409·55	1477·2	1500
	V	1477·2	1409·55	1299	1149		964·2	750	513	260·4	
2000 m	H	347·2	684	1000	1285·6	1414·2	1532	1732	1879·4	1969·6	2000
	V	1969·6	1879·4	1732	1532		1285·6	1000	684	347·2	
3000 m	H	520·8	1026	1500	1928·4	2121·3	2298	2598	2819·1	2954·4	3000
	V	2954·4	2819·1	2598	2298		1928·4	1500	1026	520·8	

Line length (vertical axis label)

H = height at angle to the horizontal (metres)   V = height at angle to the vertical (metres)

* 1 metre = 3·2 feet

permissible to have adult aid and flight supervision.

When these recommendations were issued the control-line kite had yet to become popular, and its arrival has opened up other possibilities. With the advantage of controlled positioning, the two-line kite is suitable for contests on the following basis:

1. *Formation Flight:* The event is judged when two or more control-line kites are put aloft and operated through parallel man-oeuvres in formation. They must not be connected in any way. Penalty points would be given for contact between kites, and points awarded for the duration of persistent close formation and the number of manoeuvres performed.

2. *Solo Manoeuvres:* Preferably with long streamer to aid judging. Points for the shape of circles, length of horizontal passes, touch-downs and take-offs. Multiple kites in linked formation can be entered.

3. *Target Area:* A marked area at 180 ft (55 m) distance is established as a landing point. Kites to be given a fixed-duration period of, say, two minutes before landing under control. Points given for distance from the marked area (in feet or decimetres) and seconds over and above 120 seconds from start signal to touchdown. The competitor with the least points wins.

4. *Balloon Bursting:* Kite has a pin at each lateral spar end and attacks balloons on 36-in. (1-m) sticks set vertically in a clear area downwind. Points given for balloons burst within two-minute attack period.

Polish kite rally, Swieto Latawca, *held annually at Krakow; design is as important as flight for points in this contest.*

5. *Picket-Line Pick-Up:* Pins in ends of lateral spar are used to pick up tissues supported on sticks 36 ins (1 m) high and spaced at 20-ft (7-m) intervals over 100 ft (30 m) across wind. Points for each pick-up. More points may be given for tissues at extreme ends of the line. The flyer must remain stationary.

There are other ideas in prospect, some of which could be used to involve the whole family, e.g. parachute release and recovery contests, or Le Mans-style races to be first in the air after the teams have been given dismantled kites and a ball of line to put on a reel. The possibilities are manifold.

Contests are a fine means of bringing people together as long as no one takes them too seriously. If that happens, then a degree of professionalism comes into the picture and all the merits fly away in the wind.

Treat the contest as a social occasion. Use the messenger to spill lightweight sweets over the spectators and let the kids know what is about to happen. Encourage onlookers to feel a sense of participation. Share your kite lines, help those who are obviously new to kiting, and the resulting pleasure makes it all worthwhile.

FIVE

Control-line Kites

Writing in *Kite Tales* in spring 1972, Harold B. Alexander stated: 'Recommended only for those who are proud of their EKG traces [Electro Kymo Graph biological analysis], there is the control-line flying of a Glite, equipped with a tail, and a pair of 50-ft [16-m] wingtip streamers, all three preferably crêpe paper or very light plastic. If your pulse does not pound with the excitement and beauty of that, you'd better find another hobby.' That sums up the sheer thrill of control-line kiting which has revolutionised the hobby in the 1970s, though the concept is far from new.

In 1899, Orville and Wilbur Wright were flying a biplane kite with 'joysticks' linked by pairs of lines to upper and lower tips at each extremity. As the sticks were moved fore and aft, the changing tension on the control lines twisted the wings. This warping technique was later used on the Wright brothers' gliders and the famous Flyer of 1903. This control could be said to be the very origin of control design for aeroplanes as well as kites.

The first evidence of two-line control for sideways manoeuvres is that concerning J. Woodbridge Davis, who in 1894 was operating a star-shaped kite designed for life-saving operations. Separate bridles and the use of variable tension on the two lines made the Davis kite the first in the field with a control system that has been revived over seventy years later.

In World War II, the US Navy adopted a Target Kite designed by Paul E. Garber, assisted by Lloyd Reicher and Stanley Potter. Garber was a lieutenant-commander in the Special Services Division of the US Navy Bureau of Aeronautics. He had long been a devotee of kiting and, before the war, as curator of aviation in the Smithsonian Institution in Washington, he had been custodian of one of the world's finest collections of historical kites. On his return to the Smithsonian after the war, Garber was instrumental in establishing the present National Air and Space Museum, and instituted the Washington Kite Carnivals on the Mall each spring.

The Target Kite (Fig. 53) took a full year to develop, and as a basis it used the configuration of the William Eddy bowed Malay. Since the kite had to weave from side to side, or to provide a quickly moving target for machine gunners, a ventral fin and rudder were fitted to control direction. Two lines from a long spreader bar held by the flyer led up to a duplicated bridle on the kite. As either was pulled, it swung a bridle stick which was held at its centre point in a central bridle. The bridle stick acted as a spacer, and regulated the pull on tiller lines which ran to the rudder tiller. So when the flyer used the spreader bar in the manner of an aeroplane rudder bar, the rudder on the kite moved in proportion. At the centre of the spreader bar, two reels held a 200 yd (180 m) line each. They were ratchet-

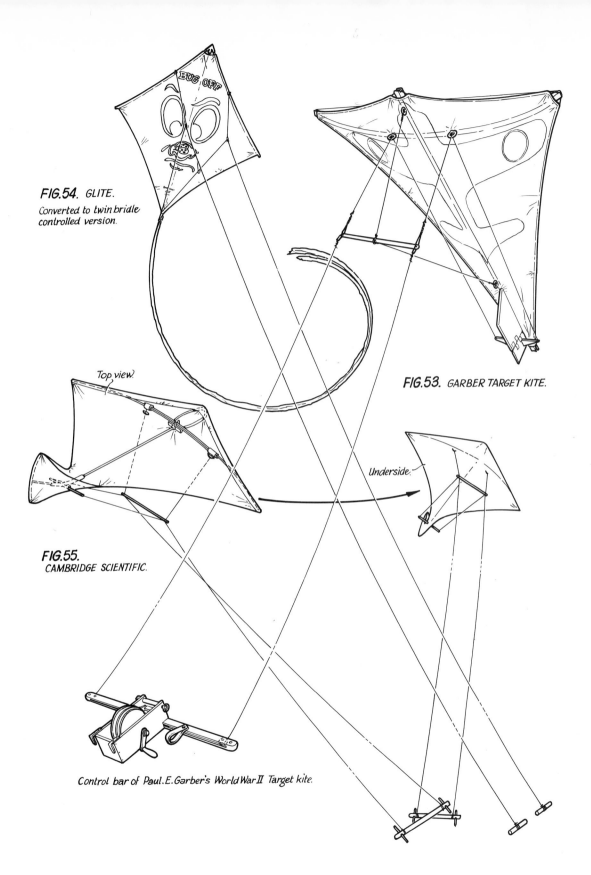

FIG.54. GLITE.
Converted to twin bridle controlled version.

BUG OFF

FIG.53. GARBER TARGET KITE.

Top view.

Underside.

FIG.55.
CAMBRIDGE SCIENTIFIC.

Control bar of Paul.E.Garber's World War II Target kite.

restrained to enable the flyer to equalise the line length, and handles permitted the line to be reeled in while the whole unit was hooked to a belt on the flyer's waist.

Demonstrations to the US Army and Navy resulted in an initial order of 1,500, and subsequently 125,000 were delivered by the sports goods manufacturers A. G. Spalding & Bros.

The Garber Target Kite of the 1940s was made to be shot at. The spars were bulky: the main boom was $\frac{3}{4}$-in. (2-cm) square spruce and the lateral bar was $1\frac{3}{4} \times \frac{3}{8}$ ins (45 × 10 mm). Altogether 61 ins (1·5 m) tall, it had a span of 60 ins (1·5 m) and was covered with plastic-treated rayon. It could be flown from a ship's deck or on a firing range, and the manoeuvres were unlimited in the plane of a hemisphere. Sideways loops, zig-zags, figures of eight, dives and climbs were part of its evasive repertoire. An aeroplane silhouette, coupled with the Japanese red spot insignia, completed the picture.

In every way this kite pre-dated all the subsequent commercial developments of two-line kites, although none of the more recent control-line kites has made use of the hinged rudder. There is little doubt that it was not the rudder alone which gave such effective directional control on the Garber Target. As each line was pulled, it applied a tension on the kite surface and deflected the angle of the kite to displace the lift distribution. It is the latter attribute that is utilised in most commercial kites that have appeared since.

GLITES

The original 'Glite' was a clever semi-flexible kite based on the Rogallo shape, created by Charles H. Cleveland of Bend, Oregon, USA, and manufactured by North Pacific Products Inc. It followed the Rogallo scheme of being cut as a square, then having two leading-edge spars swept back a few degrees to obtain dihedral of about 15° and to allow the covering to billow up into two conical cambered aerofoils. As designed and patented (US 3,276,730) in 1964, the Cleveland Tailless Kite or Glite was unusual in having the kite line fixed direct to the centre boom. There is no requirement for a bridle on a Glite unless it is adapted according to the instructions for controlled flight.

Glites are marked on their leading edges at 10 ins (25·4 cm) from the central (patented) plastic socket which accepts the three spar booms. One end of a 48-in. (122-cm) line is tied to each of these two leading-edge points, and the other ends are joined to the extremity of the central boom at the rear. Instructions advise on the bridle arrangement, which gives line attachment about 2 ins (50 mm) behind the normal central tie point. If the Glite tends to fly too high and does not keep the lines tight when stunting, the front bridle lines have to be lengthened, and if the Glite moves slowly and is unwilling to climb, the rear bridles have to be lengthened (Fig. 54).

Flying on lines 100–125 ft (30–38 m) long, the Glite is spectacular when carrying streamers at tip and rear. It can be parallel-bridled so that up to four can be flown on one set of lines, with the Glites 6–8 ft (2–3 m) apart. Also, being light, though about 9 sq ft (1 m²) in area, it will perform aerobatics in light breezes. Sadly, because the Glite does not arrive with a prepared two-line bridle, very few flyers bother to operate it in this way.

THE CAMBRIDGE KITE

During 1975 another twin-bridle design arrived which offered a different approach from that of its predecessors, and in turn a flying pattern that had a distinctive feel when compared with other control-line kites. It is the Cambridge Scientific Aerobatic kite. In shape it is a blend of the Asian fighter, with curved lateral spar and no dihedral, and the original Garber Target Kite. The rudder, which is not hinged, is on the upper surface in the form of a drogue, or pocket, which is twisted to one side or the other by tension on the bridle line from a harness bar (Fig. 55).

Assembly is a matter of linking pieces of bamboo and dowel with plastic tube, one of which becomes a horseshoe-shaped nose-buffer which stretches the double nose pocket of plastic sail to a pointed leading edge. The twin bridle links to each end of the harness bar, where the flying lines are tied, and the maker suggests using a wooden steering bar which is held by the flyer.

Flying the Cambridge kite is the nearest people in the Western world can get to being in full control of an Asian fighter. This kite flits rapidly; it is sensitive, light on the line and fast to change direction. These features are caused by its flat shape and the effective rudder control. Certainly it is the safest to fly of all control-line kites, for its inertia on impact with any solid object is insufficient to break any of its parts or to do physical damage. The Cambridge comes in two sizes, 43-in. (110-cm) and 30-in. (76-cm) wingspan, and the instructions include the delightful clause that 'if your kite is wrecked by a tree or a fierce dog we will rebuild it . . .'

THE DUNFORD KITE

Meanwhile in Oxford Squadron Leader Donald Dunford had been experimenting since the 1960s with a control-line aerobatic kite shape that was wholly different from the Rogallo-form Glite or the Garber Target Kite. It uses a bridle stick to link a pair of two-line bridles (which Dunford calls the 'control bar') as on the Garber, and in plan form it has a vague similarity to a Conyne winged box; but in fact the Dunford is as original as can be (Fig. 56).

Its distinction is the coupled use of a deep, v-shaped centre box or channel with a cutaway to admit airflow, and two cambered wings or sails either side. The three longitudinal spar booms are tensioned by the shape of the sail, the bridles, and a centre spacer. The spacer was originally a block of balsa wood but was changed to plastic tube for mass production. Tension in these spars gives them an aerodynamic curvature. The sail adopts the section of a cambered profile not unlike that of early aeroplanes. Porous cotton sailcloth is used as a fabric, which is easily collapsible when the kite is dismantled. A key to the stability is the bow in the lower boom which gives a butterfly-tail effect on the rear v.

Dunford's kite was tested in the wind tunnel at Hatfield Polytechnic in England, and provided a most interesting analysis of the longitudinal stability which is one of its strongest attributes.

Owing to the cambered surfaces, the Dunford kite generates significantly greater lift than its contemporaries and is rarely at an angle which might be termed 'stalled'.

This kite has a weight problem. The five spars, spacer, bridles, clips, rigging and sailcloth add up to an unusually heavy weight for the area, so that you really do need a steady breeze of over 10 mph (16 km/h) to get the full effect. The British average wind speed of 17 mph (27 km/h) is ideal.

Flying a Dunford is best expressed by a quotation from the instructions: 'Try to imagine you have the kite on a long pole with a steering wheel at your end.' Personally, I prefer the image of motorcycle handlebars. When control of the Dunford is second nature to you, you can manoeuvre it with incredible precision. Don Dunford can pick a lady's hat off her head, burst a balloon or perform aerial chain-mail circles as well as all the other stunts in a control-line kite repertoire. For greater ·spectacle, smoke canisters, or streamers at the tips are sometimes carried.

THE WIND PLANE

Early in 1974, Joe Butler of Weatherford in Texas started marketing what the originators called the Wind Plane. Designed by the Wheat brothers, this kite is actually a near scale model of a World War I SE5 fighter moulded in styrofoam (polystyrene). The three brothers, Bob, Jim, and Roy Wheat, must have been experienced aeromodellers since they had many difficulties to overcome in making an aeroplane shape into a kite. Their experience must have taught them that the bridle position had to be low and well forward, with long, well-spaced bridle lines. As I have already explained, model gliders can only 'kite' on their towlines when wind speed is equal to or greater than the normal flight speed. Otherwise the model glider has to be kept in motion, either towed forwards or circling.

A three-dimensional version of a biplane will present even greater problems with its higher drag and shorter wingspan. It seemed that the Wind Plane had little chance, but

these determined brothers devised a two-line control system unlike that used by Dunford, Cleveland or Garber. One line is anchored and fixed in length. The other, on a reel, is hand-held. Variable tension on the reeled line enables the flyer to bank the Wind Plane in either direction, to dive or climb, and even to come down to a landing.

Wings, fuselage and tail assembly are moulded in styrofoam. Struts and wheels are of balsa wood, and a free-wheeling wooden propeller completes the illusion. A wingspan of 40 ins (1 m) makes the scale approximately one-sixth. The total weight is just over 1 lb (500 g).

Similar, but not made from plastics, are the Biplane Kites by Hiness of Japan. They can be decorated either as a Japanese Willow or an

The Hiness Willow, a huge, rigid aeroplane kite weighing 2¾ lb (1.2 kg). This Japanese control-line kite is made from a kit, using corrugated card for its construction.

American Kaydet trainer, and are made of corrugated cardboard, spruce and paper covering. They are not sold as control-line kites, and are suggested for long (6-ft (2-m)) yoked bridles to a single line. But their weight ($2\frac{3}{4}$ lb (over 1 kg)) and bulk (too large for anything but a big estate car or van to carry them in one piece) make them a far better proposition, in my experience, for the Wind Plane two-line technique. They highlight the real advantage of the sail kite – its portability. Desirable though they may be, simulated model kites are awkward to carry about, and can be difficult to make from kits.

THE POWELL KITE

Chronologically next to arrive *en masse* were the kites of Peter Powell. These have made a great impact on kiting wherever they have appeared in Britain, Canada, the USA and Japan.

Peter Powell is a lifelong kite flyer; he once sent his grandmother aloft on a swinging seat beneath a train of big Eddy kites to prove a point. For six years he struggled to perfect the details of his Stunter, which achieved fame in 1975. It was awarded the Silvergilt Diploma at the Fourth Salon International des Inventions et des Techniques Nouvelles in Geneva, and was the subject of considerable television publicity. As a result the Powell Stunter, sometimes called the Skymaster or Stunter, was rapidly popularised and for good reason.

In general shape the Powell resembles a Rogallo, with a centre boom and two leading-

Assembling a Powell Stunter. Attaching the line to the bridle.

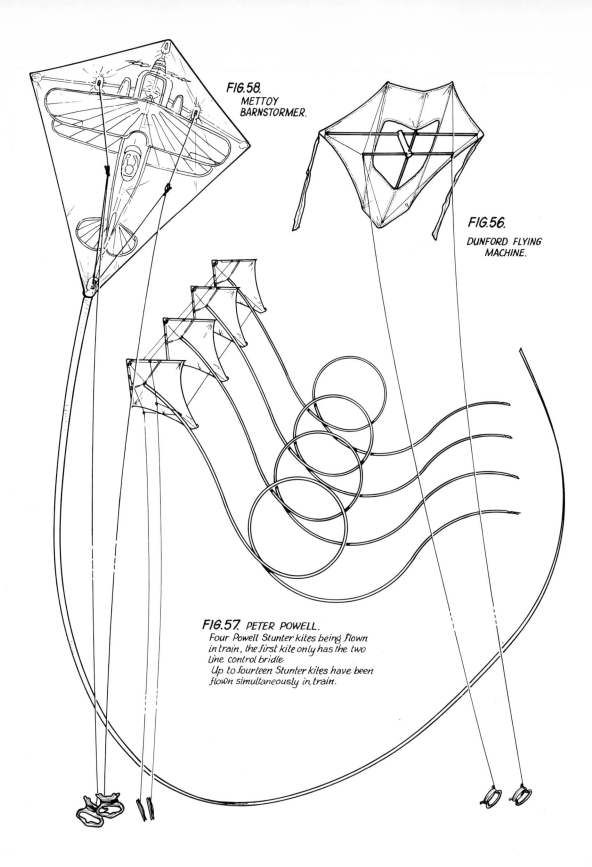

FIG.58.
METTOY
BARNSTORMER.

FIG.56.
DUNFORD FLYING
MACHINE.

F16.57. PETER POWELL.
Four Powell Stunter kites being flown
in train, the first kite only has the two
line control bridle
Up to fourteen Stunter kites have been
flown simultaneously in train.

edge spars, which give dihedral and sweep back for the sail form. It is larger than its contemporaries, with a 46-in. (117-cm) span and 48-in. (122-cm) length, and is not a square but slightly elongated. The real distinctions came in the use of lightweight alloy tubing for the spars (since replaced by fibreglass rods), heavy-gauge translucent plastic sail material, and a steel wire sprung cross brace which makes the Powell incredibly strong yet flexible enough to absorb strong pressures. Its final difference is its tubular tail which slips over the centre spar where it picks up a pressure point. Over 65 ft (20 m) of colour tube soon fills with air under pressure and this tail follows gracefully through each manoeuvre.

Two bridles are arranged as on the Cleveland-designed Glite, and a deep bow in the centre spar enhances stability. Because it is

larger ($6\frac{1}{4}$ sq ft/0·58 m²) and braced, the Powell can be flown in a wide range of wind speeds and can be spectacularly fast in its dives. It was the first kite to be widely demonstrated in multiple trains. Two, then four, then fourteen Stunters have been linked by Powell with about 7 ft (2 m) spacing between (Fig. 57). He says that the pull on the lines can be tremendous.

SKITE, SKY-RIDER, AEROBAT, RED ARROW, SKY-CAT, ACE, AERO-KITE, GLOSTER, Etc.

Inevitably, the success of the Powell kite drew similar competitors, one of which is the Skite produced by the Frisbee Co. Ltd. Smaller and lighter (the span is 41 ins (104 cm) and the length 42 ins (106 cm)), the Skite also has alloy

Powell Stunters controlled to move horizontally to the right.

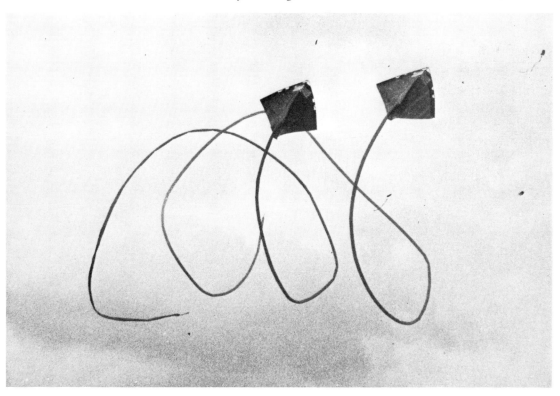

tube spars with a deep centre bow, and its bridle is of the same Cleveland-designed Glite style. It has no tail. The Skite arrives in a stout tube with an armband which enables it to be carried about easily. In flight it has characteristics which are typical of the Rogallo form, and since it is lighter and smaller ($5\frac{1}{4}$ sq ft/0·48 m²), it has no cross brace, relying instead on a very robust steel wire system in the nose joints of the three tube spars.

Other developments on the same theme are the Sky-Rider and the Aerobat, with a further twist to the idea in the Red Arrow. The first of these, produced by Sky Sports Ltd of London, was arguably the most manoeuvrable of all the control-line kites at the May kite festival held by the British KFA on 2 May 1976 at Old Warden. The design has a more flexible frame

than most others and the struts are preformed in an outward curve. It has a 75-ft (22-m) streamer. The Aerobat is 48 ins (122 cm) long, has a 42-in. (106-cm) span and a wire cross brace to withstand strong winds; the Red Arrows (first by Schofield, later by Mettoy) are distinguished by having a pointed nose extension and a Dayglo silhouette of a Red Arrow Gnat on the sail. Innumerable variations in structure, shape and decoration have appeared (as listed in Chapter 6), the most original being the Flexifoil – perhaps the most manoeuvrable of all.

THE METTOY BARNSTORMER

Under the brand name of 'Wembley', more kites are claimed to be sold by the Mettoy-

Sky-Rider control kite in flight.

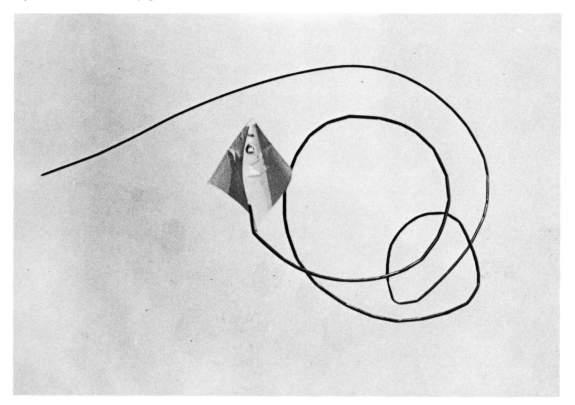

Playcraft Co. than by most others in Britain, and it was a logical commercial progression to produce in 1976 the first Wembley control-line kite. It uses the two-bridle system as created for the Glite, but the application is totally different. Called the Barnstormer (Fig. 58), with a coloured plan view of a Pitts biplane on clear polythene sail plastic, it uses the Mettoy-Playcraft umbrella assembly and erects as a dihedralled Malay shape. A novel plastic fitting slides up and down the centre dowel spar, and as it is pushed towards the nose it forces each of the two side spars out at right angles to push against the tips where the spars fit in plastic reinforcements. At the same time the monofilament bridle slides into position through reinforced sail slots, so that from folded state to erection the Barnstormer

is ready in seconds. Two handles are provided, and a roll of flat polythene plastic which unrolls to make a 'smoke' trail.

You might be excused for thinking that a Malay kite with flat centre spar and straight, though dihedralled, side spars would hardly be a candidate for the commercially competitive aerobatic kite market. But flying it soon dispels any doubts. The use of two lines transforms this otherwise simple design into a stunt flyer which offers yet another kind of 'feel' in flight. It will turn rapidly, recover from a vertical dive, and trace circles in the sky with its long tail. The radius of action may not be the same as one of its more aerodynamic companions, but as it comes complete in a colourful presentation box, from a source which has a large slice of the market, it has

Formation aerobatics by Tom Chapman with a team of Barnstormer kites which he designed for Mettoy-Playcraft. The kites are linked by their bridles.

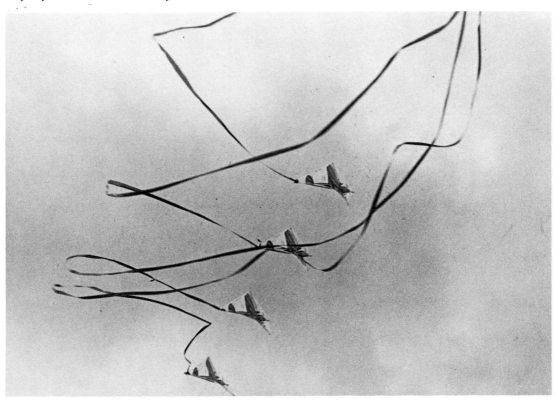

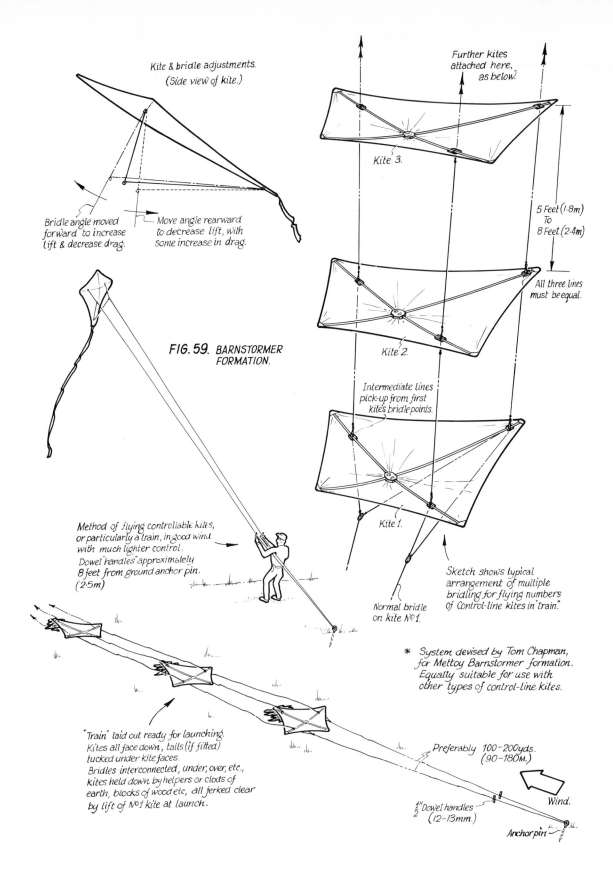

Kite & bridle adjustments.
(Side view of kite.)

Bridle angle moved forward to increase lift & decrease drag.

Move angle rearward to decrease lift, with some increase in drag.

FIG. 59. BARNSTORMER FORMATION.

Further kites attached here, as below.

Kite 3.

5 Feet (1·8m) To 8 Feet (2·4m)

All three lines must be equal.

Kite 2.

Intermediate lines pick-up from first kite's bridle points.

Kite 1.

Method of flying controllable kites, or particularly a train, in good wind with much lighter control. Dowel "handles" approximately 8 feet from ground anchor pin. (2·5m)

Sketch shows typical arrangement of multiple bridling for flying numbers of Control-line kites in "train."

Normal bridle on kite Nº1.

* System devised by Tom Chapman, for Mettoy Barnstormer formation. Equally suitable for use with other types of control-line kites.

"Train" laid out ready for launching. Kites all face down, tails (if fitted) tucked under kite faces. Bridles interconnected, under, over, etc., kites held down by helpers or clods of earth, blocks of wood etc, all jerked clear by lift of Nº1 kite at launch.

Preferably 100-200yds. (90-180м.)

½" Dowel handles (12-13mm.)

Wind.

Anchor pin.

done much to introduce two-line flying to the casual kiter, and has made 'formation' aerobatics with multiple kites a relatively inexpensive proposition (Fig. 59).

FLYING CONTROL-LINE KITES

Each of the kites described in this chapter operates on the principle that when the pressure distribution on the kite is displaced, the kite is manoeuvred into variable attitudes. Bridles are spaced apart, either as independent yokes, or (as in the Dunford and Cambridge), where structure demands, on a control or harness bar. As unequal tension is applied on the flying lines, so the kite is angled. Pull on the left line and the kite moves left. To arrest such changes of direction, pull on the right line and hold the tension. It is easy to sustain horizontal flight.

Use the full stretch of your arms. You must keep the lines equally taut. Crossed nylon lines slide on one another. It does not matter if you have a dozen right-hand twists and cannot unwind with twelve left-hand turns: you should still have control. To make the kite go up, lift your arms over your head. To dive, push down. The motions come quite naturally after a while. Practice makes for perfection and the self-launch or 'touch and go' is a mark of an experienced control-line kiter.

Each of the kites described has a different 'feel'. The aerodynamic-sectioned Dunford will fly through greater arcs in the downwind hemisphere than any other, owing to its design. It also has a more constant speed. The flat Cambridge flitters like a demented midge and, like the Mettoy Barnstormer or Skyrider, will spin like a top on one line. In between, the trio of Rogallo shapes, Glite, Skite and Powell, offer precise control through stunts that can build up incredible speeds. To speak of the noise of a kite may sound a little odd, but the plastic sails on a control-line Rogallo are exceptionally loud, and the additional swish of a long tubular tail adds to the thrill.

DOs	DON'Ts
Select a clear area.	Fly recklessly.
Wind lines separately.	Use stretchy line.
Keep lines equal in length.	Attack single-line kites.
Check assembly before launching.	Tie with slip knots.
Use swivels and brass ring connections.	Scare livestock.
	Move your base – stay put.
	Use lines longer than 150 ft (45 m).

SIX

Off-the-peg Kites

The number of kites sold in Britain in 1977 exceeded four million. Will Yolen, the New York-based kite flyer, is quoted as saying that the equivalent figure for the USA was no less than 35 million, which is a lot of kites by any standard. There is no denying that, for some factories, kites are big business, and manufactured kites satisfy at least 95 per cent of all kiters.

The sections at the end of this book confirm the size of the kite-making trade, though they only account for Europe and the USA, and other plants in India, Japan and South America would possibly double the list. What follows is by no means a complete catalogue of kites that are commercially available in Europe and North America. It is my own collection of information, since there is no trade association to link kite manufacturers, and apologies are offered in advance to those who are not included.

BRITAIN

Aerobat

One of the 1975 introductions to the control-line kite ranges was that by Aerobat, a mail-order house based in Stratford-upon-Avon, Warwickshire, England. This kite measures 4 ft × 3 ft 6 ins (122 × 107 cm). It is an extended Rogallo shape with a cross brace which resists collapse through wind pressure. The plastic sail is decorated with a bat silhouette and is spread over an alloy tube frame. The kite appears to be available only by mail order.

Aero-Kite

Aero-Kite announced their two-line controlled kite at the 1977 trade fairs. Of similar size and structure to the others, being the standard 4 ft (122 cm) in length, and with a 65-ft (22-m) tubular tail, it has a polythene sail, and glass fibre spars joined with moulded nylon fittings. One main difference between the prototypes and other brands is that the cross brace goes tip to tip to give a Malay shape.

Albatross

These kites must be among the few that are made on a site where they could be regularly flown. The St Albans factory is on a farm and produces a range of quality kites for the enthusiast, all with rip-stop nylon sails. In general they are winged box-cell kites, with two exceptions which I shall deal with first.
Soaring Delta: an 8 ft-6 in. (260-cm), or a larger size 11 ft-4 in. (345-cm), span flexible delta with a keel. Each is capable of soaring in light winds and the larger 11 ft-4 in. (345-cm) version has quite a strong lifting force.
Hexagonal: the only Albatross kite for which a tail is essential. The span and length of the kite are each 4 ft (122 cm), and the cotton tail is 30 ft (914 cm) long. Smaller and larger variations have been available.

Surveyor: a large double box kite with side wings and a separating sail between the cells. Because the two boxes are set diamond fashion with vertical centre dividers, there are multiple cells and the lifting capacity of the large area (48 sq ft/4·45 m²) makes it suitable for carrying a camera. The span is 6 ft (183 cm).

Skylark: has the same span as the Surveyor but has one central box, triangular in overall section though vertically divided to make four cells, two at the front and two at the rear.

Phantom: similar to the Skylark but does not have the box divider membrane and is smaller at 60 ins (152 cm) span. Each of these kites has a sail plan form which makes up a shape of a combined 'wing and tail' as though it were an aeroplane.

Dodge: differs in two ways. The sail plan is more traditional. The shape is a conventional double box, each box being made of fore and aft triangular cells. The second difference is that the Dodge can be single- or two-line controlled; it is among the largest of this type, at 60 ins (152 cm) span and with as much as 25 sq ft (2·3 m²) of area.

Eden: a central box with three cells at front, centre and rear, plus a conventionally shaped pair of side sails to a 60-in. (152-cm) span. The box is triangular in cross section, like most of the Albatross designs.

Cody: a 4 ft-3 in. (130-cm) version of the famous design.

Ariel

At the 1977 trade fairs Ariel introduced three sizes of two-line stunt kites in progressive standards of size and detail.

Sky Lark, Sky Weaver and *Sky Rider* (see also under Sky Sports later) are produced for a division of the huge London Rubber Industries Co.

Atalanta

This is a kite brand that has not been obtainable for many, many years. So why include it? Simply because, in its time, the Atalanta range was supreme. It educated the parents of today's readers in the art of flying kites in all weathers, and with all sorts of fun attachments. Atalanta kites were hexagonal, proofed tissue-covered, collapsible framed kites that came in three sizes – 18, 30 and 36 ins (46, 76 and 92 cm). There was also a Baby non-folder and a small square kite, but the larger three were the key to Atalanta's success. A bridle-attached tail, made of thin tissue ribbons attached to a thread, acted as a stabiliser, and the Atalanta could be flown steadily at a constant height while the flyer sent up accessory messengers, parachutes or buzzers.

Unhappily when their creator, Sophocles Xenophon Pantcheff, died, his kites ceased production, though Sprinko's of Eastoke, Hayling Island, made them for a while with PVC covering.

Brookite

Next, to the longest established of all kite companies, Brookite, run by S. N. Harrison in Tufnell Park, London N19. Founded by Thomas and Walter Brooke who made the famous aerial-carrying kites for Marconi, this company maintains the old tradition of using selected porous cotton cloth for all its kites. While some of the sixteen shapes have not changed since the name of Brookite was first registered in 1906, the company also manufactures some more modern designs.

In the American bicentennial year, 1976, the AKA endorsed the large delta shape as a symbol of the occasion, and Brookite included an 88-in. (224-cm) monster. They also added a train of Malay bowed kites designed to fly on a common line.

The complete Brookite range covers fifty different cloth kites in a wide variety of colours. All their kites are collapsible. Control-kites are being planned, including at least one of unique shape.

Delta: a 1976 introduction following the craze

79

for large (88 in./224-cm) deltas in the USA. The key is the trailing edge apron and unbraced nose. It looks like a hang glider with a keel, and flies almost overhead (Fig. 60).

Cutter: seven different sizes of traditional two-stick kites with a cloth keel, which Brookite call a fin, and a tail. They need a +10 mph (16 km/h) wind; their tails tend to wind up. The largest is 48 × 58 ins (120 × 147 cm) (Fig. 61).

Bluebird: a Brookite special in two sizes, with curved-shape wings on a triangular box centre. The larger one is 31 × 38 ins (78 × 96 cm) (Fig. 62).

War: eight different sizes of Conyne, Blériot or winged triangular box. They are very reliable in all winds. The largest is 68 × 66 ins (172 × 167 cm).

Box: four sizes, with Brookite collapsible design using cross struts. Follow the instructions carefully, and you will find that these are the most robust box kites available. They need strong winds and are very stable. The largest is 46 ins (117 cm) long × 18½ ins (47 cm) square (Fig. 63).

Hawk: five sizes of developed kite shape, with fluttering wing slaps and a tail. The largest is 48 × 75 ins (122 × 190 cm).

Master: four sizes of winged double box, the

Underside of an Atalanta 30-in. (76-cm) Hexagon with a PVC *sail. Made by Sprinko's.*

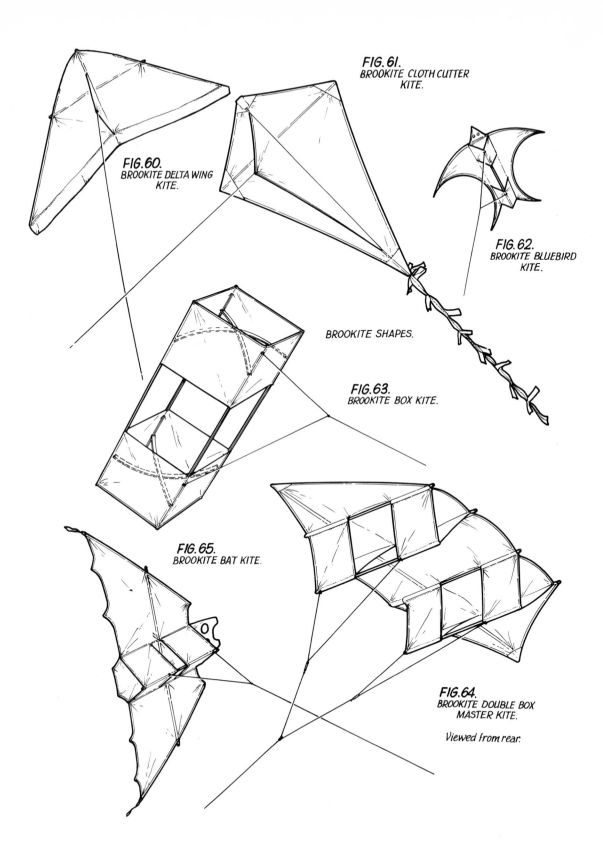

FIG. 61.
BROOKITE CLOTH CUTTER
KITE.

FIG. 60.
BROOKITE DELTA WING
KITE.

FIG. 62.
BROOKITE BLUEBIRD
KITE.

BROOKITE SHAPES.

FIG. 63.
BROOKITE BOX KITE.

FIG. 65.
BROOKITE BAT KITE.

FIG. 64.
BROOKITE DOUBLE BOX
MASTER KITE.

Viewed from rear.

pride of the range. The largest is 64 × 100 ins (163 × 254 cm), and is the most expensive and majestic of all Brookites. It is extremely well made and will last for many years. It tends to be unstable until the line is at steep angle, when it pulls hard and is quite majestic (Fig. 64).

Aero: three sizes of four-winged box, making a unique Brookite. It needs careful bridle trim, but flies well. The largest is 50 × 51 ins (127 × 129 cm).

Oceana: three sizes of hexagonal, up to 33 ins (84 cm) across. Fly it in light winds. It is very manoeuvrable, and thoroughly recommended.

Bat: three black bat-shaped deltas with centre box, up to 34 × 74 ins (86 × 187 cm). They tend to wheel about, but are impressive. They are easily collapsible (Fig. 65).

Malay Train: three kites on one line with opposite bow on lateral and centre spars – a novel idea. The sizes are 29 ins (74 cm), 35 ins (89 cm) and 40 ins (102 cm).

Wing Box: two sizes of box with wings to help in 'normal' winds when a standard box is difficult. The larger size is 40 × 43 ins (102 × 110 cm).

Chang: a screen-printed 22-in. (56-cm) hexagon with a trailer tail.

Square: two sizes of simple square kites. The larger is 24 ins (61 cm). It can be used as a 'header'.

Flying Mouse: a novelty-printed keel triangular kite with mouse head symbols. It is 22 ins (56 cm) long.

Sky High: the only Brookite that comes absolutely complete with twine, parachute or message release etc., wrapped in a sales pack with cutter-shaped kite.

Accessories: as would be expected of this leading manufacturer who caters for the true kiting enthusiast, there is a full range of twines and winders. The lines are made of linen, flax or plaited nylon. Brookite once included ply reels in their lists but these have become too expensive to produce. The lines range from 12 lb (5·5 kg) to 97 lb (44 kg) breaking strain.

Condor

From oldest to youngest, next come Condor of London Colney, Hertfordshire, who introduced their range of toys in 1976. Unfortunately this was a short-lived venture, for the company ceased trading from 1 April 1977. The products may still be in circulation, however.

Magpie and *Condor:* two printed plastic sleds with triple vent holes, linked to the television character promotions. They fly in light to moderate winds, and are inexpensive.

Cambridge Leisure

This firm produces the control-line kite (Fig. 55) described in Chapter 5.

Combat Kite: two sizes of two-line aerobatic kite with a harness bar to warp a vertical drogue rudder. They come in Indian or Malay fighter shape, with a 30- or 43-in. (76- or 109-cm) span. The earlier products had wooden spars, the later ones have plastic. They are fast and twitchy kites. (See also Chapter 5.)

W. R. Davies

Southend, Essex, is a long-established kiting centre where regular activities take place in the parks. One of the local manufacturers is W. R. Davies who make Sharon Lee products including kites, among which is an inflatable.

Aerjet: a rocket-shaped inflatable with side wings and a two-line bridle, it comes with a winding reel and tail streamers. It is not widely known, and is sold mostly as a toy item.

Don Dunford

The preceding chapter on control-line kites has already introduced Don Dunford whose products are marketed by Cochranes of Oxford.

Flying Machine: three sizes, with 41-, 51- and

61-in. span (also known as 1000-, 1250- and 1500-mm sizes) of the unique Dunford cloth (a special material is used for the sail) control-line kite. The most precise and expensive of its contemporaries, it is the Rolls-Royce of kites. Adventurous pilots used to need to buy spare dowel spars owing to high stresses on this efficient kite, but later versions have a special triangular-sectioned glass fibre frame and Dunford cloth. Once flown – never forgotten (Figs 31 and 56).

Flying Fighter: an extremely clever, apron-shaped Malay two-line kite produced for the 1977 market. The sail is tensioned by buckles which clip to the spar ends. They enable you to replace a torn sail or even to change the material. A special feature produced to meet requests from the export market is the free-wheeling airscrew on the nose (with protecting frame) and the undercarriage with wheels. The axle for the wheels doubles as a control bar, and the Fighter is thus fully aerobatic (Fig. 66).

Flying Dixie: a simplified variant without the wheels or airscrew, but it is not as controllable when rigged for two lines which attach to a bridle which links all the spar extremities. This is done very cleverly by the use of cleats which are part of the sail buckle assembly (Fig. 66).

DY

Kites are sometimes made for practical purposes as opposed to a leisure pastime. The Stirling Clothing Co. of Oldham sell Walter Young's DY design for mountain-rescue work.

DY Kite: a message- or line-carrying Eddy bow with an extendable third line and bridle to adjust the kite to the optimum angle of attack. It can be aluminised to reflect radar for rescue work. One was used by the mountaineer Chris Bonington on his Annapurna and Everest expeditions. The nylon sails are coloured international orange for high visibility. The sizes are 30 and 36 ins (76 and 92 cm). It has aluminium spars (Fig. 67).

Empey

The 1975–6 boom in kite flying, especially of the centralised types, brought many new manufacturers into the field. This is one example of the new products.

Empey Ace: a red or blue striped sail of 37 ins (94 cm) span and length over a very light-weight aluminium channel section frame. It is fully aerobatic. Later versions have fibreglass rod spars. Also known as the *Airsport Ace.*

Frisbee

The Frisbee Co., better known for the American-originated flying saucer-shaped discs, produced several designs.

Skite: a Rogallo-frame design, two-line aerobatic with three aluminium spars and a plastic sail with shallow camber. It has no tail. It is light for its area, 41 × 42 ins (104 × 106 cm), it flies in light wind, and comes in a tube carrier. It is sensitive in flight, well made and robust.

Red Bat: introduced in 1977 as a Malay-type aerobatic with a red sail.

Black Bat: the Rogallo equivalent of the Red Bat.

Gloster

Unique quick-assembly fibreglass spars in this control-line kite which arrived in 1977. Malay shape, has differing sail decorations.

Hammoco

Some kites, though off-the-peg, come in kits. Hammoco of Solihull go one better and provide two kites in one kit. They are Indian fighter shape and are sold with full instructions, and parts.

Fighting Kites Kit: two 18-in. (46-cm) square, tissue-covered fighters with coloured tissue supplied for a pattern overlay. They have a wire curved lateral and a bamboo centre spar. They come with tail material and two reeled lines. This excellent design is well presented. By comparison with the original Bombay

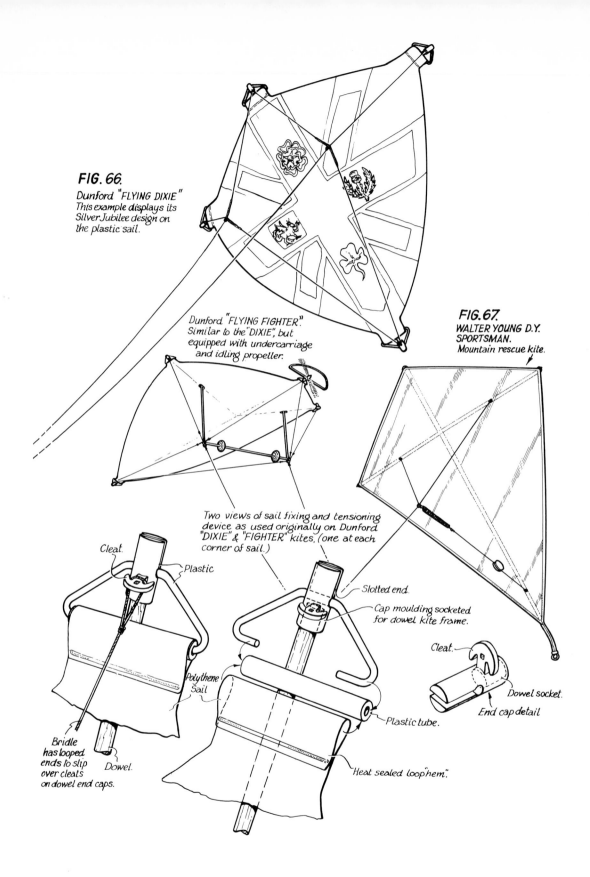

FIG. 66.
Dunford "FLYING DIXIE"
This example displays its
Silver Jubilee design on
the plastic sail.

Dunford "FLYING FIGHTER".
Similar to the "DIXIE", but
equipped with undercarriage
and idling propeller.

FIG.67.
WALTER YOUNG D.Y.
SPORTSMAN.
Mountain rescue kite.

Two views of sail fixing and tensioning
device as used originally on Dunford
"DIXIE" & "FIGHTER" kites, (one at each
corner of sail.)

Cleat.

Plastic

Slotted end.

Cap moulding socketed
for dowel kite frame.

Cleat.

Polythene
Sail

Dowel socket.

Plastic tube.

End cap detail

Bridle
has looped
ends to slip
over cleats
on dowel end caps.

Dowel.

Heat sealed loop "hem".

'fighting kites' these are rather heavy and need a fair breeze.

Kite Workshop

This London company produces numerous special designs, for example:

Flexifoil: a 72-in. (183-cm) span 'wing' which fills with air taken in through a mesh leading edge. Being cellular with ribs of aerofoil contour, the wing becomes reasonably efficient as a lifting surface. The leading edge has a tapered glass fibre rod in it – the only rigid part of the assembly. In flight this curves as the tension is taken on its ends by the two control lines. When the wing is sent into a dive or made to do fast circles it builds up speed at an exceptional rate. The Flexifoil rolls around its control bar and will travel easily – it fits a Boeing 747 luggage locker perfectly!

Ambrose Lloyd

Kite enthusiasts sometimes take the opportunity of turning their hobby into business, and Ambrose Lloyd of London has specialised in the sled type. He designed the kite for the British Standards Institution's 1974 schools competition, and a similar design of his is produced by Condor.

Zammo: a flexible polythene patterned sled kite with two bamboo spars. It is inexpensive and very easy to fly in all winds. It has a 36 × 17 ins (91 × 43 cm) centre panel with triple hole vents (Fig. 68). (See also Condor kites.)

Mettoy-Playcraft (Wembley)

Possibly the largest volume seller of kites in Britain, if not in Europe, is the Mettoy-Playcraft Co., known by their brand names of Corgi and, for kites, Wembley. The range uses a clever 'umbrella' assembly with a plastic fitting that slides along the centre spar to erect the collapsible plastic sail. The hinge gives a rigid dihedralled Eddy shape with extra area obtained by curving the outer lines of the lower sail.

Wembley: a pattern-printed plastic, two-line

bridle Eddy with plastic sockets for dowels. The range includes Skydiver, Witch, Helicopter, Spacewalker, Osprey, Dragon, Devil and Hot Air Balloon designs, all of 41 ins (104 cm) span, and 30 ins (76 cm) long. No tail is needed, and a line is provided. The Wembley is a very steady flyer.

Pocket Kites: all-plastic mini-kites which can be carried in the side pocket. They are a toy line. The designs are called Spiderman, Superman and Batman.

Barnstormer: a control-line Eddy as described in Chapter 5. It has a 60-ft (18-m) flat polythene tail, a 34-in. (86-cm) span, and is 36 ins (91 cm) long. It represents excellent value, is precise in control over a smallish area, and comes with lines and handles (Fig. 58). (See Chapter 5.)

Red Arrow: a Rogallo-frame design, two-line aerobatic kite originated by Schofield, with an extended triangular nose and a Dayglo silhouette of a Red Arrow Gnat trainer jet on the otherwise translucent plastic sail. It was demonstrated in triple kite linked formation; it is slightly larger in area than most control-line kites and has curved trailing edges. Wembley Kites (Mettoy) took it on in 1977, keeping the same name (Fig. 69).

Falcon: a hang-glider model which can be flown as a kite or as a glider, and a plastic *Boxkite* 40 ins (103 cm) long with clever quick assembly were also introduced in 1977.

Peter Powell

If anyone could be said to have put kites on the map in the 1970s, it would be Peter Powell of Cheltenham. His adaptation of the Rogallo frame to a shallow camber sail for two-line control, and the linking of multiple kites for formation with long tubular tails of varying colours, attracted more publicity on television around the world than any other kite known.

Stunter (also *Freedom Stunter*): a control-line Rogallo shape but without deep camber, cross-braced with a wire torsion bar, it originally used specially developed aluminium spars by

Minalux but these were later replaced by glass fibre. It has a 46-in. (117-cm) span, and is 48 ins (122 cm) in length plus a 65-ft (20-m) tubular tail which follows the flight pattern. It needs a 10 mph (16 km/h) wind, and is better on 100–125-ft (30–38-m) lines for manoeuvres in light wind. It is extremely well made, strong and resilient. A great experience, fast in dives, quick to turn, it is also easy to dismantle and carry (Fig. 70).

Multiflite

A north of England company, Multiflite, engaged staff at the University of Newcastle to develop a variation on the Rogallo concept for a controlled kite. The result was:

Concorde: a glass fibre rod spar assembly with a sail pattern that is almost bird-shaped. The main portion is of high aspect ratio, tapering to a narrow tail end. A trailing tube forms a stabiliser, but the actual attachment is not well defined in the instructions. It must be on the underside, where pressure is greatest (Fig. 71).

Merriam

Giant kites have a fascination and a specialist manufacturer in Britain is Merriam:
Nimbus: a 74-in. (188-cm) delta with an extended tail and a silver calendered rip-stop nylon sail over a black alloy tube frame. A whistle device is also supplied by Merriam, which fits other kites as well.

Wembley Skydiver – the design is printed on transparent plastic and the kite erected in the same way as an umbrella.

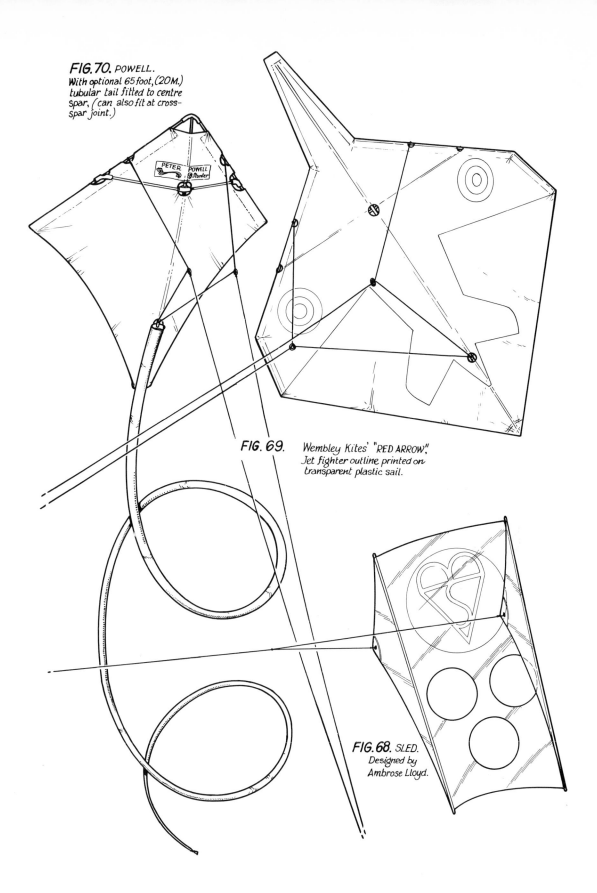

FIG. 70. POWELL.
With optional 65 foot, (20 M.)
tubular tail fitted to centre
spar, (can also fit at cross-
spar joint.)

PETER POWELL
Stunter

FIG. 69. Wembley Kites' "RED ARROW",
Jet fighter outline printed on
transparent plastic sail.

FIG. 68. SLED.
Designed by
Ambrose Lloyd.

Sampson

Another Southend manufacturer is Sampson, who have a range that rivals Brookite for its variety, but the majority of the designs have plastic sails. There are signs that more cotton kites will be added to the Sampson range following the success of their excellent cloth colour-printed Giant Eagle which is one of my favourites for reliability.

Swift: a square plastic kite with a two-line bridle, it measures 12 × 12 ins (30 × 30 cm), and has a helicopter-printed pattern.

Space Pirate: square, as above, but 18 × 18 ins (46 × 46 cm) with a skull and crossbones on a black sail. The same kite also comes with a *Welsh Dragon* pattern.

Magic Roundabout: as above but 22 × 22 ins (56 × 56 cm), with Florence and Dougal pattern.

Jet Flyer and *Uncle Bulgaria:* two Malay cutter kites, 19 × 27 ins (48 × 68 cm) with tails.

Butterfly: a collapsible two-stick Eddy with extended lower sails as a large apron and a printed butterfly pattern on transparent plastic. It measures 32 × 22 ins (81 × 56 cm).

Stunt Flyer and *Giant Eagle* (Fig. 72): two unusual wide-span kites with printed patterns using an Eddy dihedralled basic form but with a large apron. They are 48 ins (122 cm) span, and 23 ins (58 cm) long. They are well named in a third variant: *The Wombles Flying Carpet.* Double dowels at the centre are wise strengtheners.

Box: a nylon kite (there is also a cotton version) supplied in two sizes – 20 ins or 25 ins long (51 cm or 63 cm).

Cutter: a 24 × 30 in. (61 × 76 cm) nylon Malay shape of robust construction for all weathers.

Cutter: four sizes – 18, 24, 30 and 33 ins (46, 61, 76 and 84 cm) long – in porous, coloured cotton fabric; it is supplied with plastic tails.

Bat Shaped: a black cotton kite with a 40-in. (102-cm) span, 18 ins (46 cm) long. It is rather tricky, but fascinating.

Box: a cotton kite for strong winds. It is not too large at 27 ins (68 cm) long and 10 ins (25 cm) square.

Giant Eagle: not to be confused with the plastic kite of the same name, this is a 48-in. (122-cm) span cloth shaped kite with two lateral spars and a triangular centre box. The screen printing of the eagle is of a high standard and the flight characteristics cannot be bettered for anyone seeking a kite that goes up, stays up, and looks good in the air. Sampson call it the 'kite of the century', which is taking praise a little too far, but nonetheless it is a kite to be thoroughly recommended (Fig. 72).

Giant Python: a Malay dragon kite with a triangular framed head and a 30-ft (9-m) trailing broad tail 13 ins (33 cm) wide. Printed as a snake on the delta head, it gives excellent performance and is comparatively cheap when set against similar dragons. See Chapter 7 for a typical shape. Also sold as *Red Devil* with RAF aerobatic-team decoration.

Bird Dual Control: the first Sampson for aerobatics. Measuring 36 × 30 ins (91 × 76 cm), it was put out as a Sugar Puffs Honey Monster promotion in 1977.

Accessories: Sampson make reels and winders and supply twine and rayon on spools.

Scale Craft

Promotional ideas on kites are not new. On the European continent the printed slogan or logo has been frequently used to advertise products on kite sails. One company that has developed kits for publicity in Britain is Scale Craft, who launched a range of Football Team kites, each striped in team colours and supplied with cut-out stick-on letters to place the name of your favourite team under the 'I support' line.

Dragon and Ghost: two vented sleds with egg-shaped sails and printed patterns. They have PVC tube spars.

Football Teams: five different colour stripings on egg-shaped sleds, 37 ins (94 cm) high with

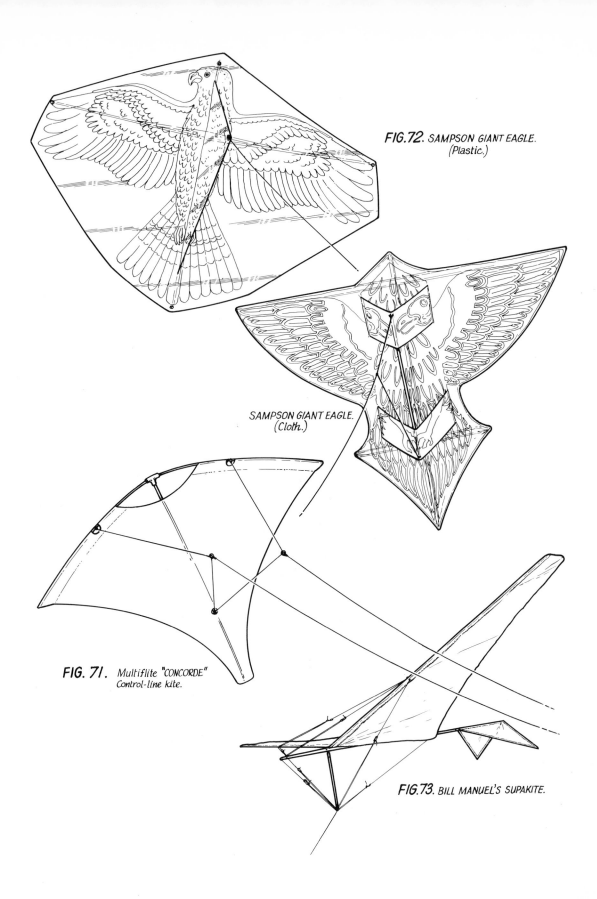

FIG.72. SAMPSON GIANT EAGLE.
(Plastic.)

SAMPSON GIANT EAGLE.
(Cloth.)

FIG. 71. Multiflite "CONCORDE"
Control-line kite.

FIG.73. BILL MANUEL'S SUPAKITE.

two PVC tube spars. They have triple hole vents (see Lloyd). The colours are those of thirty-two different League Football teams and the printed pattern is of a leaping goalkeeper. They fly very steadily in light breezes, and fill out well with air pressure. The curved tail depresses and stabilises.

Tornado and *Hawk:* two aerobatic designs introduced in 1977.

Seamer Products

A long-established kite company at Hull is Seamer Products whose trademark is a Leprechaun. This company also imports and distributes the German Tosta range (see below).

Cutter: two sizes of cloth sail Eddy with tail in porous, coloured cotton.

War: a winged box type with cotton sail, also in two sizes. This long-established design is robust.

Sky Cat

Another comparatively recent introduction to the aerobatic ranges comes from the west of England where Sky Cat make extruded PVC spars for:

RCW1-Parawing: has rectangular-section spars, a polythene sail and a 75-ft (23-m) ribbon tail.

Sampson's cloth Giant Eagle, a beautiful flyer in all weather.

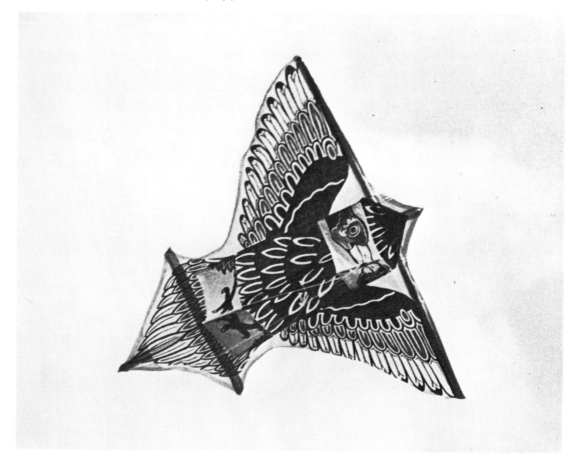

Sky Sports

These kites were introduced at the heyday of the aerobatic kites with:

Sky-Rider: a Rogallo-frame design with triple spars, and what is referred to as a Superflex design with a two-stage sprung nose. Twin-control lines in polyester link to a double yoke bridle, as with most other control-line kites, but the 75-ft (23-m) streamer tail attaches to the rear bridle point, as distinct from the cross brace on the Powell kites. This kite is remarkably manoeuvrable, and can spin rapidly or recover quickly. It normally has a yellow sail and black streamer. (See *Ariel* kites.)

Plans and One-offs

Apart from the kites made *en masse* by the manufacturers mentioned above, a number of kiting enthusiasts will supply plans or make kites to order. The plans are usually for highly original designs such as Alex Pearson's Roller (Fig. 147), Bill Manuel's Supakite (Fig. 73) or the Kensington Gardens bird shapes as illustrated in Chapter 7. If you have the opportunity, it is an investment to purchase one of these expertly made kites. They last for ages, and often change hands at little more than the cost of the materials.

Imports to Britain

Apart from its own domestic products, Britain has an eager market for imported kites. Details of these are given under the headings North Pacific, Wepa, Pax, Tosta, Top Flite, Gunther and Synestructics in the sections that follow.

HOLLAND AND GERMANY

There is a strange lack of large-scale kite marketing in Europe except in Holland and West Germany. Designs also appear to have stagnated. Almost all the factories are turning out fold-up apron and Eddy designs with printed patterns on clear polythene sails. So much so that when a long-tailed dragon kite was announced at the Nuremberg Toy Fair it was described as *Die Neue Drachen-Generation* – and this with a design that is centuries old, not only in Malaysia but also in Germany itself.

The following list, again in alphabetical order of manufacturer, is not claimed to be complete but represents a fair assessment of kites in production.

Conacord

A specialist firm in Germany, Conacord, manufactures fifteen different printed plastic apron-style two-stick variants of the Malay kite. Typically, over half are printed with birds of prey. If you look closely at the types of pattern applied to these continental plastic kites they fall clearly into bird, butterfly, aeroplane or Red Indian categories, which does not make for much variety.

Indian: the only Malay diamond-shaped kite in the range. At 18 × 22 ins (45 × 55 cm) it is a toy line.

Butterfly: the smallest of the apron shapes; 22 × 18 ins (55 × 45 cm).

Buzzard and *Tortoiseshell:* medium-size apron kites, 18 × 27 ins (45 × 70 cm), they fly well in light winds.

Jet bomber: 21 × 26 ins (55 × 65 cm); *Falcon* 31 × 20 ins (50 × 80 cm); *Butterfly, Batman* and *Hawk* 31 × 23 ins (90 × 60 cm); *Skyraider* 35 × 30 ins (90 × 75 cm); *Condor* 39 × 24 ins (110 × 60 cm); *Osprey* and *Golden Eagle* 43 × 30 ins (110 × 75 cm); *Sea Eagle* 49 × 33 ins (125 × 85 cm). All these are two-stick apron shape with transparent or translucent white backgrounds and two-line bridles. Dowel spars fit plastic sockets for assembly.

Drako

One company which departs from the standard shape is Drako of Hamburg who have revived the Malay Dragon:

Spermy: a 48-ft (15-m) long metallised Mylar Dragon shape tapering from a rounded head to a pointed tail. Supplied in a silver or gold base colour with black overprint, it flies in jerky motion with the tail fluttering, giving the impression of embryonic life. This is one type that must be kept well away from overhead cables as the material will conduct electricity. The material was in fact changed for 1977 to a yellow plastic.

Dux

A toy firm well known for its ready-to-fly model aeroplanes is Dux. They combined their inventive talents to produce a helicopter kite in 1974. They also manufacture other kites but these are unknown to me.

Rotokite: all plastic, with a five-sided kite rotor above a moulded fuselage, an aeroplane-style tail assembly and wind cups on the five dowel spars to rotate the kite surface. It is heavily loaded, and only useful in strong winds. The ingenious part is the transparent film used for the kite: it has printed rotor blades to make it look like a real helicopter (Fig. 74).

Paul Gunther

The outstanding exception to stereotyped kite design in Europe are the products of Paul Gunther, a specialist in all kinds of outdoor leisure toys and hobbies. Gunther introduced the printed aeroplane pattern on otherwise transparent kite sails, and he maintains a range of these ordinary kites while producing remarkable original devices, all in plastic. They are imported to Britain by Riko.

Brazilian Butterfly, Falcon and *Vampire:* three printed-pattern, 30-in. (76-cm) apron, Malay two-stick kites.

Bonanza and *Condor:* two 36-in. (92-cm) apron Malays but with a yoked spar arrangement to spread the tail to give a wider rear end to the sail. They are excellent flyers – referred to by some as simulators because only the printed shape (especially of the Bonanza) is visible in the air.

Flexi Drachen: a 29 × 35 in. (74 × 89 cm) cartoon sled with Mickey Mouse or a similar printed pattern. The first of the European sleds, it is not vented.

Kasten Drachen: an all-plastic collapsible 29 × 48 in. (74 × 122 cm) winged box which must be the first of its kind. The use of plastic film for a large War or Blériot type must create strong line tension in any reasonable wind, but makes it possible to fly this kind of design in conditions where the heavier, porous cloth-covered kite cannot lift.

Turbino: a rotary kite of delightful simplicity that collapses into a smart, small package complete with nylon line on a winder. The basic rotor is 15 ins (38 cm) square, with red, yellow and blue swirls to add to the visual impression. Four dowels brace the rotor and have wind cups combined with spring-loaded plastic ends. The fuselage is a stick, carrying a green sheet-plastic tail assembly with a yellow kite-keel bridle. A brilliant concept, the design supports a surprising weight and will carry the Ferry messenger despite its small dimensions (Fig. 75).

Deltaplan: the nearest to a true Rogallo in all kiting. A 39-in. (1-m) span model hang glider with a pendant pilot. The glider can be kept on the kite line or released to sail down. Striped colours and clever design features made it the star of the 1976 Nuremberg Toy Fair.

Comet: a square all-plastic header for a 33-ft (10-m) snake tail is a correct but inadequate description of this brilliant design for a minimal kite. It comes in a small bubble pack with reeled nylon line and yet can be assembled and flown in minutes. Even the bridles are plastic. It is perfect for children, and extremely easy to fly in all conditions despite the fact that the header is only 18 ins (45 cm) across its diagonal.

Ferry: not a kite, but the only commercial messenger known to me which will ascend to great heights on a line, collapse its two plastic wings and slide to the flyer. It is designed just to go up and down with a propeller, and can be converted to carry parachutes etc. (See Chapter 4.)

A Gunther Deltaplan in level launch. Released as a glider from a line.

Superfly: a hang glider type, 30 × 48 ins (75 × 120 cm), this was a 1977 introduction.

Akrobat: another 1977 introduction, this is a modification of the apron Malays mentioned earlier.

Knoop

In Holland the name of Knoop is synonymous with kites and they have a huge range of the apron-shape two-stick plastic Malays with coloured overprinted patterns. They also make some cloth kites and specials for advertising. These kites are illustrated and numbered but not named in the Knoop catalogue, so the names below are my own descriptive ones, and not the manufacturers.

Butterfly: 21 × 16 ins (53 × 42 cm); *Jet Bomber* 21 × 26 ins (53 × 66 cm); and *Bird* 31 × 20 ins (80 × 50 cm) are the smaller Knoop kites, also supplemented by mixed patterns on a true Malay shape. All are collapsible two-stick models and similar to the range already described under Conacord.

Batman, Butterfly, Hawk, Owl, and *Robin:* all 31 × 23 in. (80 × 60 cm) apron Malay designs.

Skyraider, Eagle and *Condor:* 35-in. (90-cm) span larger versions of the above. The largest are the *Osprey* and *Golden Eagle,* 43 × 30 in. (110 × 75 cm) designs, again each like the Conacord series (Fig. 76).

Cloth Cutters: in 30-, 39- and 43-in. (76-, 100- and 110-cm) span variants, are of differing shapes, cotton-covered in many colours and with a triangular box in the centre, leading to a two-line bridle (Fig. 77).

Pax

Under the trademark of Pax the Schmohl firm, from Göppingen in Germany, are known for all kinds of flying models from catapult gliders to rubber power. Naturally they include kites in the range. Assembly is by Paxmatic, a fold-out-and-click system. (They are imported into Britain by A. A. Hales Ltd.)

Roto Pax: an unusual device whose wings rotate about the spars and generate lift. It comes with reel and line and is a popular seaside seller. It has a 19-in. (50-cm) span.

Filou: a mini-kite, made in pressed polystyrene (styrofoam) and printed with a clown pattern. Only 6 ins (15 cm) across, it is an Eddy-shaped children's toy.

Pucki: an extended, integral-tail Malay two-stick with a 25-in. (63-cm) span, it is 55 ins (140 cm) long, with a worm-like printed pattern.

Flimmy: a dragon-style kite, also *Tilly,* all with the long tail so popular in Europe.

Jungmeister: the best known of all Pax kites. It is a straight Eddy with dihedralled lateral spars and a two-line bridle of short attachment spacing. It measures 34 × 36 ins (87 × 91 cm).

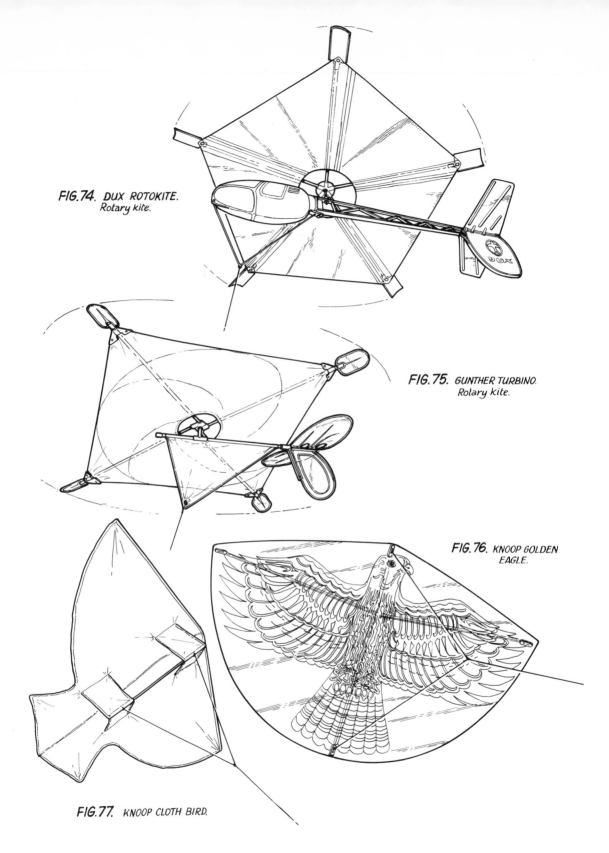

FIG.74. DUX ROTOKITE.
Rotary kite.

FIG.75. GUNTHER TURBINO.
Rotary kite.

FIG. 76. KNOOP GOLDEN
EAGLE.

FIG.77. KNOOP CLOTH BIRD.

An aerobatic two-line version is also made. There is a tendency for the Paxmatic plastic fittings to over-ride in strong winds, causing the kite to collapse.

Eagle: 30 × 36 ins (76 × 91 cm) and *Firebird* 39 × 41 ins (100 × 105 cm) also have Paxmatic fittings. Firebird has enlarged apron areas which flap. The Eagle also comes in a matched pair set for two in train. In 1977 Pax introduced a two-line aerobatic version of Eagle.

Owl: a large apron flapper, 26 × 30 ins (67 × 77 cm).

Buzzard: similar in size to Owl but more conventional in shape.

Red Milan: a giant Eagle, with a 49-in.

(125-cm) span, 36 ins (92 cm) long, with a keel bridle.

Luftikus: a hot-air balloon pattern, is a smaller version, 30 × 36 ins (76 × 91 cm).

Bobby: an apron type with a streamer at the trailing edge, it is 22 ins (57 cm) square; there is a *Butterfly* of about the same size, but with unslit trailing edges.

Parachutist and *Rocketship*, both 26 × 33 ins (65 × 83 cm) and the larger *Space Station*, 30 × 36 ins (76 × 92 cm): three straight two-stick Malay designs.

Accessories: Pax spools are perhaps the most useful, and feature a line guide in each case. There are two clever reel spools and an ingenious bobbin-type winder.

The Pax Jungmeister, a very popular German kite.

Tosta

One firm which has not wholly diverted into the apron extensions of Malay designs and still produces straight-edged diamond Malay shapes is Tosta. But they are still in line with all the rest by using birds of prey, Indians, aeroplanes etc. in their patterns. Seamer Products import them into Britain.

Moon Man, Thistlethrush, Fire Kite, Sheriff and *Aeroplane:* five patterns on 22 × 26 in. (56 × 66 cm) straight Malay shapes, each with two streamers for tails.

Owl, Buzzard, Gull, Heron and *Aeroplane:* five patterns on a diamond shape not unlike an Indian fighter. At 26 × 36 ins (66 × 91 cm) they ought to make very good flyers.

Bird of Paradise, Indian Chief, Clown and *Balloon:* four larger straight Malay shapes, 27 × 29 ins (68 × 72 cm), each without a tail.

Icarus, Heron and *Eagle:* the largest in the Tosta range, these have a novel back-to-front delta shape with a projecting triangle on the nose. They are all 29 × 46 ins (72 × 116 cm).

Accessories: Tosta reels and winders come in five different types, each with braided nylon line which is light and appears to have about 20 lb (9 kg) breaking strain.

Wepa

Another Dutch company which is well known for its kites is Wepa, and though the range is kept to ten basic sizes and patterns this company produces many other kites for special purposes and advertising. All spars are dowels, plugged into plastic sockets. RF Developments import them into Britain. All Wepa kites have two-line bridles and fly well, but there is a tendency for the sail to tear at the plastic socket area where the spars plug in and prior reinforcement is a wise precaution. (The kite names given below are my own translations from the Wepa catalogue.)

Eagle: number one in the range, and the largest at 46 × 30 ins (116 × 75 cm). It is an apron-type Malay with a greater than usual extension of the wing area, so that in flight it adopts a Rogallo curvature which is stable and graceful (Fig. 78).

Buzzard, Javelin, Parachutist and *Harlequin:* each has a maximum dimension of 31 ins (80 cm), but with quite different shapes. Each is a true flyer but the best of all is *No. 5* (the *Harlequin*) which is a large square apron type that will stay up for ever (Fig. 79). *Javelin* is an apron with a nose added, patterned after the RAF Delta fighter.

Footballer: a small, traditional Malay shape, 21 × 24 ins (54 × 60 cm).

Indian Chief: a larger version, 29 × 31 ins (73 × 80 cm).

Clown: an octagon, 29 ins (73 cm) across, which needs a tail for best flight performance.

Butterfly: 23 ins (58 cm) and 32 ins (80 cm) span, each is an apron Malay with dihedral on spar attachments.

ITALY

Quercetti

Though not well known for kites, Italy does produce the Quercetti range of kites – 22-in. (55-cm), 27-in. (68-cm) and 42-in. (107-cm) delta shapes in plastic for beach use. The swept-back spars in these designs are unusual.

JAPAN

A visit to a Japanese kite shop is an intriguing experience. The *kato* (or *dako*) is a matter of such national pride and tradition that designs, materials and decorations have changed very little in centuries. They are hand-made from selected bamboo split by skilled strokes with a long knife which looks like a chopper. The bamboo 'bones' are lashed and bound into frame shapes, covered with hand-made papers and then hand-decorated.

Off-the-peg kites hang in gloriously coloured festoons in shops such as Bingoya (69 Wakamatsu-cho, Shinjuku-Ku, Tokyo) where you can purchase all the famous traditional shapes.

(Facing page) *Top:* Beautiful Chinese silk Butterfly. *Below:* Chinese Phoenix and Dragonfly paper kites flying well in a light breeze; these two on separate lines and flown by the author's son.

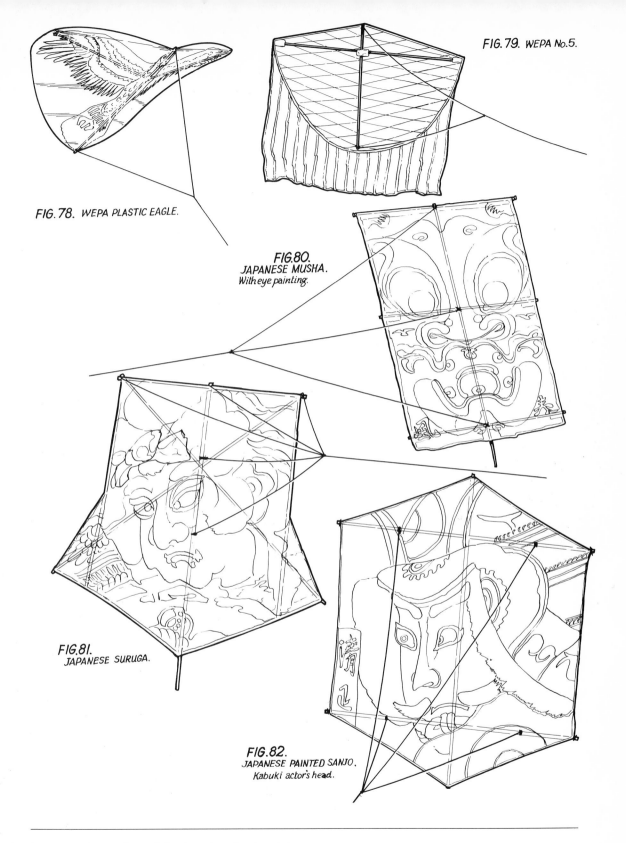

FIG. 78. WEPA PLASTIC EAGLE.

FIG. 79. WEPA No.5.

FIG.80.
JAPANESE MUSHA.
With eye painting.

FIG.81.
JAPANESE SURUGA.

FIG.82.
JAPANESE PAINTED SANJO.
Kabuki actor's head.

(Facing page) *Top:* This 15-ft (3-m) version of S. F. Cody's
seventy-year-old design is part of a train of man-lifting
kites. *Below left:* Tom Van Sant's Clown kite. *Below right:*
The gaily coloured Gunther Turbino with wind cups and
rotating plastic sail.

The full range cannot possibly be described, for the variations applied by the individual artist-kitemakers and the local characteristics make the selection enormous. The average size is 22 × 18 ins (56 × 46 cm) and all the kites are flat. They are framed, and thus fixed in shape and not collapsible. Bridles are not always provided, nor are pick-up points indicated, but excellent literature is available with many diagrams to help the Westerner understand this ancient oriental art. If you cannot obtain the books, the best advice is to bridle to all corners so that four- or five-line bridles hold the frame at a constant angle of 18°–20°. A few random samples:

Musha: rectangular with an extended centre spar, it uses a three-line bridle and flies well. The black-and-white face has a prominent eye decoration. This is the simplest of the Japanese kites; only four bamboos are used – three laterals and one centre spar (Fig. 80).

Suruga: has two diagonal bones to extend the lower corners into extra triangular areas. The brightly painted figurehead of a Kabuki actor makes this a startling kite. It needs a four-line bridle to the upper half and flies stably in a steady breeze. The Suruga is robust, being full-framed, and its extended centre spar enables you to tie a tail if conditions warrant it (Fig. 81).

Sanjo: a hexagonal shape, basically a square of about 18 ins (46 cm) with extended triangles at base and apex. As sold, only two lateral spars are fitted, so it is rather like a sled on edge and four bridle lines are recommended. My advice is not to try and fly this kite as a flexible, which would risk damaging the painting. These are usually signed by the artist and make beautiful room decorations. In my experience adding a spine, which is obviously

Japanese kite shop at Kawada, Cho, Tokyo.

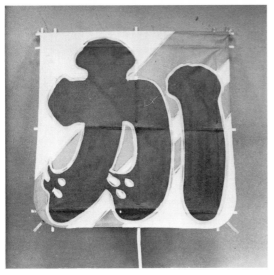

The Machi-Jirushi, a small version of the giant Hamamatsu fighting kite.

intended, though not supplied, makes the Sanjo delightfully easy to fly (Fig. 82).

Machi-Jirushi or *Hamamatsu Fighting Kite:* only about 15 ins (38 cm) square, but with its centre spar extended twice the length. It is a small version of the giant ceremonial kites flown at the annual festival in May.

Simpler Kites

If you are lucky enough to be near a Japanese arts and crafts imports shop you may be able to buy less sophisticated Japanese kites. Printed eagles and butterflies on stout paper with keel bridles, about 39 ins (1 m) span, and multiple-disked centipedes are obtainable in London, for example. But they cannot all claim to be representative of the ancient art of kitecraft as practised by the experts in Aichi, Fukuoka, Nagasaki, Shizuoka and Akita.

Japanese decorative kite – an unlikely flyer.

Hiness Kite Kit

This kite kit is a development which was announced in 1975 by the Hiness Co. This is a 60-in. (150-cm) semi-scale aeroplane which can be decorated as a Willow trainer or a Boeing Kaydet. It weighs about $2\frac{3}{4}$ lb (1·25 kg) because all the flying surfaces are of pre-painted corrugated card, and stout spruce members make a cruciform of struts for the two wings and become undercarriage legs as well. To transport the one-piece kiteplane you need an estate car or van. The recommended bridle is a long yoke to a single line. The type lends itself to the method described for the wind plane in Chapter 6. Though very impressive, it takes about ten hours to make up and problems of transport and storage tend to inhibit interest. Hiness also make an Autogyro type, which is difficult to operate

unless you have an understanding of such aeroplanes.

CHINA

While Japanese off-the-peg kites are rigid-frame, those from China are semi-flexible, and ingeniously collapsible. Made of toughened paper, and printed by hand in beautiful colours, the Chinese bird and insect kites are true works of art. At one time they were also obtainable in printed silk. I count myself lucky to have purchased one as late as May 1974 at the Chinese Arts and Crafts Store, Kowloon, Hong Kong. The shape is a butterfly (Fig. 83), perfectly painted, and it is assembled by plugging together the five bamboo bones into the network of the body and locking with small metal loops. In flight, the wings flap just like those of a real butterfly.

Chinese kite store in Kowloon, Hong Kong.

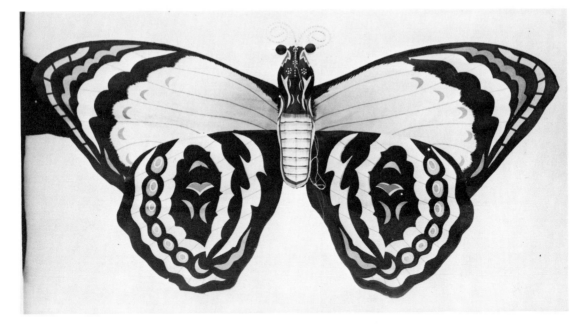

Chinese silk butterfly kite – prettiest of all.

The range of paper kites exported from the Chinese factory in Shanghai covers eighteen types. Some of these have found their way to the USA and Britain through kite shops and craft centres, but not the entire range, which is coded by numbers. My own names for the kites are given below. The whole range is known by the Hong Kong outlet for China as 54F, and this prefix applies to each of these numbers:

13. Longtailed Moth: 40 × 22 ins (102 × 56 cm) with head antennae.

14. Dragonfly: two sets of wings, and a long tail 39 × 33 ins (100 × 84 cm).

15. Locust: two sets of wings, no tail, 39 × 18 ins (100 × 46 cm).

16. Hawk: large wings, long tail, 41 × 17½ ins (105 × 45 cm).

17. Swallow: twin tail, short body, 41 × 13½ ins (105 × 33 cm).

18. Firebird: mythical red bird, 37 × 21½ ins (94 × 64 cm), good to fly.

19. Duck: predominantly white, 39 × 15 ins (100 × 39 cm).

20. Phoenix: very long twin tails, the prettiest of the series, 39 × 36 ins (100 × 94 cm).

21. Owl: squat-tailed white bird, 39 × 14 ins (100 × 36 cm).

22. Bee: two sets of wings, squat, 42 × 11 ins (107 × 28 cm).

24. Locust: long tail, single set of wings, 40 × 28 ins (102 × 74 cm).

25. Pigeon: larger tail, white bird, 41 × 20 ins (104 × 51 cm).

26. Brown Owl: large wings, longish tail, 42 × 19 ins (106 × 50 cm).

27. Mosquito: two sets of large wings, 37 × 18 ins (94 × 46 cm).

29. Pheasant: colourful, well proportioned, 40 × 18 ins (102 × 46 cm).

30. Osprey: well-feathered, 42 × 17½ ins (106 × 45 cm).

31. Flying Frog: large area tail, 33 × 45½ ins (84 × 116 cm).

32. Peacock: beautiful large tail, 39 × 26 ins (100 × 66 cm).

It would be intriguing to discover the identities of the missing numbers in the

101

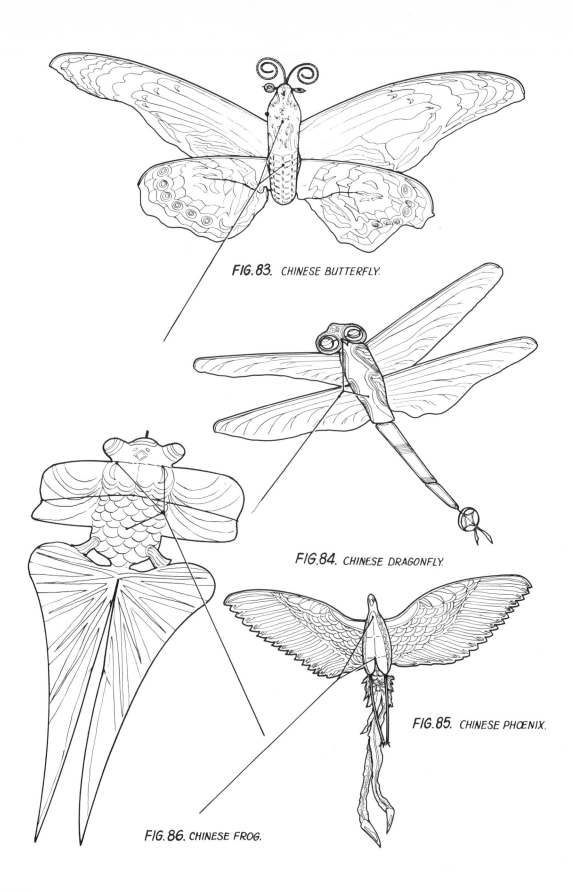

FIG. 83. CHINESE BUTTERFLY.

FIG. 84. CHINESE DRAGONFLY.

FIG. 85. CHINESE PHŒNIX.

FIG. 86. CHINESE FROG.

sequence. Each of these kites adopts a standard construction for either one- or two-winged (Fig. 84) assembly, and the majority of the birds have a similar wing shape, as sketched for the Phoenix (Fig. 85), with a curved leading edge. In all cases the bodies are a built-up framework of bamboo, and the wing trailing edges are free to flap. Because they are paper and not framed these kites should not be flown in damp conditions or blustery winds, because they may tear when weakened by moisture.

Not all the Chinese exports are flappers. There is also a framed butterfly which has a main wing kinked so that it obtains an aerofoil section, and a mandarin figure. One very attractive shape which combines the framed kite with a huge flexible tail is the *Frog* (Fig. 86) over 6 ft (2 m) long and a handful to release if it is gusty. It is impressive in the air and can be classified as aerodynamic because of the way it develops a lifting shape and makes use of the stabilising tail element.

Chinese butterfly kite with rigid outline and tassel tail.

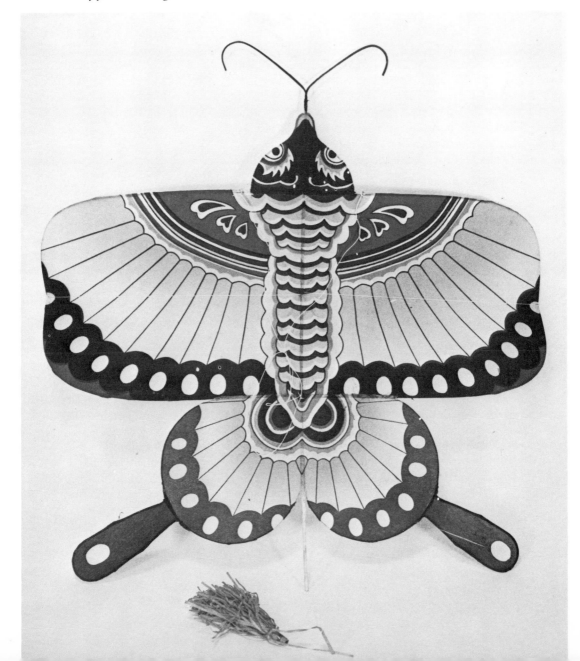

USA

The Americans are inventive people and the very broad variety of designs which are marketed prove the point. They range from the simple sled to the tetrahedral, the simulated Clipper ship to the bird-like Blackhawks, with which I shall begin this survey of American off-the-peg kites. Here, more than for any other source, I apologise in advance for inadvertent omissions. Those listed are the ones of which I have personal experience.

Airplane Kite Co.

Ray Holland Jr started his Airplane Kite Co. in 1948. An aeronautical engineer and keen kiter, he had taken out the first of his many kite patents in 1938. He produced a paper stunt kite in the early 1950s, then went over to plastics and in 1965 launched the Blackhawk, a name which was registered as his trademark. Frank Scott designed a sled type for Ray Holland to make in 1967, hence the Scott Sled, a title registered to the company and now synonymous with the flexible bag kite everywhere. Later designs on Blackhawk lines have all been patented and each of them has been the subject of aerodynamic study, making full use of Ray Holland's expertise.

They have several points in common. Wooden spars are made with dowels, many of the highly stressed spars being twin dowels, side by side, to give a horizontal figure-of-eight cross-section. These spars are bow-braced. In the Blackhawk bird simulators the peripheral bracing can be adjusted to tweak the nose to right or left for trimming the flight. All the designs are free of bridles. Kite lines join direct to the spar or keel. All fly at shallow angles. Most can be taken down on the ground and jerked up, and none of them requires a tail for stability. The covering in some cases is Du Pont Tyvek, while others have polythene covering.

Blackhawk: like the Brazilian Papagaio (see below), this design is a black bird silhouette, cut out (not printed on transparent sail) and braced by adjustable rigging string around the edge of the shape made by two bowed spars, lateral and longitudinal. It has a 46-in. (117-cm) span, it adjusts for all winds, and is remarkably steady and reliable. It is a kite to be thoroughly recommended (Fig. 87).

Spitfire: similar in structure but smaller at 35 ins span, 27 ins long (89 × 68 cm) and with a red aircraft shape. It is equally stable.

Blue Bird: larger tail area version, the same size as Spitfire but with two separate lateral spars spaced parallel to strengthen the broader wing.

Dove of Peace: has the same two-spar design as the Blue Bird, and a similar-shaped bird-like sail in pure white; 35-in. (89-cm) span.

Skyscraper: a 36-in. (92-cm)-long box kite with one black and one white cell of narrow chord. Can be joined side by side in six or eight units to build up a giant meteorological-type kite (Fig. 88).

Zenith: a 36-in. (92-cm) box kite with larger square cells than Skyscraper. It has a white covering with single line attachment, and flies apart if crashed. (See Chapter 2.)

Skyhook: a keel-bowed Eddy with extremely light construction, it features a forward attachment point for a kite line. It is orange with a blue keel, has a 36-in. span, and is 36 ins (92 cm) long. A remarkable flyer in light winds, it has been airborne when others were unable to lift. It tends to fly overhead in stronger breezes, and is very stable (Fig. 89).

Scott Sled: the original! It has three spars and a triangular vent. The centre spar stiffens the flexible $35\frac{1}{2}$ × 40 in. (90 × 102 cm) canopy against collapsing. It flies in a light breeze up to full-strength winds. It is yellow.

Space-Ship Earth: an ecology-printed motif on a Tyvek unvented sled with split trailing tails to 52 ins (132 cm) length. A novelty.

Wind Wizard: a small flexible sled, 18 × 27 ins (46 × 69 cm), which rolls up to be carried anywhere. It flies anywhere, is practically faultless and foolproof. Mine just wore

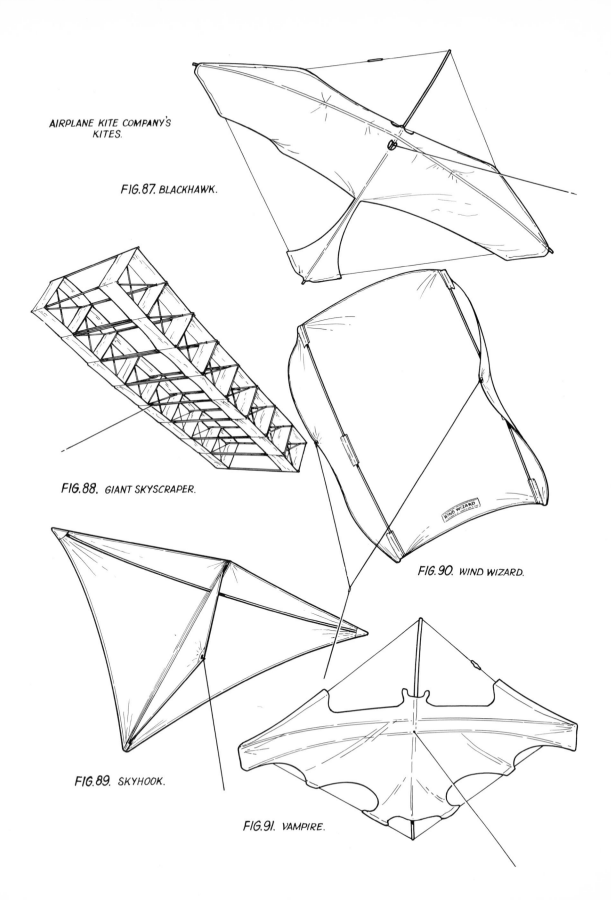

AIRPLANE KITE COMPANY'S
KITES.

FIG.87. BLACKHAWK.

FIG.88. GIANT SKYSCRAPER.

FIG.90. WIND WIZARD.

FIG.89. SKYHOOK.

FIG.91. VAMPIRE.

out with too much flying. It has no vents, and comes in mixed colours (Fig. 90).

Sky Sail: a billowing unvented sled in red polyethylene, 27 × 39½ ins (68 × 100 cm). It rolls up, is quick to get airborne, and stays put all day on a pegged line.

Vampire: a black vampire-bat profile of the same dimensions as the Spitfire, with a single lateral bowed spar (Fig. 91).

Sky Lark: a painted bird design on a lark-shaped sail to the same 35-in. (89-cm) span. It is 27 ins (68 cm) long with two parallel lateral spars (Fig. 92).

Gayla Industries

Largest of all the US manufacturers, but scarcely known in Europe at all, is Gayla Industries of Houston, Texas. They market keel delta shapes with printed patterns and use coloured plastic sails with unique square box-section flexible plastic tube spars. The shapes are similar, with differences in the decorations and the span.

Firebird: a keel delta of 54 ins (138 cm) span.

Super Bat: slightly larger, and a better performer provided you use Plasticine weight blobs to balance out the tips if there is a tendency to bank to one side. This one has a 60-in. (152-cm) span.

Sky Spy: a popular and inexpensive 45-in. (114-cm) keel delta.

Space Demon, Sky Rider and *Baby Bat:* each has a 48-in. (122-cm) span, with different patterns.

Hi-Flier

One American company that has produced the kind of quick assembly kite which is so common in Europe is Hi-Flier of Decatur (Damon Industries) who call their special device a flexhedral junction.

Hustler: an Eddy bow with umbrella assembly of printed Mylar sail, it has a single point line attachment.

Keelkite: a printed eagle on a 48-in. (122-cm) span delta with a long keel which extends on a centre spar behind a 'wing' trailing edge.

Spinwinder: the Hi-Flier name for a reel that has a line guide and reels off like a fishing-line reel. The handle has a winder arm.

Kung Flew: a 48-in. (122-cm) delta; 28 ins (71 cm) long with flexible extruded plastic leading edge spars of rectangular section, a centre spar and plastic clip braced side spars. The two tails are each 30 ft (10 m) long. A single line flyer, good in all winds, it has a coolie face caricature and black tails to look like a moustache.

Centipede: has a 54-in. (137-cm) span, and is 32 ins (81 cm) long. It has a printed, flexible plastic 'head' with an open keel bridle, plus a 30 ft (10 m) long, 15 ins (38 cm) wide tail which is brightly printed and makes a very attractive novelty that flies well.

Super Stunt: the 'Baron' kite machine has a 32-in. (81-cm) span and is 42 ins (107 cm) long with twin 30-ft (10-m) streamers. This is an American stunter with lines connected directly to the lateral spars which meet in the centre with an ingenious folding plastic joiner.

Big Brain: a huge Eddy, 45 ins (114 cm) long, it needs a bow string for stability. A low-cost purchase for casual kiting.

Kite Factory

The west coast of America has a staunch kite enthusiast in Dave Checkley of Seattle, who runs the Kite Factory and specialises in original and individual designs that would not otherwise be marketed. You could say he is offering unique kites off-the-peg for others to enjoy!

Parafoil: an original Jalbert design with triple keel and no rigid spars, made in nylon spinnaker cloth. This type is similar to a parachute with an aerofoil camber on its surface. It can lift considerable weights and has been used for various scientific experiments (Fig. 93).

Winged Box Kite: a full box centre with Blériot or War-kite style side wings in polyurethane-coated orange nylon.

Manoeuvrable Box Kite: an unusual kite, it has

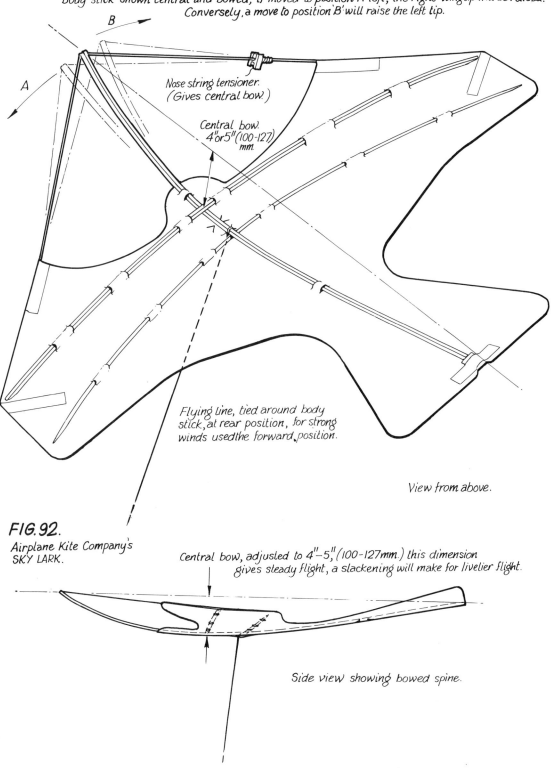

Body stick shown central and bowed, if moved to position 'A' left, the right wingtip will be raised. Conversely, a move to position 'B' will raise the left tip.

B

A

Nose string tensioner. (Gives central bow.)

Central bow. 4" or 5" (100-127) mm.

Flying line, tied around body stick, at rear position, for strong winds used the forward position.

View from above.

FIG. 92.
Airplane Kite Company's
SKY LARK.

Central bow, adjusted to 4"-5" (100-127mm.) this dimension gives steady flight, a slackening will make for livelier flight.

Side view showing bowed spine.

a central vane (called a destabiliser) in aluminised Mylar across the front cell. The kite is made in orange and blue nylon. It is flown on two lines to manoeuvre, and is a form of control-line kite.

Allison Sled: a reproduction of the first sled, with a triangular vent, in polyurethane-coated nylon.

Minifoil: a small Jalbert parafoil with a tail drogue in which the whole kite packs away.

Open Keel Delta: the bicentennial year craze. It is a nylon 60-in. (152-cm) delta with an open keel to stabilise it, and a Mylar sail.

Mylar Box Kite: consists of four wings on a box kite 36 ins (92 cm) long with a 29-in. (74-cm) span.

Bullet: Ed Grauel's combination of the Allison sled and Jalbert parafoil with drogue has a double aerofoil surface.

Accessories: the Kite Factory has many unusual and very useful accessories including a kite carrier – a zippered nylon case with leather handles, 5 ins in diameter and 38 ins long (13 × 95 cm), to carry a KF Tube; and a kite line skeiner for rapidly winding line in at a yard a time.

Lee Custom Kites

Fabric covering is a feature of Lee Custom Kites, which, as the name suggests, is a specialist house providing kites to order for a limited range of designs. All are covered with a cloth that is 77 per cent Dacron and 23 per cent cotton, and none of the designs could be described as small. Heavy-duty reels for enthusiasts are also part of the Lee service.

Super Eagle: this 6-ft (182-cm) span bird shape, with rigid leading edge, flapping trailing edges and a tail, is 40 ins (102 cm) long. It comes with a carrying case, and is a truly professional job.

National Eagle: a 5 ft 9 ins (175 cm) variant in mixed colours, partly hand painted.

Super Bat: a 6-ft (182-cm) span bat shape in black with lighter colour wings and a red body.

Bat: as above, but all black with white eyeballs.

Super Arrow: a 4 ft 8 ins (142 cm) semi-aeroplane shape with keel bridle; red and black with decorative tails.

Junior Arrow: a 42-in. (106-cm) span smaller version of the Super Arrow.

Arrow: a Mylar (metallised) variant, 30 × 19 ins (76 × 48 cm), it has a coloured tape outline with long tails.

Korean Fighter: made of Mylar with a silk-screen-printed butterfly or Korean symbol.

Marblehead Kite Co.

A range of unusual kites (for the USA) is produced in Massachusetts by the Marblehead Kite Co. These kites are made in the traditional Malay shape in cloth, with patterns sewn on in contrasting colours. There are apparently six different patterns.

Diamond: Malay-shaped cloth kite with *Locomotive, Beer Mug, Butterfly, Gull, Sailboat* (Yacht) and *Ice Cream Cone* cloth patterns sewn over. Each has a Mylar strip tail. The design is extremely durable and good for all weathers.

Nantucket Kiteman

Famous for his delta designs in the east coast area is Mr Hartig, otherwise known as the Nantucket Kiteman.

Ace and *Valkyrie:* these two basic designs of up to 6 ft (2 m) span are handmade to Hartig's patented (3,347,500) design with a deep keel and three-stick spars with a cross brace. They are made in carefully selected material with the brightest of patterns and can be rolled up or assembled in seconds. The design is very flexible and does not have a rigid nose joint. In full flight, a Rogallo form develops, but in gliding attitude, or when pressure drops, the kite edges flex independently. They are very highly recommended as easy flyers giving excellent performance. Be sure to use at least 30 lb (15 kg) strain line.

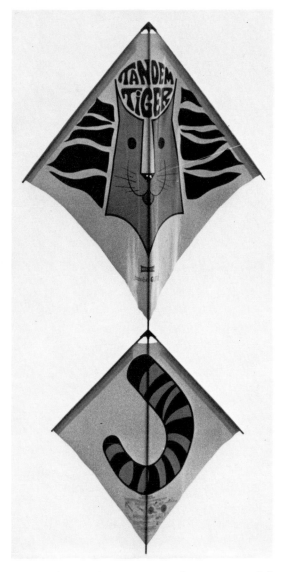

Jumbo Glite Tandem Tiger. No tail streamers needed.

North Pacific

In the north-west of the USA, at Bend in Oregon, is the highly productive plant of North Pacific which makes the world-famous series of Glites. I have already described in Chapter 5 how the Glite was the first kite with a two-line bridle for aerobatics. It also led the field for its sheer simplicity and ease of flying.

The Glite is deservedly popular all over the world and has established one more standard that is unmatched – that of consistency. The Glite is produced to such high standards that every one is identical in balance and shape, two factors which are critical to its performance. A. A. Hales Ltd import them into Britain.

Glite: a triple-spar Rogallo-frame assembly with dihedral and shallow conical camber. It is made in two sizes: $33\frac{1}{2}$ ins (85 cm) and $39\frac{1}{2}$ ins (100 cm) long over the stinger centre spar. This carries an extension for tying plastic-tape tail streamers (Fig. 94). There are nine printed patterns. The large designs are *Pretty Bird, Sky Diver* and *Red Baron* (Fig. 95). The smaller ones are *Bug Off, Eagle, Arrow, Bionic Buzzard, Aqua Lady* and *Dragonfly*. Red Baron is the most popular, Bug Off second. The *Jumbo Kite* is a twin Glite sold in two printings, *Spy Eye* and *Tandem Tiger*, each 5 ft (152 cm) long, with two sizes of Glite on a linked control spar. The Jumbo does not need a tail, and flies well (Fig. 96). All Glites lift easily in light breeze to strong wind. No bridles are required and full instructions are printed on the kite sail. These kites can be linked in train, and their stable flight characteristic is always impressive.

Rogallo Flexikites

Although I refer to the Glite and others which followed its success as Rogallo types, what is meant is that the construction is triple spar, joining at the nose with a squarish sail left to have two free trailing edges. While the sail billows up, it does not completely follow the aerodynamic principles first established by Francis M. Rogallo who is also a kitemaker in his own right, at the birthplace of powered flight, Kitty Hawk.

Flexikite: has a 15-in. (38-cm) square sail on a 22-in. (56-cm) keel with a four-line bridle to be flown on one line, but which can be flown aerobatically on two lines. Sold assembled or as a kit, it has the deep conical camber associated with the Rogallo patents.

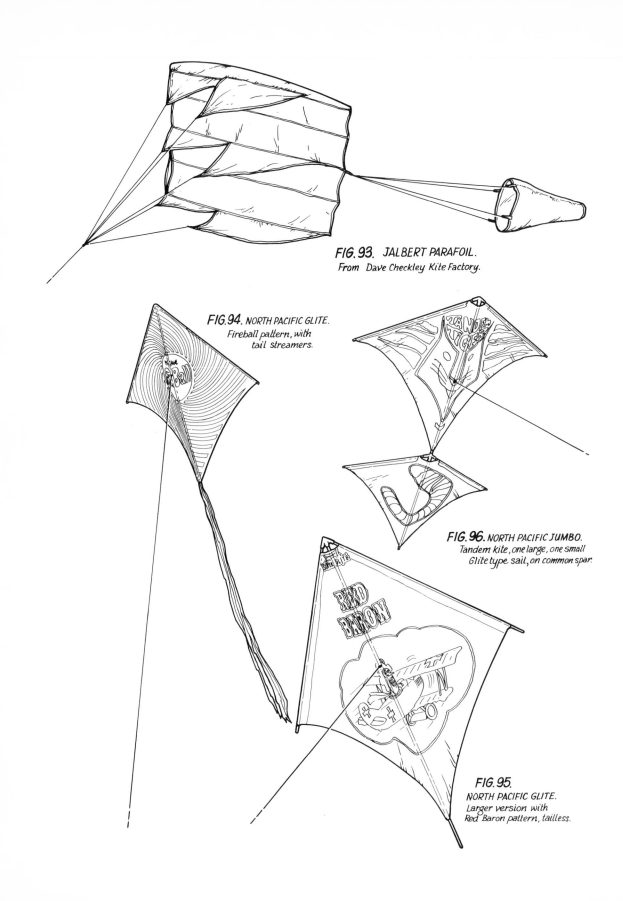

FIG. 93. JALBERT PARAFOIL.
From Dave Checkley Kite Factory.

FIG. 94. NORTH PACIFIC GLITE.
Fireball pattern, with
tail streamers.

FIG. 96. NORTH PACIFIC JUMBO.
Tandem kite, one large, one small
Glite type sail, on common spar.

FIG. 95.
NORTH PACIFIC GLITE.
Larger version with
Red Baron pattern, tailless.

Stratton Air Engineering

Kits for kites are a speciality of Stratton Air Engineering who make Squadron Kites. Craig A. Stratton designed his range of profile aeroplanes, made up from spruce strips and ingenious plastic fittings, to use his pre-printed silkspan paper covering for fuselage, wings and tail. The result is three different biplanes, a triplane and a superb Clipper ship. A quadruplane was the latest in 1976 and more are sure to be added.

The principle of the Squadron Kites is that the wing surfaces act as a kite, with the fixed leading edges to maintain shape, and a tailplane is set at a steep negative angle to stabilise the kite. The fuselage offers an excellent deep-keel surface and the whole assembly is flexible owing to the use of spruce in a cantilever arrangement. Strong wind can play havoc with the structure, but my Sopwith Camel spent many hours aloft before anything broke, and even then was quickly repaired with a replacement part from a model shop. Constructing a Squadron Kite is similar to making a model aeroplane except that an aeroplane has a flat profile and not a box. The fuselage is covered on each side with printed tissue, and the remaining parts are assembled to it.

Sopwith Camel, Fun Star, F3F-2 Helldiver: each is a 48-in. (122-cm) span biplane of similar shape, but they have different colours and insignia. They are excellent flyers which can

Squadron Kites' Sopwith Camel in flight.

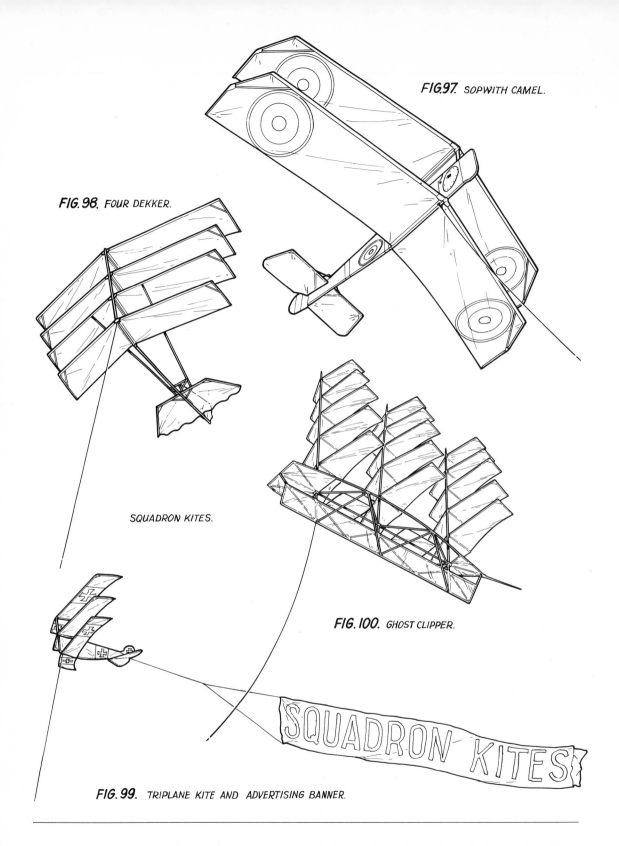

FIG.97. SOPWITH CAMEL.

FIG.98. FOUR DEKKER.

SQUADRON KITES.

FIG.100. GHOST CLIPPER.

FIG.99. TRIPLANE KITE AND ADVERTISING BANNER.

SQUADRON KITES

(Facing page) *Top:* Sale Sail novelty kite by Chris White and Simon Morice of London. *Below left:* Unique decoration using acrylic paints on clear plastic produced this 'lips' design. *Below right:* Giant sled made from black polythene using cut-out letters to convey a message.

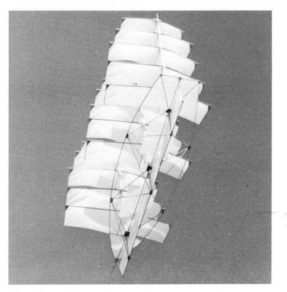

The Ghost Clipper by Squadron Kites – an inspiring sight.

be manoeuvred and landed at will. They have no bridle, and a single-point attachment (Fig. 97).

Four Dekker: a 48-in. (122-cm) span, 36-in. (92-cm) length quadruple-wing aeroplane with 1,120 sq ins (7,226 cm²) of lifting area; it weighs 5 oz (142 g), rides thermals and flies overhead of the operator (Fig. 98).

Fokker Triplane: a triple-wing version, all-red World War I triplane fighter as flown by Baron von Richthofen (Fig. 99).

Cap'n Nemos: of simple construction, a smaller version of the above, on the same principle.

Ghost Clipper: the pride of the fleet (Fig. 100). A large, heavy, three-masted clipper ship with five sails per mast; 60 ins (152 cm) long, 48 ins (122 cm) high. A stunningly original concept. The Ghost Clipper needs a wind speed of at least 6 knots (10 km/h). It needs heavy ballast, so 6 oz (170 g) of its 20 oz (566 g) constitute a balancing weight in the keel. The Clipper is remarkably like the real thing in its flying. When winds are strong, some of the topsails are removed so that it flies on the mainsails. The Clipper can be dismantled for transport

and if it ever breaks the line it actually settles down on an even keel with forward weight on to a gentle grounding.

L. G. Striegel

An American winged box kite is unusual, but there is one made by L. G. Striegel of Louisville, Kentucky, and it is the only kite they make.

Superkite: a 40 × 40 in. (102 × 102 cm) winged box War kite with Tyvek covering. It is sold for leisure flying or for carrying radio aerials etc. A 40-lb (18-kg) strain line is suggested and the instructions advise starting with 200 ft (60 m) of line laid out.

Synestructics

Alexander Graham Bell's tetrahedral experiments in Baddeck (see Chapter 1) inspired the Synestructics firm to produce plastic clip-together units to make a modern equivalent. It has led to other things, and this Californian company has a range of three refreshingly different designs, all using plug-together assembly and a build-up arrangement for multiple application of a basic unit, as designed by Toby Cowan.

Tetra Kite 4-Sail Unit: to make four vs 33 ins (84 cm) high on edge. It is flown on a single-point fixing, and no tail or bridle are needed (Fig. 101).

16-Sail Quad 'Super' Units: to make a 66-in. (168-cm) high assembly. It has red sails and a yellow plastic structure.

Skylinks: a development of the tetrahedral concept but with rectangular panels instead of triangular (except for the tails).

One-Unit: makes a single Skylink kite.

Skylinks 4: makes four separate kites or one big kite.

Skylinks 10: makes ten different kites. They can be two-line controlled, flown in train or tandem.

Air Scoop: a sort of flying garden cloche with three different decorations: *Stars and Stripes, Arrow* and *Checkerboard* (Fig. 102). Plastic rods

(Facing page) *Top:* John Fowler's Eagle kite in silk and nylon. *Below left:* A link-up of nine Flexifoils showing flags of the EEC countries. *Below right:* American Kung Flew delta kite by Hi-Flier.

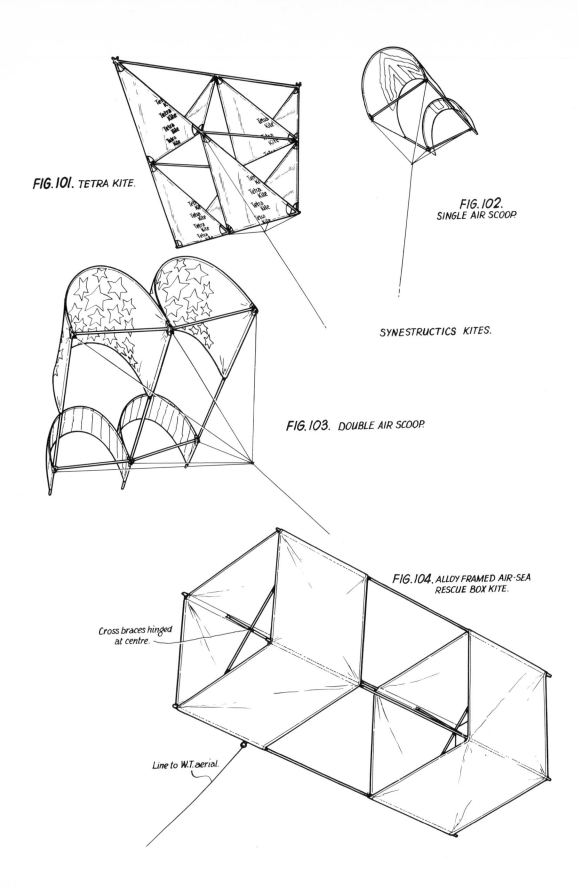

FIG.101. TETRA KITE.

FIG.102.
SINGLE AIR SCOOP.

SYNESTRUCTICS KITES.

FIG.103. DOUBLE AIR SCOOP.

FIG.104. ALLOY FRAMED AIR-SEA
RESCUE BOX KITE.

Cross braces hinged
at centre.

Line to W.T. aerial.

interconnect to form a hooped half box kite with considerable flexibility. In cooler conditions the parts need to be cemented in permanently, or the plastic frustratingly comes apart. It flies well on a four-line bridle, like a semi-rigid sled.

A Double Unit: is included in the range, with two scoops side by side (Fig. 103).

Accessories: Para Launcher is a very simple parachute release to go with the Synestructics, or other kites.

Topflite

Printed plastic Eddy bow kites are universally popular, and one manufacturer that has perpetuated the enthusiasm by producing a simple, inexpensive Eddy in the USA is Topflite. Patterns include the inevitable Indian head, but at least it has an authentic headdress. JNT models imported them into Britain.

Topflite: a one-size 33-in. (84-cm) Eddy with two flat spruce spars held by a simple staple and tensioned with peripheral string in the sail to form an automatic bow in each spar. A lightweight kite, it is a perfect flyer, calling for little or no adjustment provided that the instructions printed on the kite are followed. Possibly the best buy in kites – depending on the currency in which it is sold.

Other Manufacturers

There are several other manufacturers in the USA (Alox, Crumden etc.) of whom details have not been obtainable. Additionally, the leading kite stores Come Fly A Kite in San Francisco and Go Fly A Kite in New York each import kites from Malaysia, South America and India as well as the kites described in this chapter. Among these imports are some which would be difficult to obtain through any other source, notably:

Star of India: a multi-sided tissue kite on a bamboo frame, with trailing tassels.

Tukkai: the Indian double-winged fighting kite; decorative as well as a flyer.

Papagaio: a Brazilian bird kite from Rio de Janeiro.

Indian fighter kites: of diamond shape.

CANADA

Condor

The Condor range, produced in Victoria, British Columbia, contains just three kites, each with a difference.

Two-Cell Box Kite: a kit for a 27-in. (68-cm) long two-cell box kite that does not need a bridle.

Three-Cell Box Kite: a square kite with a long tail that can be controlled to twirl and loop by line tension.

Snake: an 18 ft (5·5 m) long tapered Tyvel snake pattern with a shaped head.

Accessories: Condor market an 8 in. (20 cm) wide, 30 ft (10 m) long red plastic tail to suit many kites.

RETAIL SUPPLIERS

Off-the-peg kites are profuse, yet often frustratingly difficult to purchase. While the USA has a number of kite shops in leading cities, this form of specialised retailing has yet to arrive in Europe. The first British all-kite retail shop was Windcraft of 36 Alma Vale Road, Clifton, Bristol, where the enthusiastic David Turner specialises in all sorts of imported and domestic products. He was quickly followed by Eric Gibson of Kites at 69 Neal Street, London WC1, and Sean Rawnsley at Rawnsley Kiting, 10 St Gregory's Alley, Norwich, NR2 1ER. Others will no doubt follow their lead in an expanding retail trade. The kite business is one which hinges on waves of enthusiasm which ebb and flow. These three 'first' shops have already seen many changes – mostly for the good – and collectively they have been responsible for a lot of kite promotion on TV and in the press. There remains one other source of manufactured kites – the government surplus store. Although rare, these opportunities occur every few years and one sometimes has the opportunity of buying a kite made for rescue signalling etc. (Fig. 104).

SEVEN

Novelties

In the kite world, nothing can be called conventional. The freedom of spirit is personified by the myriad shapes and their symbolic expression of the characteristics of the flyer. Typical of the variety are the painted kites of Japan, the condor-like shapes of the South American Papagaio, the flag-carrying Eddy kites of New York, Bell's tetrahedrals, the Chinese insects and centipedes (Fig. 105), the staid British box kite and the Malaysian Snake (Fig. 106). Now we look to the more radical kites that are regularly flown.

None are larger than the gigantic War kites (Fig. 107) made for the June Festivals in Japan. These huge rectangular sails with their network of bones and bridles measure 22 × 16 ft (6·7 × 4·8 m) and call for a whole team of *happi*-jacketed flyers to haul the monster up as they run along the bank of Nakanokuchi Canal at Shirone in Niigata Prefecture. Some kites reach as high as 500 ft (150 m) before disaster overtakes and they crash into the water. The sight of these kites and the innumerable smaller fighting kites at the Shirone Festival is breathtakingly colourful. No wonder this small town has become a legendary centre of Oriental kite enthusiasm.

Equally complex but not quite so large are the Central American circular kites made in Guatemala. Star-shaped spars brace the multi-sided, brilliantly coloured sail which has a frilled edge and bears a flag mast at its head. These kites (Fig. 108) are flown ceremoniously

Helpers in happi *jackets release a giant kite during a festival at Shirone.*
(Photo: *Japan Tourist Office*)

116

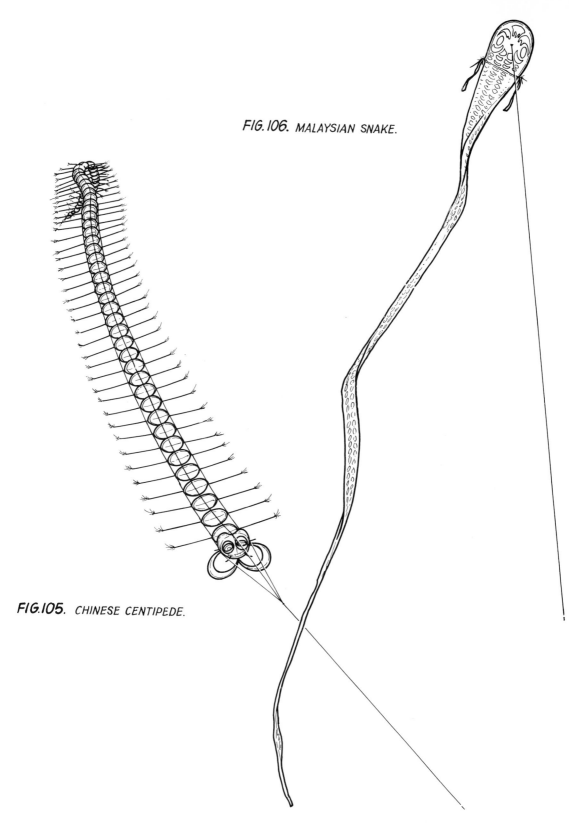

FIG.106. MALAYSIAN SNAKE.

FIG.105. CHINESE CENTIPEDE.

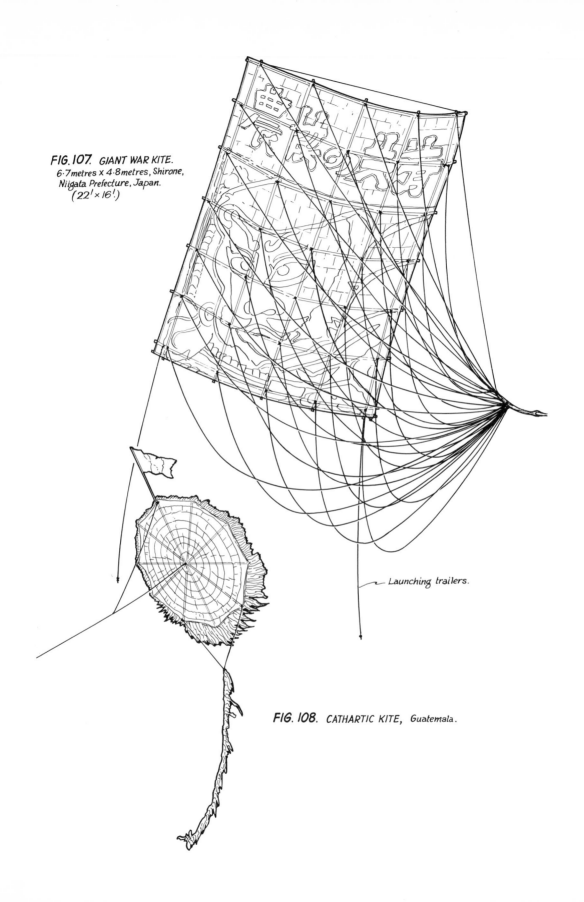

FIG. 107. GIANT WAR KITE.
6·7 metres x 4·8 metres, Shirone,
Niigata Prefecture, Japan.
(22' × 16'.)

Launching trailers.

FIG. 108. CATHARTIC KITE, Guatemala.

on All Saints Day (1 November) at the cemetery of Santiago de Sacatepequez, thirty miles from Guatemala City. Their purpose is to express the spirits of the dead, and to celebrate anticipation of good weather. Though they take months to make, with canes, reeds and paper, their life in the air is rarely more than ten minutes before they are cremated as an offering. Sizes vary from 10 to 25 ft (3 to 7·5 m) diameter, and up to ten boys are needed to heave the heavy frame into the air.

Complicated ceremonials like these are isolated examples, though there is a remarkable similarity between the Guatemalan Cathartic kite and the Star of India construction.

Much simpler is the home-constructed Tetrahedral designed by Ron Prendergraft,

which has sixty-four cells of balsa-wood triangles (Fig. 109). The thickness of the balsa can vary according to whether the builder wants a lightweight or a robust Tetrakite. One sixteenth inch (2 mm) sheet of a hard grade will equal the weight of medium grade $\frac{3}{32}$ in. (3 mm). Our choice would be soft $\frac{3}{32}$ in. (3 mm) for stoutness. As Prendergraft clearly explains in the nine stages of assembly, the Tetrakite is made up of pyramids, four cells making one unit, and sixteen units making a multiple which in turn is made four times over to produce the complete kite. Try it. Balsa sheet is easily obtained (price may govern choice of thickness) and all the joints can be made with balsa cement. If you use your metal template carefully you can use a lot less wood, provided you are prepared to assemble separate tri-

Bill Bigge assembles one of his Aeroplane kites in the Lakehurst Airship sheds, New Jersey.

Tetrahedral Kite

FIG. 109.

— By RON PRENDERGRAFT

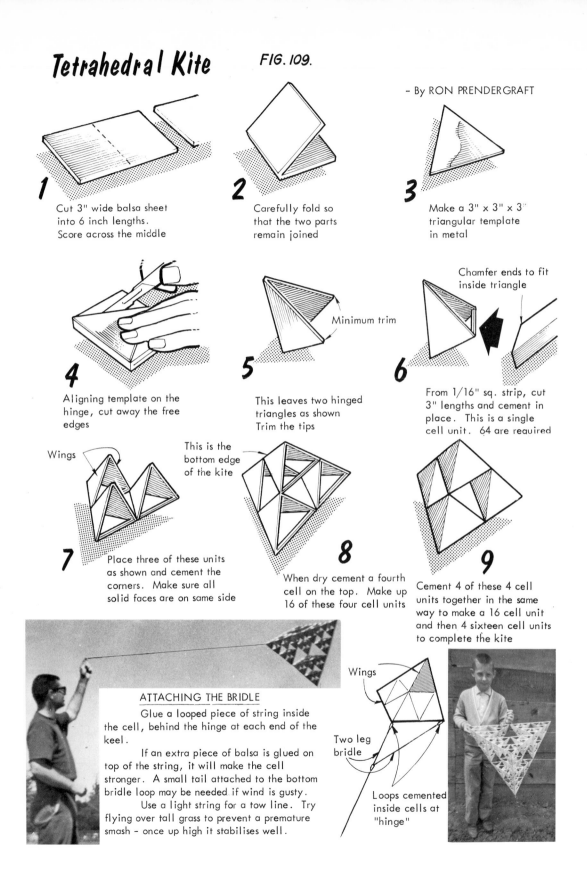

1 Cut 3" wide balsa sheet into 6 inch lengths. Score across the middle

2 Carefully fold so that the two parts remain joined

3 Make a 3" x 3" x 3" triangular template in metal

4 Aligning template on the hinge, cut away the free edges

5 This leaves two hinged triangles as shown Trim the tips

Minimum trim

6 Chamfer ends to fit inside triangle

From 1/16" sq. strip, cut 3" lengths and cement in place. This is a single cell unit. 64 are required

7 Wings

Place three of these units as shown and cement the corners. Make sure all solid faces are on same side

8 This is the bottom edge of the kite

When dry cement a fourth cell on the top. Make up 16 of these four cell units

9 Cement 4 of these 4 cell units together in the same way to make a 16 cell unit and then 4 sixteen cell units to complete the kite

ATTACHING THE BRIDLE

Glue a looped piece of string inside the cell, behind the hinge at each end of the keel.

If an extra piece of balsa is glued on top of the string, it will make the cell stronger. A small tail attached to the bottom bridle loop may be needed if wind is gusty.

Use a light string for a tow line. Try flying over tall grass to prevent a premature smash - once up high it stabilises well.

Wings

Two leg bridle

Loops cemented inside cells at "hinge"

angles instead of scoring and hinging as Ron Prendergraft suggests. Grain direction on the triangles is not important.

The Tetra is a strange sight which always attracts attention. It has the advantage of being reasonably easy to transport in one piece. In stiff breezes it is peculiarly noisy in flight owing to the airflow.

A latter-day design, by contrast, is Bill Bigge's Aeroplane kite. This in no way resembles the Squadron kites, biplanes (or Clipper Ship) described in Chapter 6, and is much more like the kind of indoor flying model which Bigge flies inside airship sheds.

A framework wing and tail are mounted on a long stick 'fuselage'. Vertical fins are fitted fore and aft, and the bridle line attaches in much the same position as it would on a glider. When covered with metallised Mylar, the aeroplane shape is very effective, especially when at 200 ft (60 m). Bigge has long strived for the zero wind kite and can fly these aeroplane shapes at walking speed inside an airship shed, but that is not the kind of facility which many kite flyers are able to utilise!

Windy weather is a positive requirement for the other kind of aeroplane kite – the Autogyro, pioneered by Juan de la Cierva. Rotary wings which 'windmill' have appeared on many commercial kites. Chapter 6 described the Dux and Gunther plastic rotor versions which currently use solid sails and wind cups at the tips of the spars. But the true Autogyro has aerofoil blades which create a lift cone as they are driven round by the wind acting on the retreating blade. All-balsa kites of this type, designed by John Sproule, were once marketed by the Solarbo Co. of Lancing, Sussex. They needed a very stiff wind, but on a hillside they usually found the right wind speed, and when out in the lift stream on the face of a steep hill they could be spectacular. In the late 1930s, Captive Flight Devices of Abington, Pennsylvania, produced an autogyro kite with a 36-in. (92-cm) diameter rotor and side wings of 40-in. (102-cm) span

The Captive Flight Devices' Autogyro kite. (Photo: *Charles E. Brown*)

(Fig. 110). The rotor had a machined shaft mounted in ballraces which could be tilted by a control arm to alter the angle of the rotor. The bridle was in effect an arm which led directly to the rotor head and so automatically adjusted the angle of flight. Rotor kites are extremely stable, and on these Autogyros a twin-finned tail assembly plus outer planes as 'wing tips' were set at acute angles to act as stabilisers. Their only limitation was the rather heavy construction which the whirling device demands for durability. Blades have to be tough. Although hinged to flap upwards, they do sometimes hit the structure and have to withstand a knock or two.

Another model/kite combination is Mervyn Buckmaster's Australian semi-box kite. Buckmaster is a keen competitive aeromodeller and was looking for a form of kite that would remain in flight upwind of his release point for models and act as a thermal detector. He devised an aerofoil cell with four trailing spars that supported a cruciform tail. The combination was rather like the front half of a box kite and the rear of an aeroplane. Constructed in balsa wood with tissue covering as for

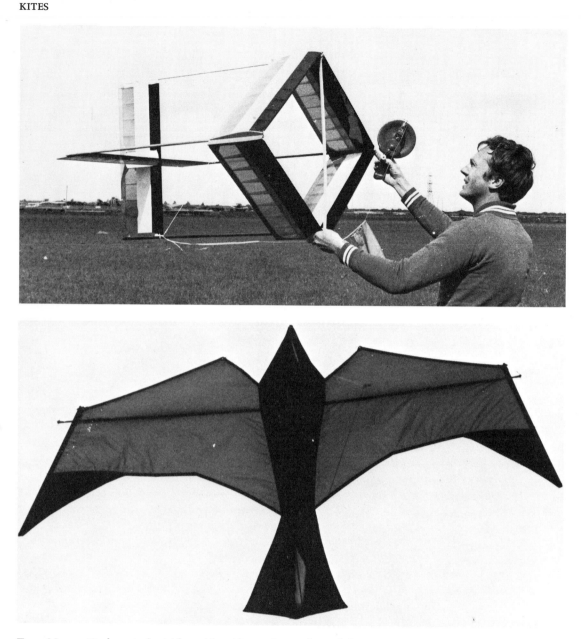

Top: *Mervyn Buckmaster's rigid semi-box kite used as a thermal detector.*

Bottom: *Pearson Bird, as flown in Kensington Gardens, London.*

model wings, the kite flew well and met all expectations. It would have been worthy of Hargrave, but Mervyn says the similarity is coincidental and nothing to do with the Australian $20 note which has drawings of Hargrave's machines on it. Many of Hargrave's early concepts could be made with balsa and plastic structures.

Eye-level view of a hang-glider sail.

From rigid to fully flexible, the Parafoil is still a stranger on most kite fields. Created by Domina Jalbert, a Canadian, the seventeenth in a family of twenty-one children, the Parafoil is only one of his many inventions. These include Jalbert ventilators for ships, multi-celled and vented parachutes, and spinnaker sails for yachts and kite balloons. Anything to do with the wind is Jalbert's province, and from his hardy upbringing at St Michel on Hudson's Bay he has spent his life with sails and kites. The Parafoil is a self-forming multi-bridled kite without any rigid structure. It is made of a rip-stop proofed nylon, shaped to form an aerodynamic curve, and when air-borne in the wind it will lift considerable weights; hence, also, the Jalbert sails which act as wind cups to trap a following wind when sailing. For its relatively light weight the Jalbert sail, Parafoil or Parasled kite is an amazing weightlifter (Fig. 111).

Though they have been mentioned in previous chapters, this section on novelties cannot pass without reference to bird kites, i.e. kites with bird-like shapes. The Papuan native straw plait kite (Fig. 112), used for fishing, is one of the most fascinating. Although heavy, it is said to fly well, and is sensibly bridled. It compares with the modern Blackhawk and Vampire with their trimmable tensioned outline cord and single-line attachment, or even that excellent flyer, the Dutch Knoop cloth bird kite. But in my experience, the Pearson Bird is the most outstanding – as any spectator at the regular kite sessions in Kensington Gardens, London, will testify. These kites are large, with about a 7 ft (2 m) span, and have rigged tips for trimming; they soar beautifully, just like a buzzard (Fig. 113).

Why not a powered kite? This was my

123

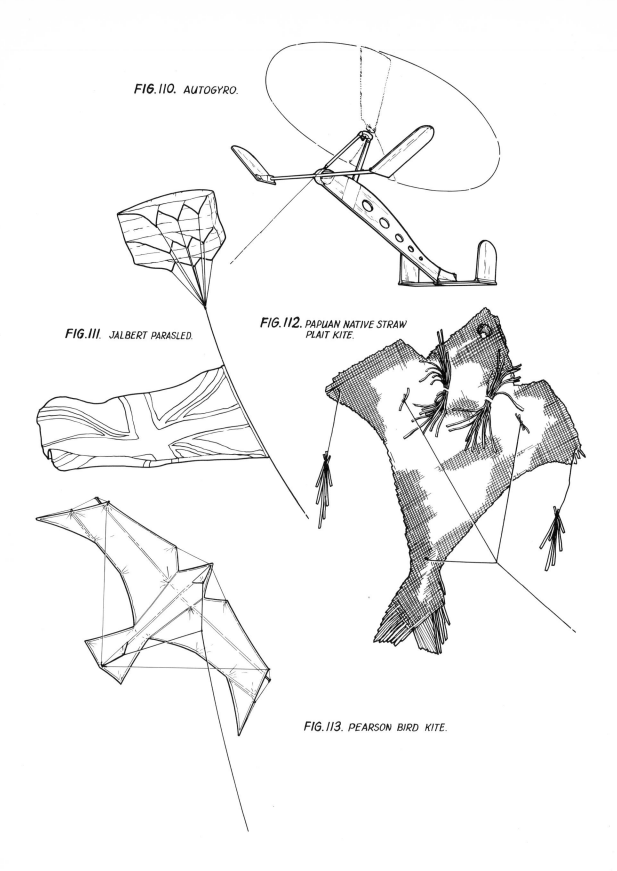

FIG. 110. AUTOGYRO.

FIG. 111. JALBERT PARASLED.

FIG. 112. PAPUAN NATIVE STRAW PLAIT KITE.

FIG. 113. PEARSON BIRD KITE.

thought in 1961 when the Rogallo wing was being used for research as a space-vehicle recovery system in the USA. The hang glider had yet to arrive, and very few daring aviators had constructed man-carrying Rogallo flex-wings as towed kites. Tom Powell of Flight Dynamics, Raleigh, North Carolina, made his Flightsail on the Rogallo principle with a platform hanging below. He was car-towed, kite fashion, along a runway, and at only 35 mph (56 km/h) was flying!

Powell was starting a craze when his Flightsail was described in *Sport Aviation*, the journal of the Experimental Aircraft Association. Since then, a whole industry has developed and the US Hang Glider Association's directory for 1976 listed no fewer than 85 different designs, all in production. The subject is so specialised that it cannot be given more than a passing mention here.

Thousands of hang gliders are flown regularly in every country where there is a reasonable degree of aviation experience. They vary in shape from the simple wing-and-tail concept to the most popular delta sail, based on the Rogallo principle. The simplicity of the Rogallo is its greatest attraction. It does not require an involved structure. It lends itself to 'model' size and, as discussed elsewhere, to the tethered kite.

Tom Powell's experiments inspired a series of model flexwings which in Britain was called Project Parasol. There were three versions, each with the same sailwing – for small engine power, rubber drive, or to be launched as a glider. Each also flew as a kite. A major difference between the Project Parasol and present-day kites was the lack of dihedral on the leading edges (as with a true Rogallo wing) and this distinction gives greater conical camber on the surface. NASA reports suggested that a 50° leading edge sweep and 15° angle of attack were ideal. The Parawing, as Project Parasol was originally called in the USA, was made from plastic gardening sheet sold as Fablothene. As Fig. 114 illustrates, model-aeroplane leading-edge section balsa was used to accept the edges as they were crimped into place by strips let into the rebates. The original 25 in. (63·5 cm) square was trimmed back to a delta shape, and the angles swept 5° at each leading edge. This allows the fabric to billow to its cone section. Two other critical factors were noted in the NASA reports. The centre of gravity was to be at 45 per cent of the wing chord from the nose, and the vertical location 33 per cent of chord below the wing. In a kite, this low centre of gravity is taken care of by the line tension, but in free flight it is something else, as all flexwing flyers have discovered at some time or other.

Project Parasol proved to be an entertaining novelty. It is just like a free-flying kite, even to its deathly pitch over and subsequent dive from which there is little hope of recovery when the sail is luffing. Fig. 115 provides the basic dimensions for construction. Flight as a kite calls for the line to be fixed on the glider hook (nose of fuselage for rubber drive), and with the small cruciform fins acting as a flight stabiliser on the rear of the fuselage, the Parasol is a most stable device. Unfortunately, it is not quickly detachable and has to be transported in one piece as a wing, with the fuselage removed so that it can be prepared for whichever version is to be flown. Such inconveniences are made worthwhile if you have the opportunity to study people's faces when the 'kite' is brought down, and then sent off in free flight! One word of warning: always make sure there is wind in the sail when launching.

Parachutes have been mentioned in Chapter 4, but few people know how to make a good one. The key to success is to make a large one, so that it will float down relatively slowly. It need only be made of tissue, with sticky-tape gussets at each shroud-like anchorage, while the edges should be doubled with hems. If the parachute seems to be too big as drawn (Fig. 116) for a 39-in. (1-m) diameter, halve all

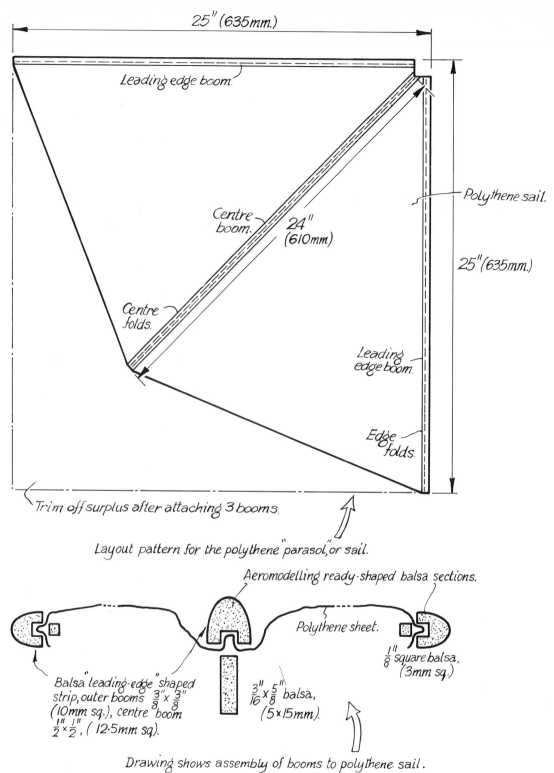

25" (635mm.)

Leading edge boom.

Centre boom.

24" (610mm)

Centre folds.

Polythene sail.

25" (635mm.)

Leading edge boom.

Edge folds.

Trim off surplus after attaching 3 booms.

Layout pattern for the polythene "parasol," or sail.

Aeromodelling ready-shaped balsa sections.

Polythene sheet.

⅛" square balsa, (3mm sq.)

Balsa "leading-edge" shaped strip, outer booms ⅜"×⅜" (10mm sq.), centre boom ½"×½", (12·5mm sq.).

3/16"×⅝" balsa, (5×15mm).

Drawing shows assembly of booms to polythene sail.

FIG. 114.

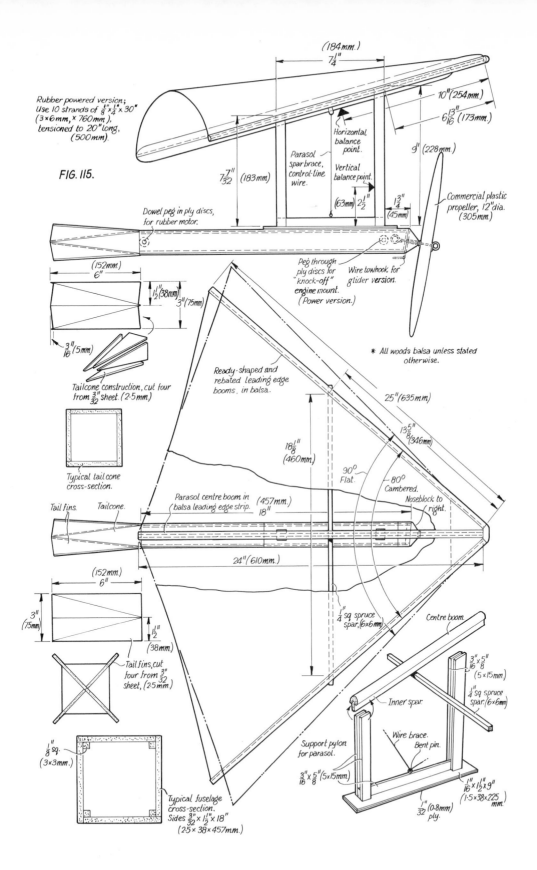

FIG. 115.

Rubber powered version; Use 10 strands of $\frac{1}{8}" \times \frac{1}{4}" \times 30"$ (3 × 6mm, × 760mm), tensioned to 20" long, (500mm).

(184mm.)
$7\frac{1}{4}"$

10" (254mm.)

$6\frac{13}{16}"$ (173mm.)

9" (228mm.)

Horizontal balance point.

Parasol spar brace, control-line wire.

Vertical balance point.

(63mm) $2\frac{1}{2}"$

$1\frac{3}{4}"$ (45mm.)

$7\frac{7}{32}"$ (183mm.)

Commercial plastic propeller, 12" dia. (305mm.)

Dowel peg in ply discs, for rubber motor.

Peg through ply discs for "knock-off" engine mount. (Power version.)

Wire towhook, for glider version.

(152mm.) 6"

$1\frac{1}{2}"$ (38mm) 3" (75mm)

$\frac{3}{16}"$ (5mm)

Tailcone construction, cut four from $\frac{3}{32}"$ sheet. (2·5mm.)

Typical tailcone cross-section.

Ready-shaped and rebated leading edge booms, in balsa.

25" (635mm)

$13\frac{5}{8}"$ (346mm)

$18\frac{1}{8}"$ (460mm.)

90° Flat.

80° Cambered.

Noseblock to right.

* All woods balsa unless stated otherwise.

Tail fins.   Tailcone.

Parasol centre boom in balsa leading edge strip.

(457mm.) 18"

24" (610mm.)

$\frac{1}{4}"$ sq spruce spar, (6×6mm).

Centre boom.

(152mm.) 6"

3" (75mm)

$1\frac{1}{2}"$ (38mm.)

$\frac{3}{16}" \times \frac{5}{8}"$ (5×15mm)

Inner spar.

$\frac{1}{4}"$ sq spruce spar (6×6mm)

Tail fins, cut four from $\frac{3}{32}"$ sheet, (2·5mm.)

$\frac{1}{8}"$ sq. (3×3mm.)

Support pylon for parasol.

Wire brace. Bent pin.

$\frac{3}{16}" \times \frac{5}{8}"$ (5×15mm)

$\frac{1}{16}" \times 1\frac{1}{2}" \times 9"$ (1·5×38×225 mm.)

$\frac{1}{32}"$ (0·8mm) ply.

Typical fuselage cross-section. Sides $\frac{3}{32}" \times 1\frac{1}{2}" \times 18"$ (2·5 × 38 × 457mm.)

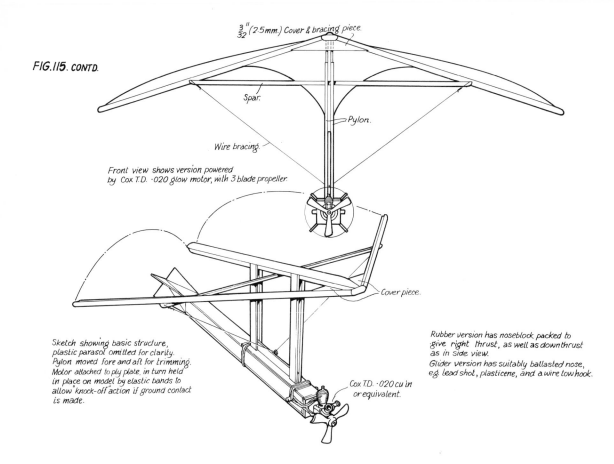

FIG.115. CONTD.

$\frac{3}{32}$" (2.5mm.) Cover & bracing piece.

Spar.

Pylon.

Wire bracing.

Front view shows version powered
by Cox T.D. ·020 glow motor, with 3 blade propeller.

Cover piece.

Sketch showing basic structure,
plastic parasol omitted for clarity.
Pylon moved fore and aft for trimming.
Motor attached to ply plate, in turn held
in place on model by elastic bands to
allow "knock-off" action if ground contact
is made.

Cox T.D. ·020 cu in
or equivalent.

Rubber version has noseblock packed to
give right thrust, as well as downthrust
as in side view.
Glider version has suitably ballasted nose,
e.g. lead shot, plasticene, and a wire tow hook.

the dimensions: but the result will not have anywhere near the same effect. The larger the parachute, the easier it will ride up the kite line on the messenger before release, if you allow part of it to act as a sail. Fourteen gores, or panels, are needed. Cut each from heavy-grade model-aeroplane tissue. The gores can be of different colours, which will make the parachute all the more attractive. In real chute practice, alternate red and white panels are often used. Mark a stiff card template to the dimensions shown, ensuring that the curves are smooth on each side in transition from each of the stations as marked. Allow a good hem

edge to project. Turn these hems over at base and apex, and hold them with a home cement or glue stick application (Uhu, Stic or Pritt). Then join the gores, using the extended hems to overlap. When the last seam has been glued, cut a 4-in. (10-cm) diameter vent hole in the apex and reinforce it with a ring from spare tissue. Fourteen rigging lines (shrouds), each 44 ins (112 cm) long, are then attached to the parachute as shown in Fig. 116. Use line that has a smooth finish so that it resists tangling, and reinforce the chute at the shroud attachments. The actual ballast weight will have to be $3\frac{1}{2}$ oz (100 g) or more, depending on the

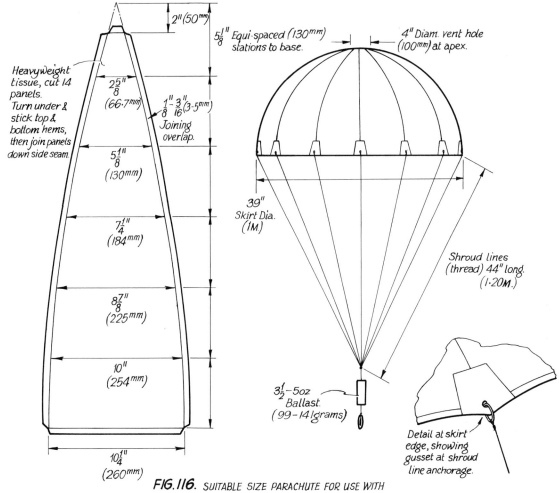

Heavyweight tissue, cut 14 panels. Turn under & stick top & bottom hems, then join panels down side seam.

2" (50mm)

$2\frac{5}{8}$" (66·7mm)

$\frac{1}{8}$"–$\frac{3}{16}$"(3·5mm) Joining overlap.

$5\frac{1}{8}$" (130mm)

$7\frac{1}{4}$" (184mm)

$8\frac{7}{8}$" (225mm)

10" (254mm)

$10\frac{1}{4}$" (260mm)

$5\frac{1}{8}$" Equi-spaced (130mm) stations to base.

4" Diam. vent hole (100mm) at apex.

39" Skirt Dia. (1M.)

Shroud lines (thread) 44" long. (1·20M.)

$3\frac{1}{2}$–5oz Ballast. (99–141grams)

Detail at skirt edge, showing gusset at shroud line anchorage.

FIG. 116. SUITABLE SIZE PARACHUTE FOR USE WITH MESSENGER CARRIERS.

intended rate of descent. A small doll, dressed as a pilot, is a suitable alternative. Parachutes can be used as kites too! If a line is attached to the shrouds in such a way that the chute is cupped to sail on the wind, it is possible to take this design up to a height, on a kite line. If light silk is obtainable, substitute it for the tissue and machine-sew the gores together for a longer-lasting and tighter-folding parachute.

It's only a short step from the parachute to the balloon. Although nothing like a kite, the hot-air balloon has been associated with kites since the time of the French Revolution. There is a curious attachment of interest, and in my

experience a vast body of kiters also share enthusiasm for ballooning though relatively few of them actually do anything about it.

Hammoco Designs, who produce the kit set mentioned in Chapter 6 for a pair of Indian fighter kites, also have a kit for a hot-air balloon if the reader wants to find a pack of parts. For those who want to start from scratch, I can recommend nothing better than Vince Redfern's six-footer (2 m high) which appeared in the pages of *Aeromodeller* magazine and has given pleasure to all who have made it.

All you need to make this particular hot-air

Heating the air in the balloon with a small butane stove.

On release, the balloon climbs away.

balloon is twenty-four tissue sheets, each measuring about 20 × 30 ins (50 × 75 cm). The adhesive used by Redfern is PVA, which is quickly absorbed by the tissue, providing almost instantaneous joints. You will also need some scrap balsa in about 10-in. (25-cm) lengths, preferably $\frac{3}{8}$ in. (1 cm) square, to make up the base octagon, a few lengths of fuse wire, and a ball of cotton wool to provide fire once it has been soaked in methylated spirits. Vince Redfern uses an ordinary blowtorch to pre-heat the balloon before the cotton wool is set alight, but you could use a variety of heating devices if you wished; a butane picnic stove, for example, is ideal.

The first stage of manufacture is to make up eight panels measuring 20 × 90 ins (50 × 225 cm), each composed of three different coloured sheets of tissue joined on the short edges. Cut the first of these into shape after

folding in half and measuring out the dimensions shown in Fig. 117. Note that the dimensions are actually for the full width and must be divided by two to obtain the half-width dimension. The lower half of the balloon is a straight taper. Once the first template is cut, lay it over the other seven prepared panels, which are then cut to shape and the joining sequence begins. This is little more than a series of concertina joins and a series of folds on alternate edges joined with PVA glue until the two last edges can be joined together to make the balloon (Fig. 118).

Don't be disappointed if you find you need the odd patch at the apex – this is quite normal and indeed acceptable because, after all, kite flyers cannot be expected to be perfect tailors! A rigid brace at the open end of the balloon is essential. Make up the octagon from the scrap pieces of balsa. Join it to the tissue, after

130

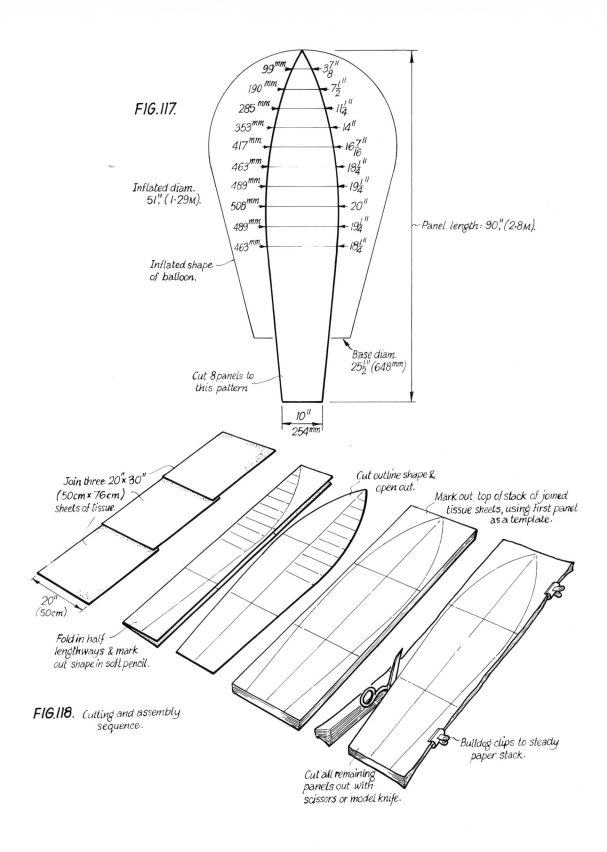

FIG.117.

99ᵐᵐ 3⁷⁄₈″
190ᵐᵐ 7¹⁄₂″
285ᵐᵐ 11¹⁄₄″
353ᵐᵐ 14″
417ᵐᵐ 16⁷⁄₁₆″
463ᵐᵐ 18¹⁄₄″
489ᵐᵐ 19¹⁄₄″
508ᵐᵐ 20″
489ᵐᵐ 19¹⁄₄″
463ᵐᵐ 18¹⁄₄″

Inflated diam.
51″ (1·29M).

Inflated shape
of balloon.

~Panel length: 90″ (2·8M).

Cut 8 panels to
this pattern

Base diam.
25¹⁄₂″ (648ᵐᵐ)

10″
254ᵐᵐ

Join three 20″× 30″
(50cm × 76cm)
sheets of tissue.

20″
(50cm).

Fold in half
lengthways & mark
out shape in soft pencil.

Cut outline shape &
open out.

Mark out, top of stack of joined
tissue sheets, using first panel
as a template.

Bulldog clips to steady
paper stack.

FIG.118. Cutting and assembly
sequence.

Cut all remaining
panels out with
scissors or model knife.

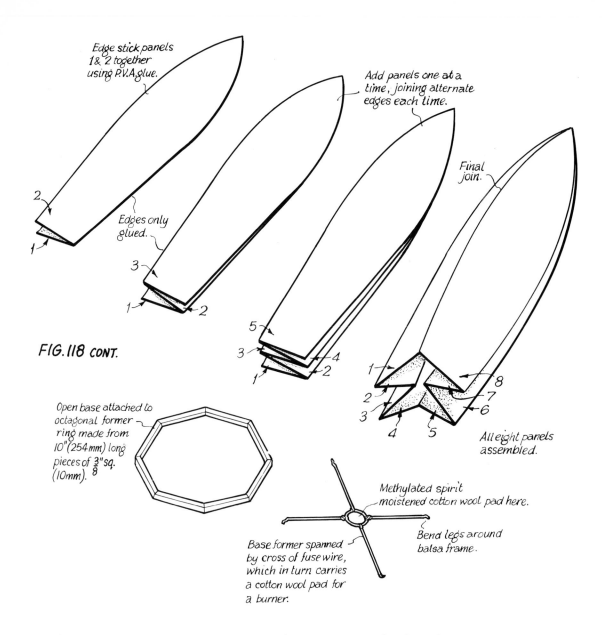

Edge stick panels
1 & 2 together
using P.V.A. glue.

Add panels one at a
time, joining alternate
edges each time.

Final
join.

2

Edges only
glued.

1

3

1

2

5

3

4

1

2

FIG. 118 CONT.

1

8

2

7

3

6

4

5

All eight panels
assembled.

Open base attached to
octagonal former
ring made from
10" (254 mm) long
pieces of $\frac{3}{8}$" sq.
(10 mm).

Methylated spirit
moistened cotton wool pad here.

Bend legs around
balsa frame.

Base former spanned
by cross of fuse wire,
which in turn carries
a cotton wool pad for
a burner.

reinforcing the joints as necessary with household pins, and wrap the tissue round, gluing firmly. The balloon should be folded for carrying and can be collapsed more or less to the shape of one panel and then rolled up, leaving the rigid base frame free. On the field, open it out, tie a cruciform of fuse wire across the opening, attaching the ball of cotton wool to it quite firmly. After gathering together a number of helpers to aid in the pre-heating, apply heat through the open space, taking care not to set the balloon on fire. When the tissue seems warm and the balloon wants to rise, pour some methylated spirits over the cotton wool, light it with a match (or blowtorch if you have been using one for pre-heating), hold on for a few moments more to build up heat and let her go!

It must be emphasised that the balloon has to be tethered if it is to be released from a heat source like this. Use about 100 ft (30 m) of line – which also ensures you get the balloon back. Safety precautions must be observed under all circumstances and it is my firm suggestion that you restrict activities to 'dry' ascents for all free flights. The balloon will rise to 100 ft (30 m) or more merely from the heat of the picnic stove or blowtorch. The balloon depends on being reasonably airtight, so always inspect the joints, creases and general surface for holes before any attempt at setting up for an ascent. It is also advisable to restrict operations to very calm conditions.

EIGHT

Making Your Own Kites

There is a certain satisfaction to be obtained from making your own kite. The product of your own endeavours flying high on the wind is a memorable sight. There are distinct advantages too. For one thing, you are not limited by what is commercially available and can enjoy freedom in shape, size and decoration. Novelty kites become a possibility. The choice of materials is a wide-open field for ingenuity, and – above all – it's cheaper.

Against these attractions, there are of course some disadvantages. Obtaining materials is for many people a great problem. Not every local ironmonger carries useful size dowels or suitable bamboo canes. The dressmaking material shop cannot always provide light-weight cloth and not all do-it-yourself shops are a treasure store of kite-making materials. But these restrictive hazards should not be allowed to dissuade the would-be kite maker. The needs are, after all, quite simple; even the tools required are ordinary household equipment. If you want special materials obviously you have to shop at the specialist kite stores which are established in many cities. See the appendices for lists of suppliers.

TOOLS

Scissors, a darning needle, pliers, a sharp knife, staple gun and a small saw are sufficient to manage practically any type of kite construction. If you want to feel that you have the best kind of workshop gear, you should visit a craft or model shop and purchase a tool chest of the X-Acto or Humbrol type. These have an assortment of handles to carry detachable scalpel-sharp blades, mini-saws and files. A sewing machine is also useful, and a hot welding iron for sealing plastic film joins on the kite sail.

As for the work space, anywhere with room on a table top or floor is a kite maker's work area. Remember when using glue that you will make less mess if you spread newspaper over the area first. And for final decoration with artists' colours newspaper is essential.

MATERIALS

For kite structures, the spars can be made of anything that is reasonably light and strong. There should be a degree of resilience in the spar, which must be of fairly small cross-section to slip into any sail pocket, or curve to a required shape.

In the early days, the favourite material in London was the U-shape channel used for umbrella ribs. A letter to the editor of *The*

Model Engineer of 25 November 1909 explained how to make box kites using eight umbrella ribs bound together in such a way that a 15 ins (30 cm) square, 52 ins (132 cm) long box kite was made that weighed only 8 oz (250 g). It would be very difficult to match that weight with bamboo or spruce spars today, and to make the original you would have to find discarded umbrellas – in 1909 it was possible to purchase spare parts.

Dependent on the size, type and shape of the kite, the materials for kites can be selected from those shown in the table below.

Assembly of these materials will call for adhesives such as cements for sealing the covering (contact cement, PVC cement, Thixofix, rubber cement etc.), where suitable, and for tapes. Adhesive tape can be put to double use by adding to the decoration of outlines – for example red or black tape to hold the covering to the rigging, or to seal joints. Two widths and colours of tape, superimposed, can become excellent decorations too.

The actual weights of the covering material depend on the size of the kite. Polyethylene sheet comes in varying thicknesses and weights, so choose your kite size and the conditions in which you will be flying. The lighter grades will satisfy most needs. Similarly, the fabrics come in various grades, and if you can purchase rip-stop nylon, you will find it better than average for very large kites. It is sometimes available from people who deal with old parachutes, but you can always find it at kite shops. Modelspan paper is a British product. It is wet-strengthened so it will stand a moderate amount of wetness before breaking up, and it will accept decoration. It is porous, but it can be sealed with model aeroplane nitrate shrinking dope; only use a diluted solution if the framework is not rigid, as Modelspan is meant to shrink! The USA equivalent is known as Silkspan.

Fabrics are advised for all the larger kites, and they ought to be porous if the kite area is 8 sq ft (0·75 m²) or over, otherwise they can be

MATERIALS FOR KITES

KITE SIZE	Small	Medium	Large
Spars	Birch dowel $\frac{3}{16}$ in. (5 mm) dia.	Alloy tube	Bamboo cane
	Spruce $\frac{1}{4}$ in. (6 mm) square	Obechi $\frac{3}{8}$ in. (10 mm)	Dowel $\frac{3}{8}$ in. (10 mm)
	Ramin $\frac{1}{4}$ in. (6 mm) square	square	dia.
	Obechi $\frac{1}{4}$ in. (6 mm) square	Dowel $\frac{1}{4}$ in. (6 mm) dia.	Glass fibre rod
	Rattan canes	Spruce $\frac{1}{4}$ in. (6 mm) square	Stout laths
		Plastic rod	Plastic tube
Covering	Modelspan	Nylon	Nylon
	Kraft paper	PVC	Cotton
	Silk	Rayon	Tyvek
	Nylon	Cotton	Sailcloth (rip-stop)
	Polyethylene	Melinex	Proofed Nylon
Rigging	Carpet thread	Braided Nylon	Twine
	Nylon monofilament	Twine	Flax
	Twine	Flax	Cord
	Flax	Cord	Seineline

quite a handful. Some nylon is calendered, having a sheen as though proofed – this material is ideal.

If you are in any doubt about the choice of material, and you have no specialist kite shop near you, pay a visit to the local model shop where there is almost always a vast fund of free and good advice to be given across the counter. Model shops are used to all sorts of questions, so don't be shy to ask about something that appears to have little to do with trains, boats or aeroplanes. If you want to make a very light kite, the model shop can supply silk or nylon model aeroplane covering in metre-square packs. Although rather expensive, this very thin material is the best quality obtainable. It is porous and, not being rip-stop, needs a seamed edge for reinforcement.

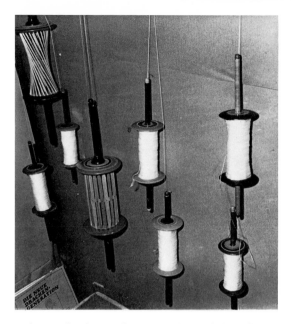

Indian reels of several types, each spool shaped.

TAILS

Almost an afterthought, the tail is a neglected part of kiting. Of course, a tail is best avoided unless it can be made aesthetically attractive, and for that reason alone it is disastrous to start with a tail that is just asking to wind itself into kinks!

On hexagonal kites and some others, it has become practice to use two tails, each with long streamers. If you use two tails with pigtail bows in them close together you are simply asking for a muddle. A pigtail with tapes of material tied across the tail line is good for producing stabilising drag, but it has to be made properly. The best way to make one is to use strong tape, of the type made to reinforce fabrics, as the centre line of the tail. Then cut coloured tail papers and sew across the centre line at right angles. These rarely tangle. If the pigtails are to be tied, always tie the line around the centre tape, not the other way about. Use a centre line that does not wind up. Tails rotate in flight action; flax or twine is soon shortened as it twirls into knots.

Crêpe paper can be made into a very useful tail drogue by folding as you would for a paper flower, then scissor-snipping many cuts to the centre core so that a full tassel develops. Tie this on the end of the line and it will act like a dragging pom-pom to keep the kite settled. Chinese kites sometimes come with this kind of tail ready made. Most important of all, remember that if you use any sort of absorbent material, the kite will pick up the dampness of the atmosphere, the dew off the grass etc., and will become heavy as well as weakened.

REELS

One necessary item of equipment, perhaps the most important, is the tether by which you are going to fly the kite. There are many commercial reels made of plastic, generally for the smaller commercial kite, where 200 ft (60 m) of 12-lb (5·5-kg) strain line is easily contained. The serious kiter looks further and may want a traditional Indian reel, which is similar to a

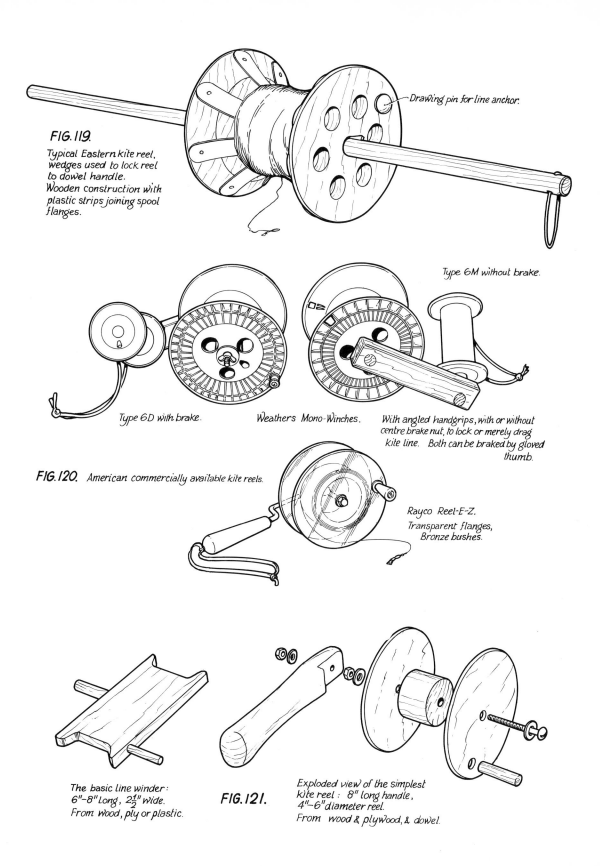

FIG. 119.
Typical Eastern kite reel,
wedges used to lock reel
to dowel handle.
Wooden construction with
plastic strips joining spool
flanges.

Drawing pin for line anchor.

Type 6M without brake.

Type 6D with brake.

Weathers Mono-Winches.

With angled handgrips, with or without
centre brake nut, to lock or merely drag
kite line.   Both can be braked by gloved
thumb.

FIG. 120.   American commercially available kite reels.

Rayco Reel-E-Z.
Transparent flanges,
Bronze bushes.

The basic line winder:
6"–8" Long, 2½" wide.
From wood, ply or plastic.

FIG. 121.

Exploded view of the simplest
kite reel: 8" long handle,
4"–6" diameter reel.
From wood & plywood, & dowel.

broadened diabolo. Two conical wood turnings are joined with slats of reed, cane, or even plastic. A central hole allows the dowel handle to pass through and the whole reel fits comfortably between thumb and forefinger to be spun in either direction (Fig. 119). These reels are perfect for fighting kites.

Larger reels of the US Rayco or Weathers types are extremely well made and will take up to 1,000 ft (300 m) of 60-lb (27-kg) line. Some of the bigger reels have handles that allow the holding hand to relax; others use a forearm strap so that the weight of the reel is comfortably taken on the arm, leaving the other free to wind in or out (Fig. 120). Several excellent reel designs are sold in British kite shops, produced by long-established experts; they are not mass-produced and are all hand-made. For straight kiting, the elementary flat winder is adequate – built from a piece of scrap ply or plastic, it can be made quickly and also works quickly. A piece of dowel in the centre at one side acts as the winder. If a free spinning reel is wanted, then the one in Fig. 121 is adequate. An old hammer handle, two-ply discs and a core (which does not have to be perfectly round) plus the centre bolt and its nuts, make an interesting little woodworking job. Of course, you can be more sophisticated. Regular kites have reels of all sizes and different kinds of mechanical ingenuity. The old favourite, Meccano, comes in very handy; and discarded cable drums, old fishing reels, first sections of sea rods and even bench grinder gearboxes can be seen at kite venues. But, in fact, gearing is neither necessary nor advisable.

PLASTIC TUBE

Before we embark on a few simple kite designs to make, let's look first at how to put the parts together. Binding is the accepted method of holding spars together, but it is not QD (quick detachable) nor is it always sufficiently flexible.

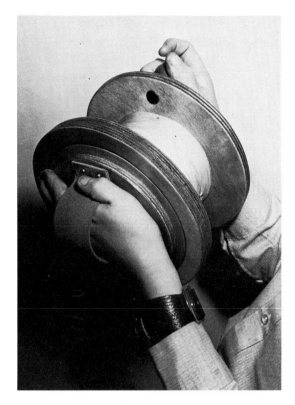

A home-built reel using a wheel bearing centre from a bicycle; note the hand band.

Commercial kites are built up around plastic, and a key factor to most of them is the use of specially moulded spar or sail fittings. Never discard these very useful fittings. Pick them off old, torn and thrown-away sails or broken spars. You never know when they will be useful on a home-built kite. Some are single sockets for dowel ends to fit to sail tips. Others use a clever buckle arrangement for sail tension, or have double or triple sockets for centre spar connections. The fitting can be cut and fashioned to suit many purposes. Some have broad bases which allow them to be stapled to the sail, if not stuck in place with contact cement. Mostly made for dowels of $\frac{3}{16}$-in. (5-mm) diameter, the plastic sockets do have a limitation when it comes to making a large kite.

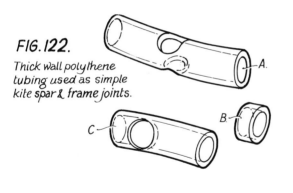

FIG. 122.

Thick wall polythene tubing used as simple kite spar & frame joints.

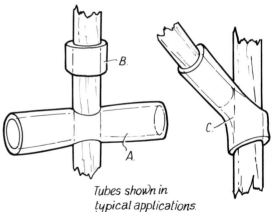

Tubes shown in typical applications.

This is where the plastic tube comes in. Thick-walled polythene tubing, sold at cycle and motorcycle shops, is flexible, transparent, very strong and an ideal medium for joints in a kite. Cut in short lengths it becomes a 'washer', or stop, on a spar. Drill or cut it through and it makes a cruciform joint for two laterals to join a centre spar. Drill one side only and it becomes a T joiner; or drill on one side near the end and it makes an angled joint (see Fig. 122). In the control-line Powell, Skite and Cambridge kites the clear polythene tube has been used as part of the mass-produced kite assembly. Glass fibre reinforced adhesive tape is recommended to hold the tube wherever a permanent fitting is required. There will be more on the use of the plastic tube later, when I shall deal with design details for home construction.

MALAY TWO-STICK KITE (Fig. 123)

This kite, being 39 ins (100 cm) high, takes fullest advantage of the spruce lengths you can get in the model shop or dowels from the hardware store. The lateral is 27 ins (70 cm), and $\frac{1}{4} \times \frac{1}{4}$ in. (6 × 6 mm). Join the spars at a point $13\frac{3}{4}$ ins (35 cm) from the top so that there is a nicely proportioned triangle at the head. Use binding thread or make a soft wire clip to go round the intersection, ensuring that the spars are at right angles to each other. Now take a length of twine and make a peripheral diamond shape by linking all the extremities of the spars. Either cut a small slot in each spar end, or tie the twine round the spar about $\frac{1}{2}$ in. (1 cm) from the end. Keep the twine tight.

The covering should be wrapped over the twine outline. If you are using cloth, use a contact cement to tack, then sew the cloth. If plastic sheet, use PVC cement to seal, or heat weld with the smoothing tip on a soldering iron. These tips are oval in shape, sold as special bits for larger irons of the electric pistol-grip type, and the plastic welds as the tip passes over it. It takes practice to perfect a continuous seal – if you do it too fast, it does not work properly; if too slow, you burn a hole. An ordinary soldering iron tip can be made to do the job, with care, but it has to be smooth. The worktop underneath the job is also important. Flat, smooth and covered with a wax paper is best. Hardboard makes an ideal base.

The two-stick Malay kite can also be covered with brown Kraft paper wrapped over the twine outline and glued. But it will not be as durable as either plastic or fabric. This kite needs a tail, which ought to be at least 10 ft (3 m) long, and the bridle has to go to all four extremities as shown in Fig. 123. The strainer line to the tail of the kite can incorporate a strong rubber band to act as a shock line, but be careful to adjust it so that it

FIG. 123.

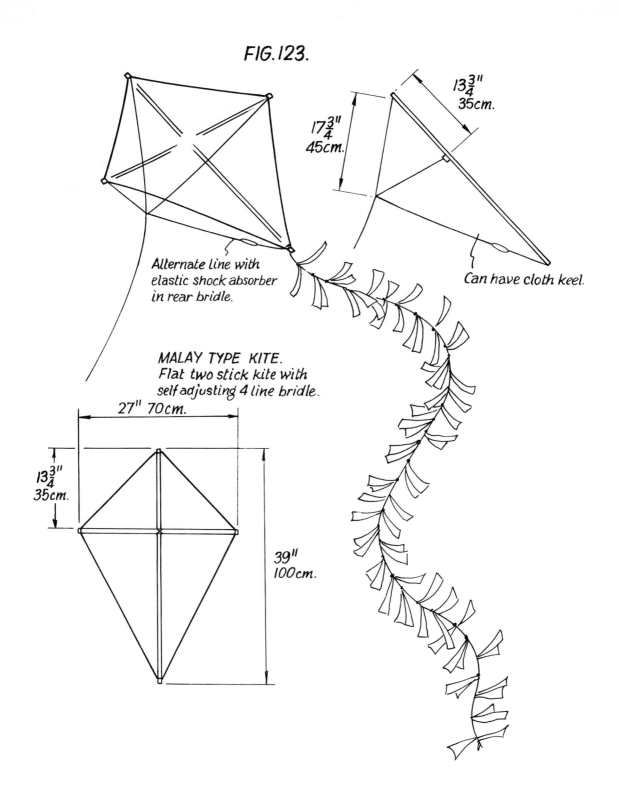

$17\frac{3}{4}"$
45cm.

$13\frac{3}{4}"$
35cm.

Alternate line with
elastic shock absorber
in rear bridle.

Can have cloth keel.

MALAY TYPE KITE.
Flat two stick kite with
self adjusting 4 line bridle.

27" 70cm.

$13\frac{3}{4}"$
35cm.

39"
100cm.

does not pull to distort the bridle profile. The pigtail as sketched is traditional for the type and most effective.

PEG TOP (Fig. 124)

This is a replica of the oldest type of kite seen in European circles. In many ways it is just like the diamond Malay described above, but its top has a curve. To form the curve, use a rectangular-section spar of $\frac{1}{8} \times \frac{1}{4}$ in. (3 × 6 mm) or $\frac{3}{16} \times \frac{3}{8}$ in. (5 × 10 mm) spruce and, with the aid of a tack, secure it to the head of the centre spar and the tips of the lateral.

Cloth covering is advised, and tip tassels on the lateral spar add to the visual attraction. Use a 10-ft (3-m) pigtail and a four-leg bridle and this peg top will fly well. Modern patterned fabrics, with floral or similar decorations, are best and achieve the most colourful effect. The curved top might give you a little trouble in getting the covering wrinkle-free. Be careful, when wrapping, to use frequent v-snips to allow the covering to adopt the curved shape.

EDDY (Fig. 125)

This is just like the Malay except that the cross is much nearer the head, or top, of the centre spar. It is also a 'square' kite, equal in breadth and length. Use a light line to make the periphery, because this kite is expected to develop curved shapes.

Plastic covering is actually better for an Eddy of this size, and it is also better to use rectangular-section spars set flat, for the curvature to develop. If the outline twine is tight enough, the centre spar should become bowed and so provide a negative camber, in which case a tail will be superfluous.

The covering can be made from large plastic carrier bags (choose ones that have attractive printed patterns). The two-line bridle ought to be arranged so that the kite line joins at a point about 12 ins (30 cm) directly below the spar crossing point. Remember – the covering is

A home-built box kite with frilled edges – an entry in a Polish kite contest.

beneath the spars, so cut a hole for the bridle to join the spars. A streamer tail of crêpe tape may be used, but is not essential.

SIMPLE RIGID BOX KITE (Fig. 126)

There are numerous ways of making a box kite, and if you want a collapsible kite, the methods can be rather complex. To avoid sewing spar pockets our 30-in. (1-m) kite is made of two frames from $\frac{1}{4}$-in. (6-mm) square sticks, or dowels, then tied with line bracing so that it forms a box frame before the two cells of plastic or fabric are applied. Plastic is preferred for lightness and easier flying in light winds. Once the frame is tied, it is rigid enough to have the covering stuck in place with two wrap-rounds, 15 ins (40 cm) apart. As this is a rectangular box it flies 'flat' and so needs a four-line bridle. The reason for this is

141

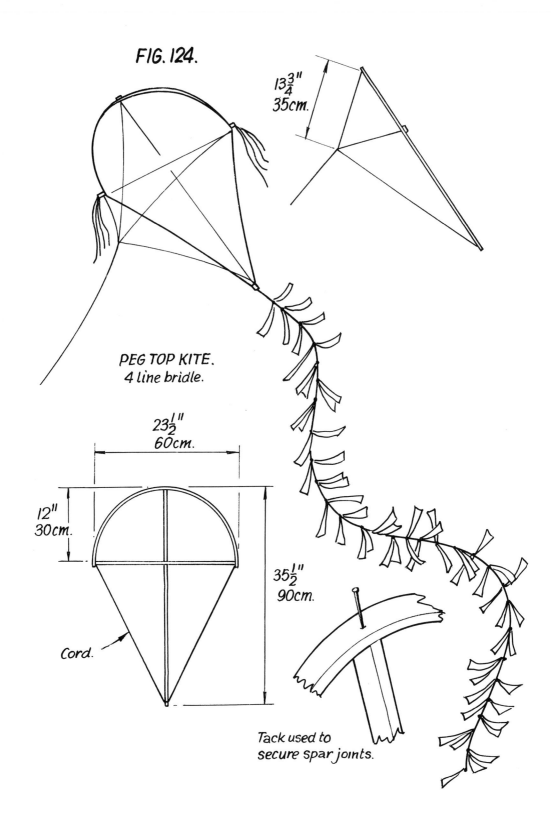

FIG. 124.

$13\frac{3}{4}''$
35cm.

PEG TOP KITE.
4 line bridle.

$23\frac{1}{2}''$
60cm.

$12''$
30cm.

$35\frac{1}{2}''$
90cm.

Cord.

Tack used to
secure spar joints.

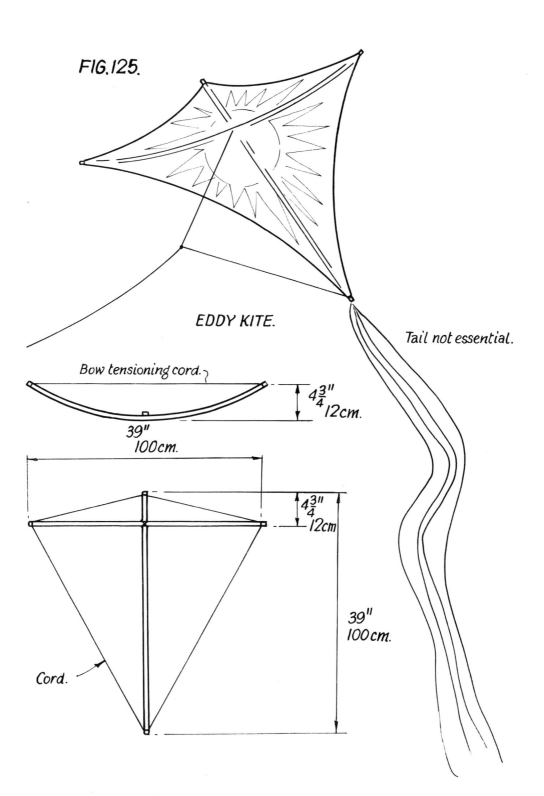

FIG.125.

EDDY KITE.

Tail not essential.

Bow tensioning cord.

$4\frac{3}{4}''$ 12cm.

39"
100cm.

$4\frac{3}{4}''$
12cm

39"
100cm.

Cord.

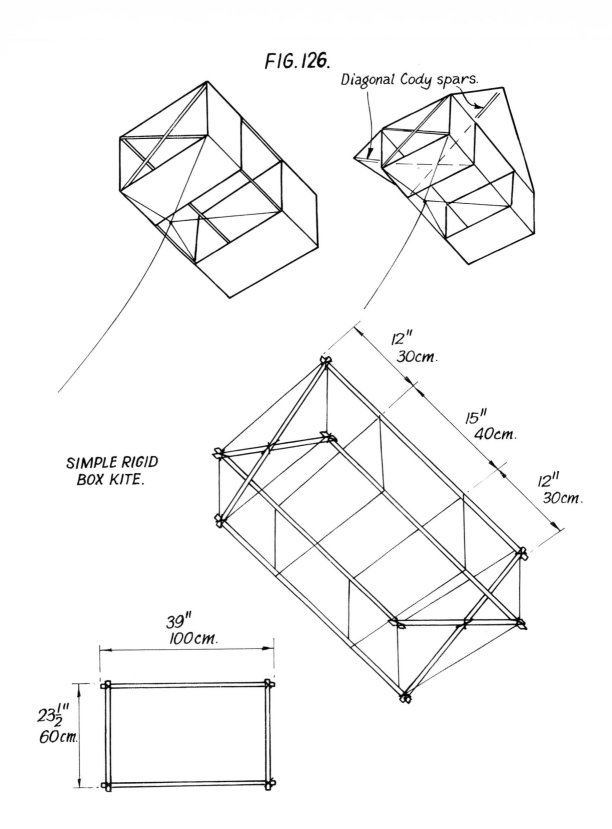

FIG. 126.

Diagonal Cody spars.

12"
30cm.

15"
40cm.

12"
30cm.

SIMPLE RIGID
BOX KITE.

39"
100cm.

$23\frac{1}{2}$"
60cm.

that a very simple conversion makes it into a Cody type with side wings. Just fit two diagonal spars in line with the end braces and you have main members for the side wings, the addition of which improves the box kite enormously. Otherwise, if for simplicity you want a 'square-celled' box, adjust the dimensions and the kite can be flown without a bridle by attaching the kite line direct to the lower spar at the rear edge of the front cell. Then the box kite flies 'on edge'. No tail is required for the box kite and the one precaution which should be observed is to keep the weight as low as feasible for strength.

SIMPLE HEXAGON (Fig. 127)

Take three sticks, each $\frac{3}{16}$ in. (5 mm) square, and trim to equal lengths, about $27\frac{1}{2}$ ins (70 cm). Drill a $\frac{1}{16}$-in. (2-mm) hole through the centres, and join with a thin bolt, or piece of wire. Slot the ends of the spars. Now make a pattern for the hexagon in paper, plastic or fabric and wrap the edges over a loose cord outline. The cord should be free to move in each seam and project in a loop at each of the points of the hexagon. Make a hole dead centre in the sail before fitting it to the spreader spars. Each loop of cord should slot into the end of a spar. Pull the peripheral cord tight and knot it when the sail is spread flat. Remember that the frame is on the back of the sail.

The bridle is made by three equal-length lines, one from the centre through the hole in the sail and two from the spar tips. The tails trail from opposite ends as shown. You now have a kite that will surprise you with its control and ability to fly in the slightest breeze. Moreover, if made carefully it can be disassembled between flying sessions. The tails, if two are used as sketched, should be streamer-type, about 30 ft (10 m) long. If you prefer a single tail, it should be a pigtail with multiple bows tied over a central tape about 40 ins (102 cm) long.

FLYING NIGHT OWL (Fig. 128)

Cane or flexible spars are essential for this shaped semi-flexible kite which is formed by three spars joined in curves. Tension in the cord from tips to the body and legs is important, and so is the selection of a good light fabric for equal flex on either wing. White cotton is ideal, since it can be painted to resemble owl feathers. Nylon is less easy to paint but possibly lighter in weight. Use acrylic dyes for the brightest paint effect.

These shaped kites are suggested as second projects after you have gained experience with a more simple design. Note the bridle points for three lines at the semi-span points, and base of the body. Trailing streamers are advised, and if vari-coloured narrow bands of crêpe paper, plastic or light fabric are used the effect is most attractive.

FLYING FISH (Fig. 129)

This is a straight-line variant with only a small section of the outer wings having a flexible trailing edge – largely for effect. Use selected (matched) sticks of $\frac{1}{4}$ in. (6 mm) square obechi or similar wood and bind each crossing firmly, with a tack of glue between the spars. The cross spar is there to prevent a folded collapse, so don't leave it out.

Bridling the fish depends largely on the size of the tail triangle. Equal lines from each of the four main diamond ends will give a good start. Coloured plastic-film tapers streaming from each of the wing and tail tips are extremely effective, and for an improvement in stability try a lateral brace across each diagonal of the centre diamond. This gives depth to the shape, plus dihedral and negative camber.

SLED (Fig. 130)

We are indebted to Dave Checkley and *Sunset* magazine for this sled, made to the Scott pattern from an ordinary plastic dustbin liner. Keep the bag folded and measure off the

145

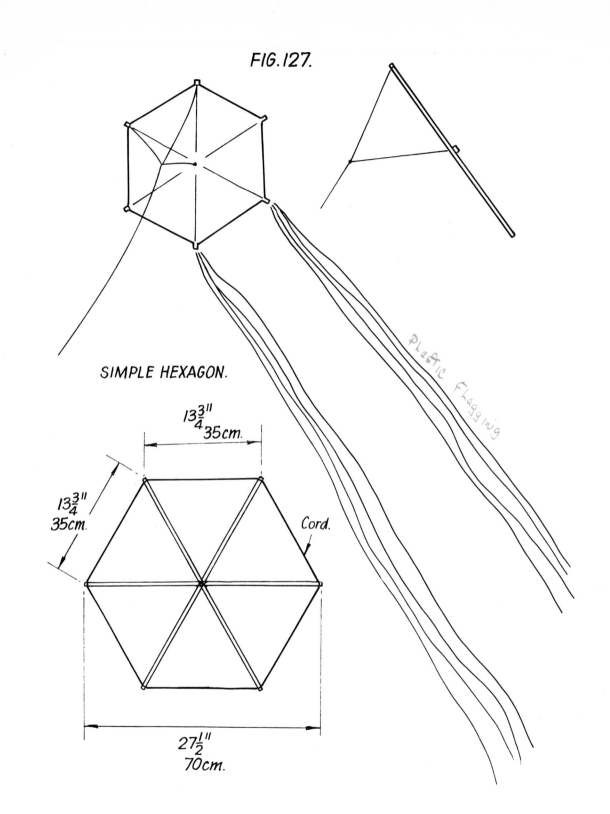

FIG.127.

SIMPLE HEXAGON.

Plastic Flagging

$13\frac{3}{4}''$ 35cm.

$13\frac{3}{4}''$ 35cm.

Cord.

$27\frac{1}{2}''$ 70cm.

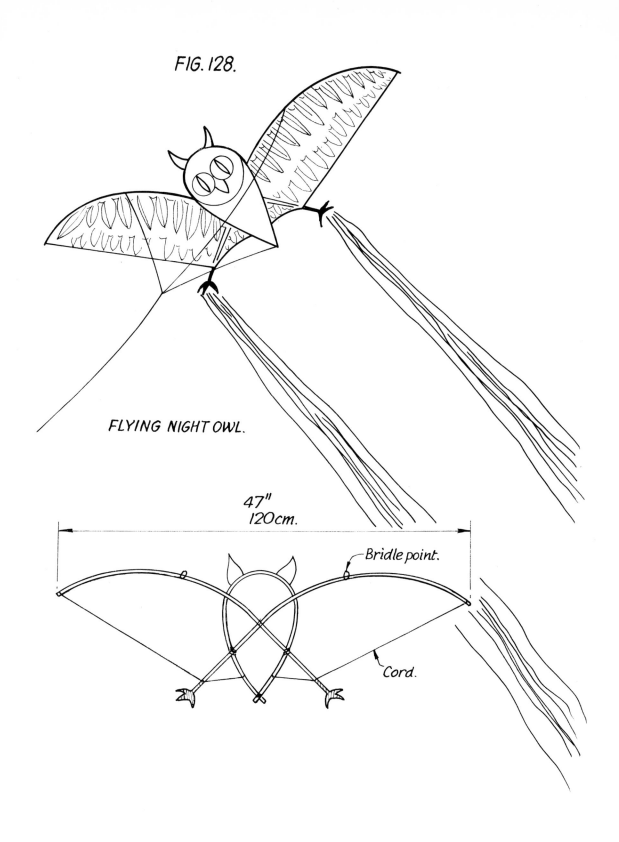

FIG. 128.

FLYING NIGHT OWL.

47"
120cm.

Bridle point.

Cord.

FIG. 129.

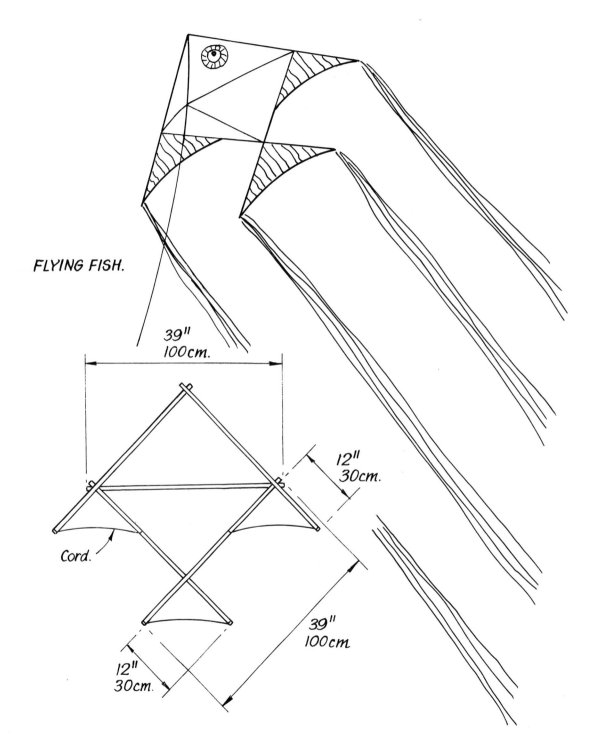

FLYING FISH.

39"
100cm.

12"
30cm.

Cord.

39"
100cm

12"
30cm.

FIG. 130.

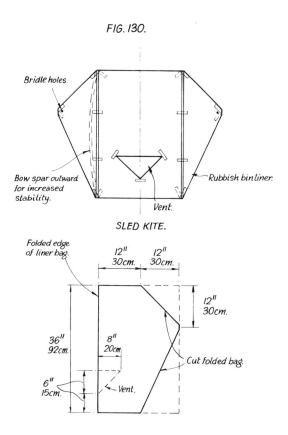

Bridle holes

Bow spar outward
for increased
stability.

Rubbish bin liner.

Vent.

SLED KITE.

Folded edge
of liner bag.

12"
30cm.

12"
30cm.

12"
30cm.

36"
92cm.

8"
20cm.

Cut folded bag.

6"
15cm.

Vent.

dimensions. Cut away at one side, slit the base and open out to the full shape. Reinforce with sticky tape at each corner and fit a couple of cane spars. Eyelets for the bridle tie points and tape reinforcement at the corners of the triangular vent are advised. If the cane spars are bowed as they are held in place, the sled is less likely to collapse and turn inside out.

This is the simplest of all kites and yet it out-performs many of its more complicated counterparts. A long two-leg bridle is suggested, with each line 6 ft (2 m) long from the bridle hole to the junction in the kite line. It is possible to vary the shape of the vent(s), for example to cut a pair of eyes and a mouth shape, or two circles. The triangular vent is a basic feature which works well.

INDIAN FIGHTER KITE (Fig. 131)

The traditional Indian kite has always been the subject of great curiosity. Neutrally stable, it is not in any way conventional to fly by Western standards, and it demands careful construction to ensure that the shape is both symmetrical in form and balanced in weight. Between 1975 and 1977 Indian fighting kites were introduced in quantity. Indian-born demonstrators showed that it is possible to fly these kites even when there is no apparent wind. As long as sufficient line can be paid out, and then pulled in to elevate the kite, it will fly, even indoors. Start by making the two spars, one just under 2 ft (61 cm) for the centre, the other longer, 30 ins (75 cm), and tapered in section over its outer 11 ins (28 cm) or so. Use bamboos of about $\frac{1}{4}$ in. (6 mm), and taper them to a slender tip by stroking the wood with a stiff-backed razor blade or very sharp knife to shave the thickness. The spars are cross-bound at 4 ins (10 cm) from the forward part of the centre spar, and an outline of cotton thread is tied around the four extremities. This must be so tensioned as to pull the cross spar back in a curve of almost a semi-circle. Use sticky tape to lock the cotton thread to the tapered ends of the spar. When the attractive semi-ogival shape is achieved, wrap light tissue covering over all the edges and seal with a glue stick (Pritt or UHU Stik). Make a delta-shape 'tail' or stabiliser, with two bamboo sliver strengtheners as shown, and all that remains is the bridle which is the simple two-line yoke.

The technique of flying this kite was described in Chapter 3. Remember always that the Indian fighter needs a pull to climb, and will twirl when the line is slack. It will move in whatever direction it is heading when the line tension is taken up – and that also means downwards if it is pointing that way, so be warned!

JAPANESE FIGHTER KITE (Fig. 132)

Closer to the Malay or Eddy shape, the

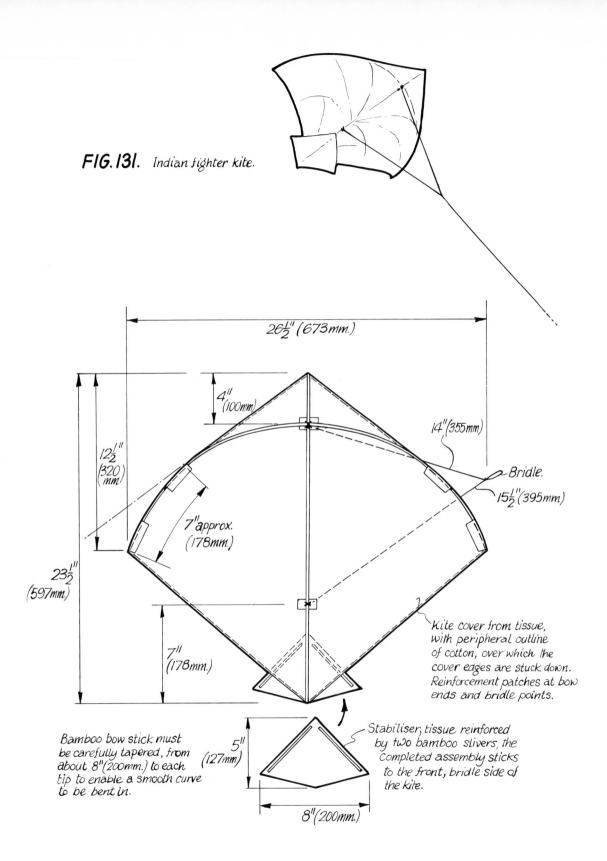

FIG. 131. Indian fighter kite.

$26\frac{1}{2}''$ (673 mm.)

$4''$ (100 mm.)

$12\frac{1}{2}''$ (320 mm.)

$14''$ (355 mm.)

Bridle.

$15\frac{1}{2}''$ (395 mm.)

$7''$ approx. (178 mm.)

$23\frac{1}{2}''$ (597 mm.)

$7''$ (178 mm.)

Kite cover from tissue, with peripheral outline of cotton, over which the cover edges are stuck down. Reinforcement patches at bow ends and bridle points.

$5''$ (127 mm.)

Bamboo bow stick must be carefully tapered, from about 8" (200 mm.) to each tip to enable a smooth curve to be bent in.

Stabiliser, tissue reinforced by two bamboo slivers, the completed assembly sticks to the front, bridle side of the kite.

$8''$ (200 mm.)

Japanese diamond kite is longer in proportion and generally larger than its Indian counterpart. Construction is identical, except that, as indicated in Fig. 132, the tapered lateral spar has less bow and the bridle attachment points are different from the Indian. Note also that tassel tips are used to balance the drag and stabilise the kite. Tissue covering is not easy to obtain in very large sheets, so I suggest that you make strips of contrasting colour and join them to provide a diagonally striped sail.

WEST INDIAN DIAMOND KITE (Fig. 133)

No sooner had the Indian fighter arrived on the scene in the mid-1970s than miniature versions began to flit around. These were not from the East, but came instead from Jamaica and Barbados in the West Indies. A typical size is 12 ins (30 cm) square, with identical construction to that described for the Indian, although using much thinner bamboos. Due to the size, a streamer tail 9 ft (3 m) long is essential for stability, and it can have pigtailed crosspieces attached over the first 3 ft (1 m). A steady breeze of moderate strength will take this small kite up quickly, and bring it down again just as rapidly. The size makes it extra-sensitive and for that reason the West Indian diamond can be lots of fun to make and fly. One make which has become popular in Britain is known as KiskeeDee.

BERMUDAN THREE-STICK KITE (Fig. 134)

Distinctive in its extended hexagonal form, the Bermudan kite is very stable and has been the subject of successive claims for world duration records. Maritime winds in Bermuda are constant in force for long periods. This enables local experts to leave their kites aloft all day. Though the point of the exercise will be obscure to the kite flyer who seeks activity, the three-stick has a lot going for it if you are seeking something that offers trouble-free flight.

The spars of split bamboo, spruce, or beech dowel are tied together with a thread wrapping at a point midway on the horizontal spar and approximately $8\frac{1}{2}$ ins (22 cm) from the top ends of the diagonal spars. The actual dimensions are not at all critical. The advised size of 20 ins (50 cm) width and 26 ins (66 cm) diagonal spar lengths can be varied, particularly if a buzzer is to be fitted on extensions as illustrated.

The major difference between this kite and the hexagonal in Fig. 127 is that the Bermudan is a permanent assembly. Its asymmetry makes quick folding a difficult prospect. The thread outline can be tied firmly to the ends of each spar. Then the tissue cover is folded and pasted with a moderate overlap all round. The tissue should be reasonably tough, and can even be decorative gift-wrap paper.

Tie a three-point bridle to the top ends and through the cover, to the intersection of the spars. The lines can be about 12 ins (30 cm) and a spare line is tied across the bottom ends of the diagonals to use as a tail bearer. This is a prerequisite and though the streamer need be only a simple strip without pigtails, it should be at least 6 ft 6 ins (2 m) long.

Buzzers are made using any hard, thin-grade paper that can be wrapped over a taut line. Some toilet tissues are good for this, producing a steady 'zizz' when vibrating under tension.

EASTERN SNAKE KITE (Fig. 135)

If you have access to long lengths of thin plastic sheet, the snake (or serpent) is one of the easiest kites to make. About 25 ft (7·6 m) is needed to make a reasonable snake – more if possible. The plastic should be tapered from the $16\frac{1}{2}$-in. (42-cm) head width to an extreme point at the end, and if reinforcement is thought advisable, lay a strip of glass fibre parcel tape down the centre line. The head can be square, five-sided or the traditional hoop shape. Use a bamboo 43 ins (110 cm) long to

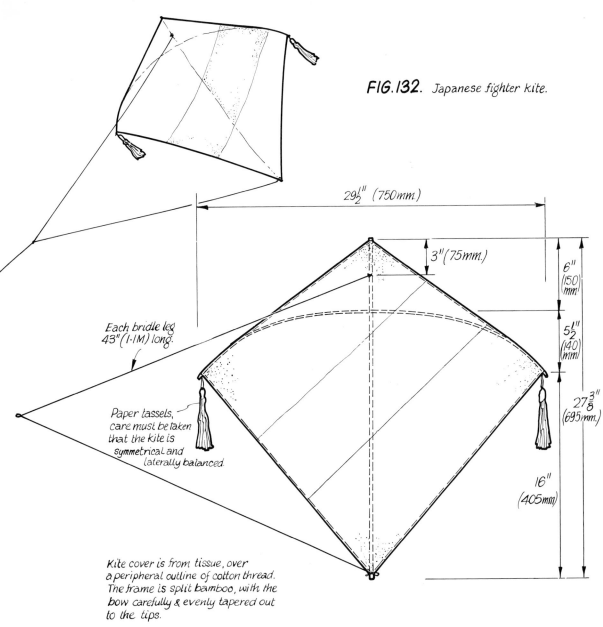

FIG. 132. *Japanese fighter kite.*

$29\frac{1}{2}''$ (750mm.)

3" (75mm.)

6" (150 mm)

$5\frac{1}{2}''$ (140 mm)

$27\frac{3}{8}''$ (695mm.)

16" (405mm)

Each bridle leg 43" (1·1M) long.

Paper tassels, care must be taken that the kite is symmetrical and laterally balanced.

Kite cover is from tissue, over a peripheral outline of cotton thread. The frame is split bamboo, with the bow carefully & evenly tapered out to the tips.

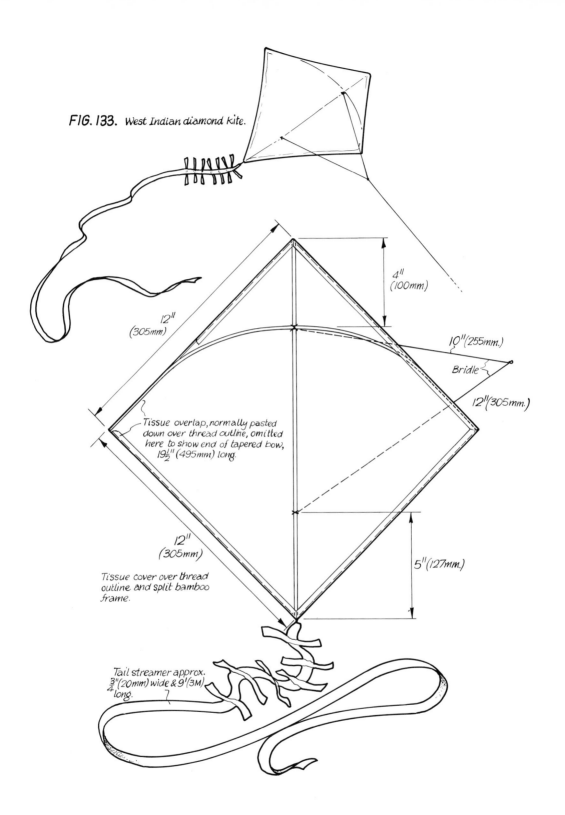

FIG. 133. *West Indian diamond kite.*

4″ (100mm)

12″ (305mm)

10″(255mm.)

Bridle

12″(305mm.)

Tissue overlap, normally pasted down over thread outline, omitted here to show end of tapered bow, 19½″ (495mm) long.

12″ (305mm)

5″ (127mm.)

Tissue cover over thread outline and split bamboo frame.

Tail streamer approx. ¾″ (20mm) wide & 9′ (3M) long.

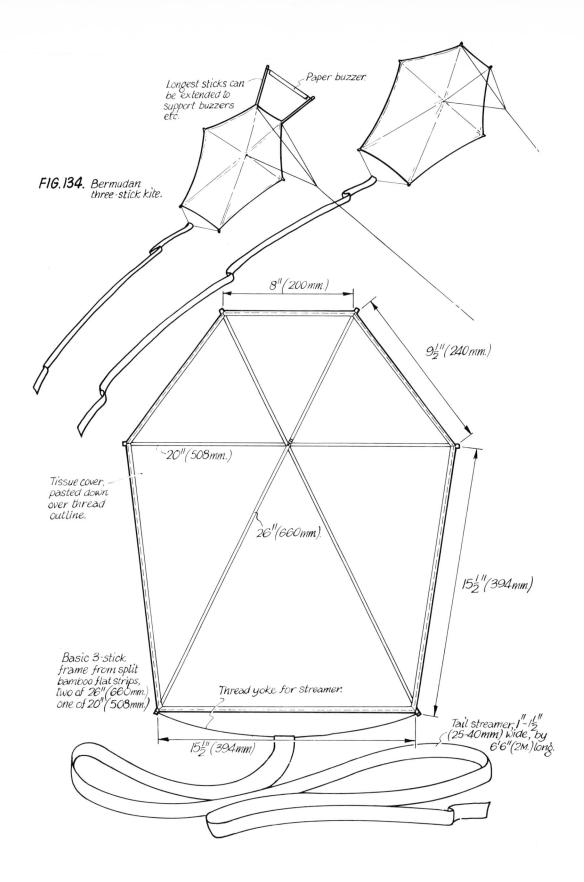

Longest sticks can be extended to support buzzers etc.

Paper buzzer.

FIG.134. Bermudan three-stick kite.

8" (200 mm.)

9½" (240 mm.)

20" (508 mm.)

Tissue cover, pasted down over thread outline.

26" (660 mm.)

15½" (394 mm.)

Basic 3-stick frame from split bamboo flat strips, two of 26" (660 mm.) one of 20" (508 mm.)

Thread yoke for streamer.

15½" (394 mm.)

Tail streamer, 1"-1½" (25-40 mm.) wide, by 6'6" (2 M.) long.

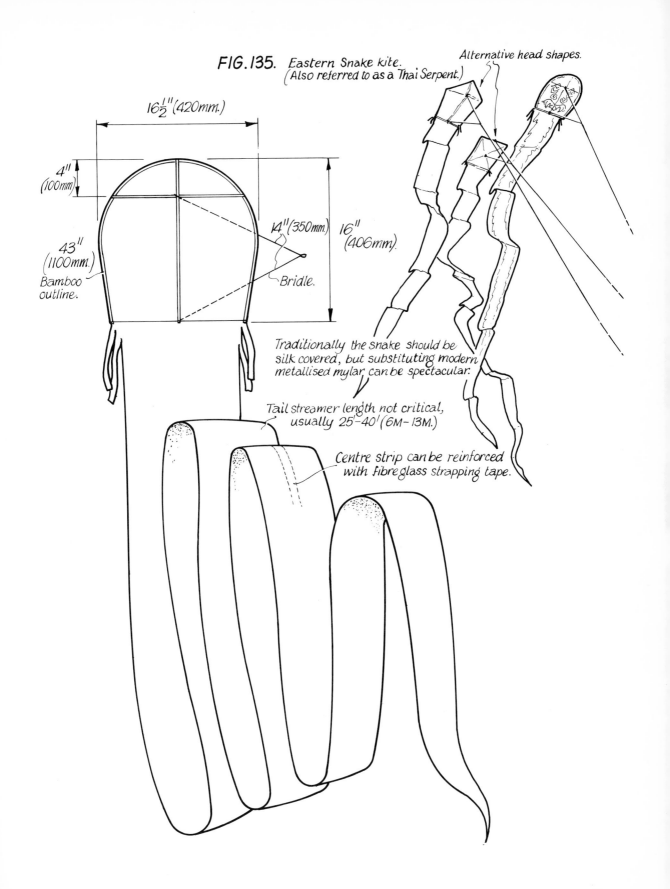

FIG. 135. Eastern Snake kite.
(Also referred to as a Thai Serpent.)

Alternative head shapes.

16½" (420mm.)

4" (100mm)

14" (350mm.)

16" (406mm.)

Bridle.

43" (1100mm.) Bamboo outline.

Traditionally the snake should be silk covered, but substituting modern metallised mylar can be spectacular.

Tail streamer length not critical, usually 25'–40' (6M–13M.)

Centre strip can be reinforced with fibre glass strapping tape.

make the curved head outline. Some snakes have been made with stout reed instead; but whatever is used a cross piece of strong sticks is needed in the centre. Tie a strong thread line across the open side of the hoop, and secure the centre spar in the middle of the line. This then forms one anchor point for the two-line bridle, the other being at the cross point of the spars. Scissor-cut streamers at the sides of the snake immediately below the head. These will flap and rustle in flight. Now paint the decoration on the head and you have one of the most attractive kite shapes and one which gets aloft on the slightest breeze. Be warned, however, not to use metallised plastic anywhere near overhead electrical cables. The silver finish looks fine in sunshine; but accidents with power lines in the USA and Germany have led to the prohibition of snakes made with this material. Incidentally, the name given to this shape varies from Dragon to Spermy.

CHINESE CENTIPEDE KITE (Fig. 136)

If the snake is easy, this centipede is the exact opposite; but if flown well, it is a real show-stopper. Basically a train of disc kites linked to a common line, the centipede becomes a pictorial essay in motion as it oscillates along its length in flight. But setting up the bridle, and linking the elements with triple tether lines, is not for the kite flyer who wants quick results. For one thing, the centipede is not one, but many kites. Each of the discs is a kite in itself which needs side stabilisers in the form of outriggers with tassels, bobbles or feathers at the ends to act as balancing 'hands'.

Tom Van Sant, an American sculptor of considerable merit, arrived in Britain for a display of his kites in mid-1976. Van Sant had taken to kites while working in the Far East, and he returned home to California with a fresh outlook on the use of modern materials for traditional designs. Among his first major works was a centipede, and it was this kite which attracted so much attention at the Institute of Contemporary Arts in London, where his kites were exhibited. Van Sant used glassfibre fishing rods, nylon covering and decorative feathers for his latter-day centipede. Film of his flights, taken from the ground, as well as from a helicopter which provided an unusual viewpoint, stimulated kite flyers enormously. As will be shown in subsequent descriptions (Figs 137, 140, 141, 142 and 143), Van Sant developed many applications for the glassfibre rod so his influence was far-reaching. Tom's big centipede possibly cost over £250 to make, but the materials for a smaller version, as sketched, could be bought for much less.

Rattan can be wound into the 11-in. (28-cm) diameter circle for an outline. Its ends can be butted, glued and wrapped with parcel tape and the 42-in. (107-cm) stabilising rod bound to its intersections with the circle to help hold shape. A vertical spar completes the first element. Alternative materials range from the glassfibre rod to split bamboo while the tassels can be of any light material that looks attractive. It is very important to ensure that the stabilisers balance. Don't let one side be heavier or bulkier than the other. Use light material or tissue for covering. The number of elements is a free choice which ought to start at eight and perhaps be as many as thirty. On the 11-in. (28-cm) disc centipede you should ideally reduce the distance between elements progressively by $\frac{1}{2}$ in. (13 mm) at each stage so that, with eight discs, and starting with the first two 9 ins (23 cm) apart, the last pair are 5 ins (12 cm) apart. Tail streamers should be fixed to a cross brace spar on the rear disc, otherwise the only other disc which may need the cross brace is the foremost one.

Flying a centipede is quite different from other kiting. The extreme tail tends to climb, then drops as the wind fluctuates in strength and the discs blanket the airflow over one another. The result is that the centipede oscillates about a more or less horizontal attitude. Ideally it needs constant moderate wind.

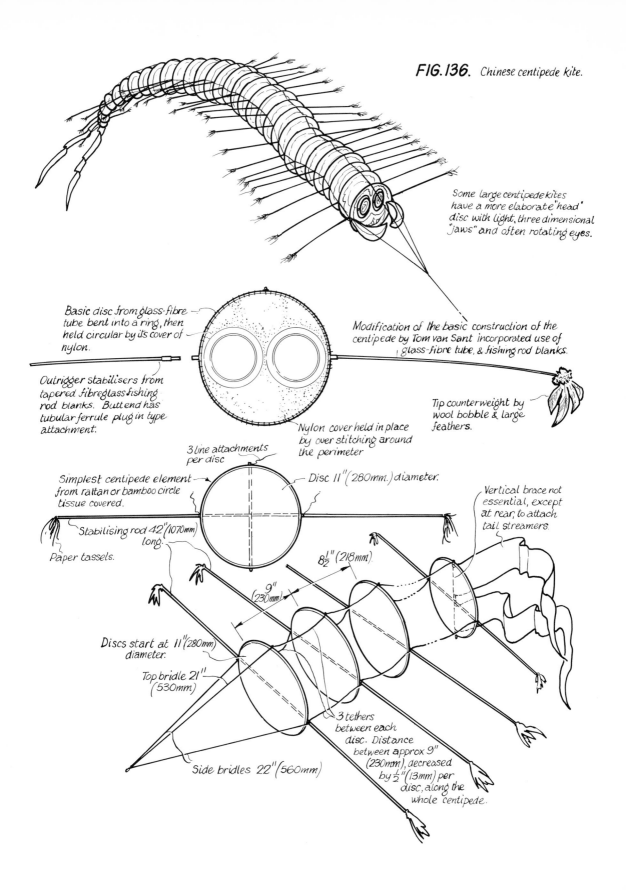

FIG.136. *Chinese centipede kite.*

Some large centipede kites have a more elaborate "head" disc with light, three dimensional "jaws" and often rotating eyes.

Basic disc from glass-fibre tube bent into a ring, then held circular by its cover of nylon.

Modification of the basic construction of the centipede by Tom van Sant incorporated use of glass-fibre tube, & fishing rod blanks.

Outrigger stabilisers from tapered fibreglass fishing rod blanks. Butt end has tubular ferrule plug in type attachment.

Tip counterweight by wool bobble & large feathers.

Nylon cover held in place by over stitching around the perimeter

3 line attachments per disc

Simplest centipede element from rattan or bamboo circle tissue covered.

Disc 11" (280mm.) diameter.

Vertical brace not essential, except at rear, to attach tail streamers.

Stabilising rod 42" (1070mm) long.

Paper tassels.

$8\frac{1}{2}$" (218mm).

9" (230mm)

Discs start at 11" (280mm) diameter.

Top bridle 21" (530mm)

3 tethers between each disc. Distance between approx 9" (230mm), decreased by $\frac{1}{2}$" (13mm) per disc, along the whole centipede.

Side bridles 22" (560mm)

DELTA SHAPES (Fig. 137)

Created by Mr Hartig and others in the USA, the Delta kite with flexible leading-edge spars which are not rigidly connected to the centre spar or keel is very much an American product. The Delta comes in many guises, and the most popular is the apron type as typified by the standard design of the American Kitefliers Association seen in I. This is a large area cloth kite, so the first essential is to find lightweight, colourfully patterned material of moderate porosity.

Rip-stop nylon is excellent for this purpose, especially as it often comes in widths sufficient to cover the 45×92 ins (115×235 cm) dimensions for chord and span. This large rectangle is folded in half, and the sleeve for the centre chord dowel is sewn by machine. Do this by measuring $2\frac{1}{2}$ ins (6 cm) from the centre fold line, and sewing a first run on a line this distance from and parallel to the folded edge. A $\frac{1}{2}$-in. (12-mm) dowel 40 ins (102 cm) long is slipped into what is now an oversize pocket, and the fabric pulled around the dowel so that a second machining can be made to tighten up the sleeve. This will leave a projecting double-thickness hem between the folded edge and the dowel sleeve, which is then used to take the keel attachment.

Having fixed the centre dowel by sewing the sleeve end at front and rear of its length, 40 ins (102 cm), the kite material is unfolded out flat and marked for cutting the outer triangles away. Allow 2 ins (5 cm) for a hem to form the sleeve for 48-in. (122-cm) leading-edge dowels of $\frac{1}{4}$-in. (6-mm) diameter, noting that the sleeves end, and the dowels with them, 11 ins (28 cm) from the extreme nose. The dowels can be sewn in permanently. Trim the rear-edge apron so that there is a 5-in. (12-cm) wide flap which can either be left as two 'elevators' with a central v cutaway, or snipped at 1-in. (25-mm) intervals to create a line of streamers. Pinking shears, rather than scissors, are advised to prevent fraying, and improve the finished appearance.

All that remains is the centre keel which is double-surfaced, cut from one of the two scrap pieces of fabric and made strictly to the dimensions shown. Eyelets for alternate line-connection points should be large in diameter and strong enough to accept tension without tearing the surrounding fabric. Along the upper edge of the keel, the two thicknesses should be left free to be sewn along the full length, over the hem left on the centre dowel sleeve. The main kite is now finished: but it requires the vital spreader which attaches to the leading edges.

In the case of the AKA Delta, the spreader is 36 ins (92 cm) long and it joins the leading edges 24 ins (61 cm) from the extreme nose. The actual method of joining is a matter of choice. Figs 157 and 158 illustrate the most popular arrangements which permit the Delta to be rolled, for carrying.

A 'soaring' Delta is shown in II. This is a type which Will Yolen recommends for high flying, almost overhead, especially in sea breezes. All the machining methods previously described for I apply here also but there is no apron, and the shape and size are such that Yolen's Delta can be made out of narrower material (30 ins/76 cm). One reason why Yolen calls this a 'soaring' kite will soon be evident at first test flight. A characteristic of these American Deltas is the way the halves of the kit fluctuate independent of each other. The leading edges pivot about the spreader connection, and as the kite adapts itself to changing winds the leading-edge dowels will tilt at varying angles. Surface loading is low and the shape approaches, but is not identical to, the Rogallo, so the Delta has a better lift coefficient than most others and thus flies frequently up and over the operator. If these Deltas are made with non-porous (plastic) sails they fly best in low wind speeds, and can be reeled out from a self launch, being stable even in ground turbulence. For moderate winds, however, the cloth Delta comes into its own.

Figs 137 III and IV illustrate Tom Van Sant's

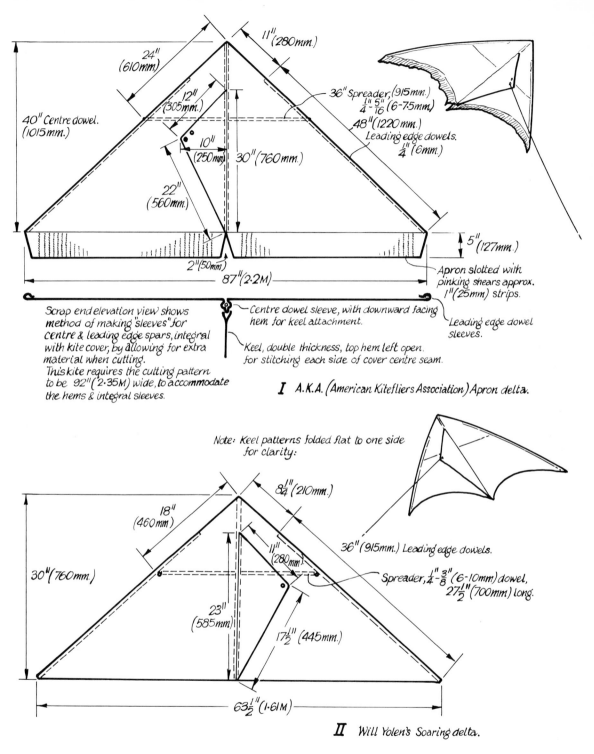

24" (610mm)

11" (280mm)

12" (305mm)

40" Centre dowel. (1015mm.)

36" Spreader, (915mm.) ¼"–⁵⁄₁₆" (6–7·5mm)

48"(1220mm.) Leading edge dowels. ¼" (6mm.)

10" (250mm)

30"(760mm.)

22" (560mm)

5" (127mm.)

2"(50mm)

87"(2·2M)

Apron slotted with pinking shears approx. 1"(25mm) strips.

Scrap end elevation view shows method of making "sleeves" for centre & leading edge spars, integral with kite cover, by allowing for extra material when cutting.
This kite requires the cutting pattern to be 92"(2·35M) wide, to accommodate the hems & integral sleeves.

Centre dowel sleeve, with downward facing hem for keel attachment.

Keel, double thickness, top hem left open, for stitching each side of cover centre seam.

Leading edge dowel sleeves.

I   A.K.A. (American Kitefliers Association) Apron delta.

Note: Keel patterns folded flat to one side for clarity:

8¼" (210mm.)

18" (460mm)

30"(760mm.)

11" (280mm)

36" (915mm.) Leading edge dowels.

Spreader, ¼"–³⁄₈" (6–10mm) dowel, 27½" (700mm) long.

23" (585mm)

17½" (445mm.)

63½" (1·61M)

II   Will Yolen's Soaring delta.

FIG. 137.

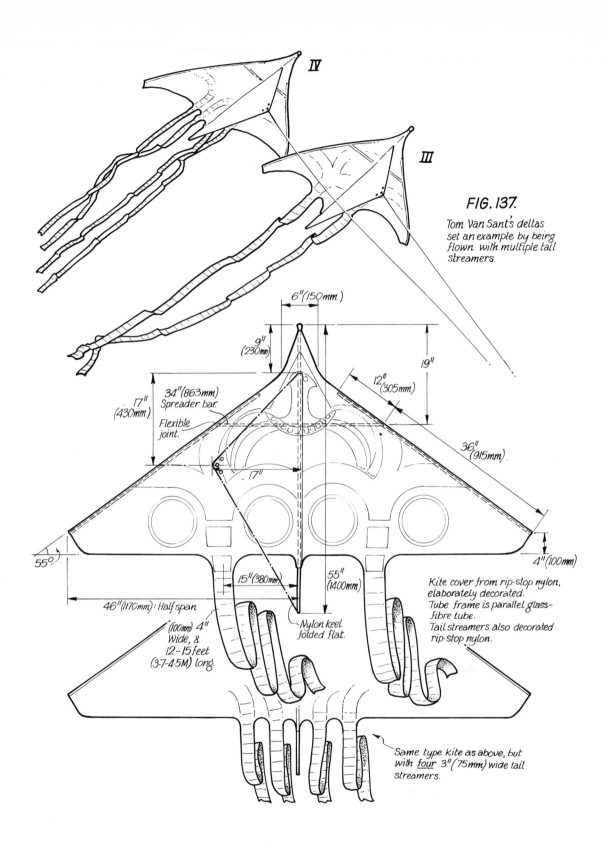

IV

III

FIG. 137.

Tom Van Sant's deltas
set an example by being
flown with multiple tail
streamers.

6" (150mm.)

9"
(230mm)

19"

12"
(305mm)

17"
(430mm.)

34" (863mm.)
Spreader bar.

Flexible
joint.

36"
(915mm).

17"

55°

4" (100mm)

15" (380mm)

55"
(1400mm)

46" (1170mm): Half span

Kite cover from rip-stop nylon,
elaborately decorated.
Tube frame is parallel glass-
fibre tube.
Tail streamers also decorated
rip-stop nylon.

(100mm) 4"
Wide, &
12-15 feet
(3.7-4.5M) long.

Nylon keel
folded flat.

Same type kite as above, but
with four 3" (75mm) wide tail
streamers.

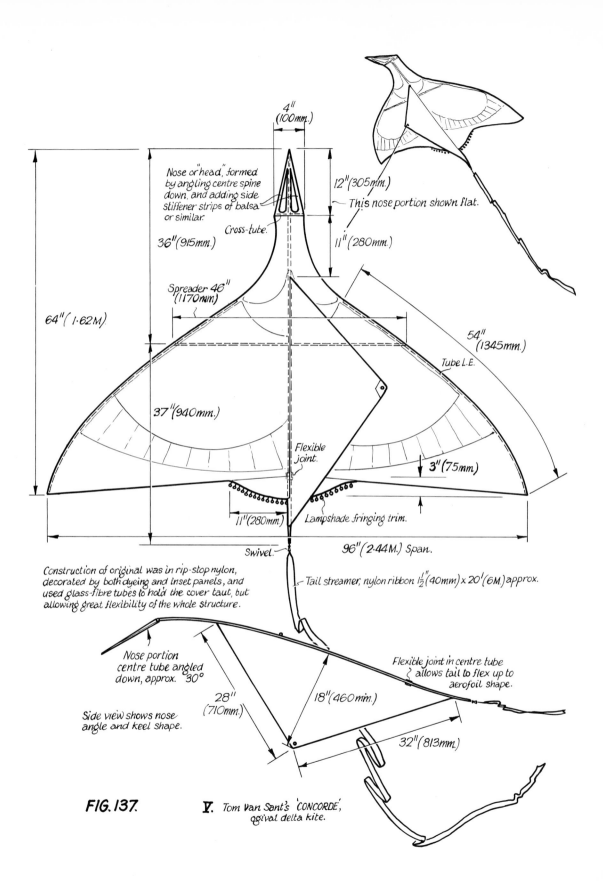

4" (100mm.)

Nose or "head," formed by angling centre spine down, and adding side stiffener strips of balsa or similar.

Cross-tube.

36" (915mm.)

12" (305mm.)

This nose portion shown flat.

11" (280mm.)

Spreader 46" (1170mm)

64" (1·62M)

54" (1345mm.)

Tube L.E.

37" (940mm.)

Flexible joint.

3" (75mm.)

11" (280mm.)

Lampshade fringing trim.

Swivel.

96" (2·44M.) Span.

Construction of original was in rip-stop nylon, decorated by both dyeing and inset panels, and used glass-fibre tubes to hold the cover taut, but allowing great flexibility of the whole structure.

Tail streamer, nylon ribbon 1½" (40mm) x 20' (6M.) approx.

Nose portion centre tube angled down, approx. 30°

Flexible joint in centre tube allows tail to flex up to aerofoil shape.

28" (710mm.)

18" (460mm.)

Side view shows nose angle and keel shape.

32" (813mm.)

FIG. 137.

V. Tom Van Sant's 'CONCORDE', ogival delta kite.

multiple-tailed variants, each of which have an intriguing Aztec-style decoration. Van Sant changed the plain Delta into a bird-like shape by extending the centre dowel into a beaked nose, and rounding off the trailing-edge tips. The material used was rip-stop nylon painted with special plastic dyes, and all of the spars were glass fibre tubes joined in pairs side by side. It was only natural that Van Sant should have developed these designs to Fig. 137 v as the Concorde with a curved outline, original in shape and sophisticated in the way the fabric tension is employed to keep the outline. This one example would have been enough to show kite flyers in 1976 that there was still room for design initiative, but as we shall see in Figs 140, 141, 142 and 143 his innovations were diverse in their novelty.

To make a Van Sant Concorde it is essential to have flexible glass fibre tubes for the leading edges. These are curved by the shape of the hem sleeve, and they pull the nylon cover tight as they resist the bending tension. The Concorde is large, with an 8-ft (244-cm) span and it has an equivalently large keel. This, too, is shaped to an aerofoil curve on its upper line where the keel is sewn to the centre sleeve. A flexed line, with positive curvature developing to negative, forms the sail into a powerful lifting wing. To complete the Concorde effect Van Sant adds a rigid 'droop snout' beak nose which is purely decorative, as is the humorous touch of a lampshade fringe for a fluttering tail. Again, all the machining required follows the instructions given for Fig. 137 i and the decoration is made with plastic dyes.

OPEN-KEEL DELTA KITES (Fig. 138a)

While the standard AKA Delta enjoys great success, some people think that what is called an OKD or Open-Keel Delta is an improvement. In principle the sail remains a flexible shape with unlinked leading edges pivoted on the tips of a spreader, but the vertical element

forms a windsock. This open-front keel (Fig. 138a) does have practical advantages at the expense of longer construction time, because machining is a little more complicated. The mainsail has a centre sleeve for the dowel, and, as described for the AKA Delta, the leading edges are sewn into sleeves. But the keel is sewn to the sail outboard of the centre line and this helps to pull a curved shape into the sail when the kite is in flight. The machining has to be symmetrical and firm. Commercial kites began to appear in 1977 using the same concept, made in plastic rather than the light cotton fabric recommended for the design as sketched.

From the OKD we move to Fig. 138b, the Owl as created by John Loy. This has many distinctions. The huge apron, full-length leading-edge spars, lack of a keel, triple-line bridle and the billowed centre make Loy's Owl an exceptional Delta. Note that the design shows a division or join line for the fabric or plastic used to make the sail. This may not be necessary but it might otherwise be difficult to find material 36 × 60 ins (92 × 153 cm). Hem edges, with sleeves at the leading edges, are quite normal. Two spars at the centre are, however, slightly tricky. You have the option of machining sleeves as for the centre spine on a standard Delta, or having these spars outside. In the latter case, they can be on the upper side of the sail, linked together at the rear, and in turn attached to the centre point on the sail. At their fore ends, the spars must be connected to the leading edges; similarly a spreader attaches to control the span, and then the shape of the Owl is left to bridle tension.

When in full flight, the triangular area between the centre spars will billow upwards, so forming a central tunnel to straighten the airflow which is otherwise directed by a vertical keel. Dimensions for the Owl are typical. Larger versions have been made but you are advised to avoid increasing the apron width, otherwise the 'luffing' effect of a flapping trailing edge spoils the stability.

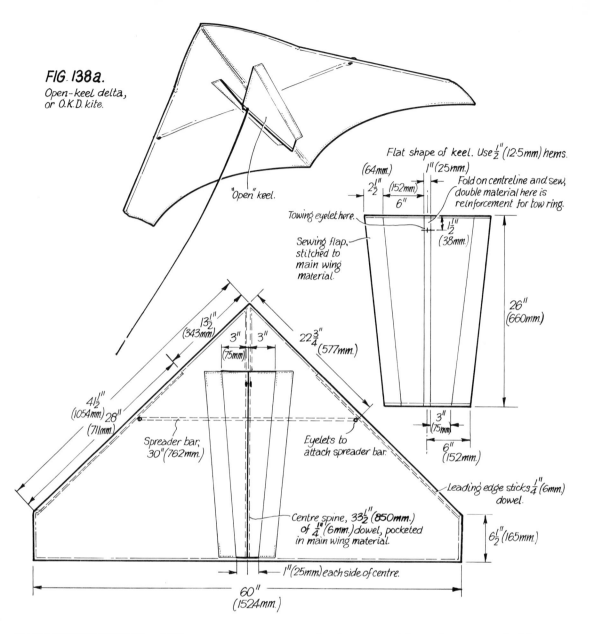

FIG. 138a.
Open-keel delta,
or O.K.D. kite.

"Open" keel.

Flat shape of keel. Use $\frac{1}{2}''$ (12·5mm) hems.

(64mm.)   1" (25mm.)

$2\frac{1}{2}''$ (152mm)   Fold on centreline and sew,
double material here is
reinforcement for tow ring.

6"

Towing eyelet here.

$1\frac{1}{2}''$
(38mm.)

Sewing flap,
stitched to
main wing
material.

26"
(660mm.)

$13\frac{1}{2}''$
(343mm.)

3" | 3"
(75mm.)

$22\frac{3}{4}''$
(577mm.)

$4\frac{1}{2}''$
(1054mm.) 28"
(711mm.)

Spreader bar,
30" (762mm.)

Eyelets to
attach spreader bar.

3"
(75mm.)

6"
(152mm.)

Leading edge sticks $\frac{1}{4}''$ (6mm.)
dowel.

Centre spine, $33\frac{1}{2}''$ (850mm.)
of $\frac{1}{4}''$ (6mm.) dowel, pocketed
in main wing material.

$6\frac{1}{2}''$ (165mm.)

1" (25mm) each side of centre.

60"
(1524mm.)

PARACHUTE KITE (Fig. 139).
Ed Grauel is one of the pioneer members of the
AKA and an authority on design origins. This
one is highly original – a flexikite without
spars, having holes or vents for stability, and
operating in much the same way as a 'para-
scender'. The silk or nylon material is laid out
to make a 43-in. (55-cm) diameter circle. This is
then divided as the dimensions show, to make

a duodecagon with twelve unequal sides. A
paper pattern is advised for trial-and-error
layout first.

The key to the operation of the Parachute
kite is the shroud arrangement which Grauel
provides in the table in Fig. 139. Each point on
the periphery of the chute (which ought to
have a hemmed edge) is marked by a sewn loop
of strong thread. The points are numbered,

163

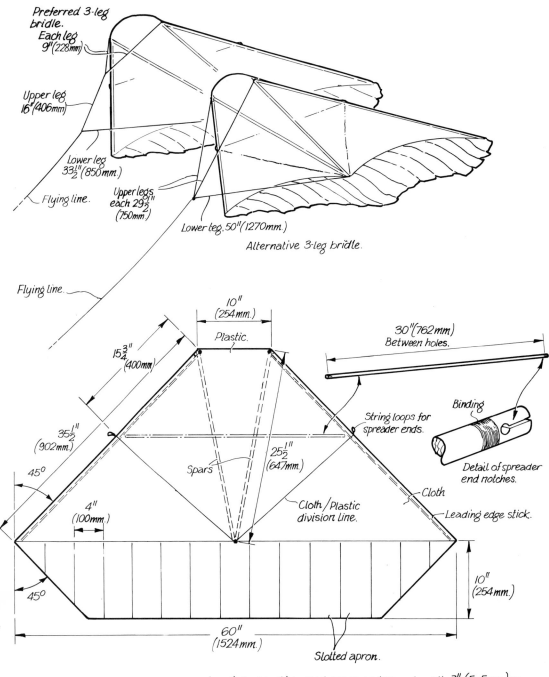

Preferred 3-leg bridle.
Each leg 9" (228mm)

Upper leg 16" (406mm)

Lower leg 33½" (850mm.)

Flying line.

Upper legs each 29½" (750mm)

Lower leg. 50" (1270mm.)

Alternative 3-leg bridle.

Flying line.

10" (254 mm.)

Plastic.

15¾" (400mm)

30" (762mm) Between holes.

Binding

String loops for spreader ends.

35½" (902mm.)

Spars

25½" (647mm.)

Detail of spreader end notches.

45°

Cloth / Plastic division line.

Cloth

Leading edge stick.

4" (100mm.)

45°

10" (254mm.)

60" (1524mm.)

Slotted apron.

Leading edge sticks and spars and spreader, all $\frac{3}{16}$" (5×5mm.) sq. or $\frac{1}{4}$" (6mm.) diameter dowel.

FIG. 138 b.   John. W. Loy's "OWL No.1." Delta kite.

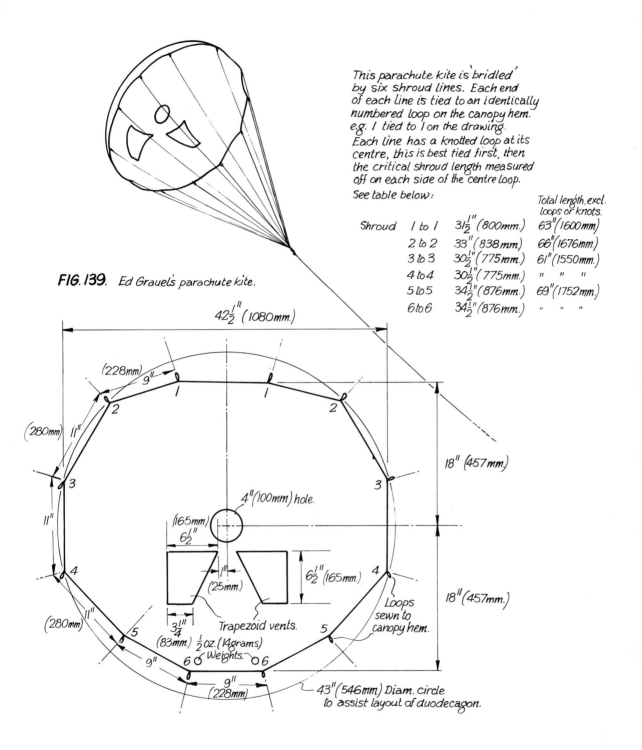

FIG. 139. Ed Grauel's parachute kite.

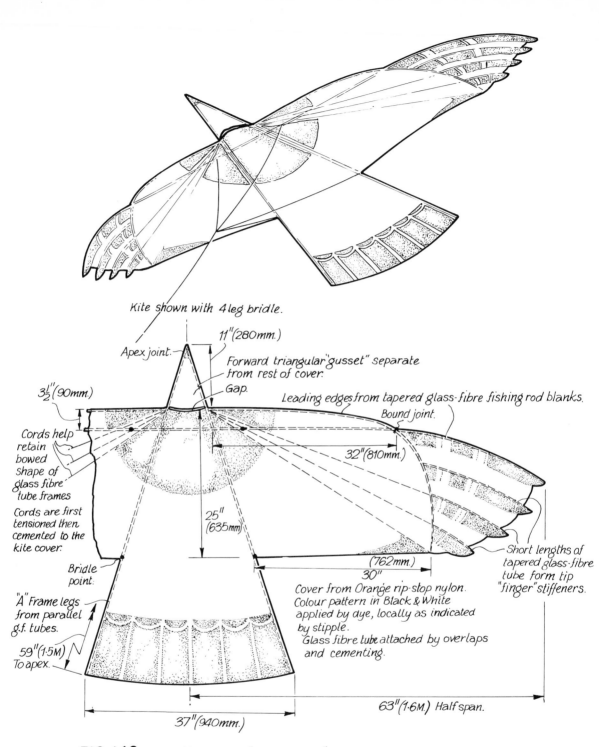

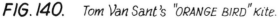

FIG. 140. Tom Van Sant's "ORANGE BIRD" Kite.

and each shroud line is tied to paired number points. The table quotes the dimensions for the full length of the shroud line and its ultimate 'half length' from chute to bridle attachment. Don't skimp the vents, since they provide the stability which prevents the kite from spinning on the line. It is quite an exercise to set up the shrouds for the first time, but once done, the Parachute is a kite that can be rolled into a neat, small package.

ORANGE BIRD (Fig. 140)

Included because Tom Van Sant's original was among the most strikingly different kites at the 1976 London exhibition, the Orange Bird is a big lightweight that uses rip-stop nylon covering and glass fibre spars. The central triangle has two rigid glass fibre spars, locked at their angle by a solid joint at the apex. There are two sets of lateral spars, each from glass fibre fishing rod blanks. One set extends through to the tip feathers, the other is curved through 90° and held in that position by three threads which are, in turn, cemented to the sail. Extra lengths of spare glass fibre are used to simulate more tip feathers, and the whole bird then has a four-point bridle. The cover or sail is sewn and cemented to the frame. In itself, the cover is part of the structure and contributes to the shape of what is an enormous kite of 10 ft 6 ins (3·2 m) span! Not cheap to make, nor in any way conventional, the Bird is a 'stopper' for the local field – otherwise it is too large to transport.

WHITE PLANE (Fig. 141)

Striking for simplicity, yet so effective in its radical appearance, Tom Van Sant's 7-ft (2·1-m) span aeroplane symbol is a perfect example of latter-day thinking and materials. It calls for three tapered glass fibre fishing rod blanks, one parallel tube and rip-stop nylon, plus a ball of wool.

The centre spar is the stouter and longer rod

end, over 57 ins (1·45 m) long, tapering from about $\frac{3}{8}$ in. (10 mm) to a point. To this are fixed two junction tubes (either as Fig. 149 or 150) at 3-in. (75-mm) and 20-in. (51-cm) stations from the front end. These accept the leading edges for the 'wings' which are bound to the tubes by loops of wool. The shape of the wings is used to hold tension in the spars, and as it is cut by using a hot soldering iron, the nylon edge needs no further protection from fraying. A combined Open and Vertical Keel (OVK) is fixed to the forward wing by sewing, and to the centre spar by a hemmed sleeve. Then a bobble of wool completes the White Plane with a stabilising puffball at the tail.

In flight this kite seems sensitive to flexure of the spars in the turbulent air nearer the ground, but at height it is a majestic sight.

ELLIPTICAL KITE (Fig. 142)

In many ways a progression from the White Plane and Orange Bird, this Open Keel Elliptical (OKE) is a rigid design with a novel characteristic. Each edge is a tapered fishing rod blank in glass fibre, overlapped with its neighbour at the tips and with a wool bobble for appearance and stability. The centre spar is extraordinarily long, made of more than one rod joint with a total length of approx. 6 ft (2 m), and carries a 'tail' in the shape of a triangular sail as well as a bobble end. To the extremity is attached a stabilising drogue which, like the open keel, has a blanked end. The result is a light, robust kite which rides the gusts in a strange, perhaps unpredictable way for, as the wind force increases, the ellipse tends to stretch or distend. This change produces a curvature in the sail which is observed to be like an aerofoil section. Van Sant joins these kites in train by lines connecting the tips, and each unit adjusts itself in curvature and section to meet the wind gradient. The comparatively small span of 54 ins (137 cm) makes the Elliptical kite

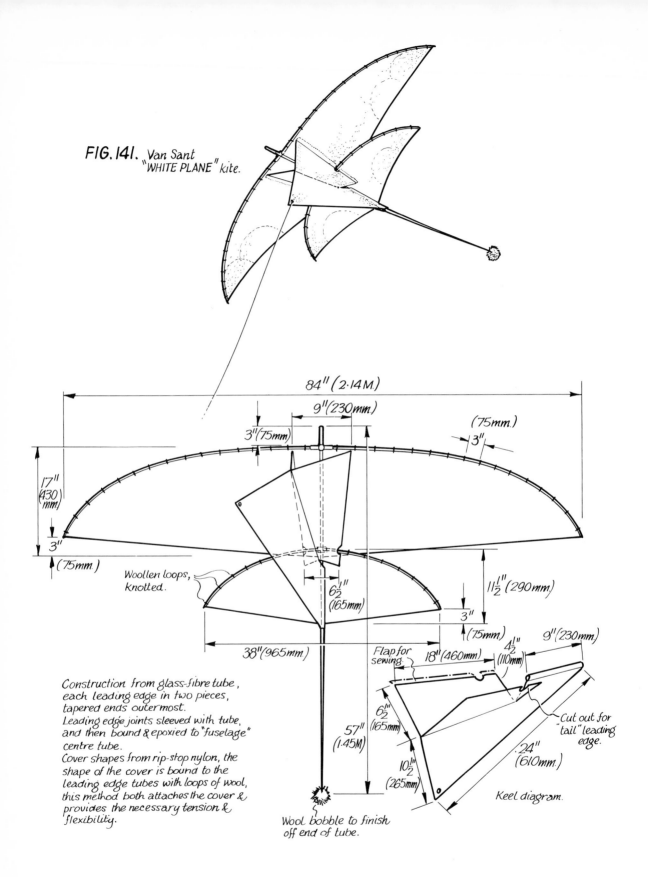

FIG. 141. *Van Sant*
"WHITE PLANE" *kite.*

84" (2·14M.)

9" (230mm.)

3" (75mm.)

(75mm.)

3"

17"
(430)
mm.)

3"

(75mm.)

Woollen loops,
knotted.

$6\frac{1}{2}$"
(165mm)

11$\frac{1}{2}$" (290mm)

3"

(75mm.)

38" (965mm.)

Flap for
sewing.

18" (460mm)

$4\frac{1}{2}$"
(110mm)

9" (230mm)

$6\frac{1}{2}$"
(165mm)

Cut out for
"tail" leading
edge.

57"
(1·45M)

$10\frac{1}{2}$"
(265mm)

24"
(610mm.)

Keel diagram.

Construction from glass-fibre tube,
each leading edge in two pieces,
tapered ends outermost.
Leading edge joints sleeved with tube,
and then bound & epoxied to "fuselage"
centre tube.
Cover shapes from rip-stop nylon, the
shape of the cover is bound to the
leading edge tubes with loops of wool,
this method both attaches the cover &
provides the necessary tension &
flexibility.

Wool bobble to finish
off end of tube.

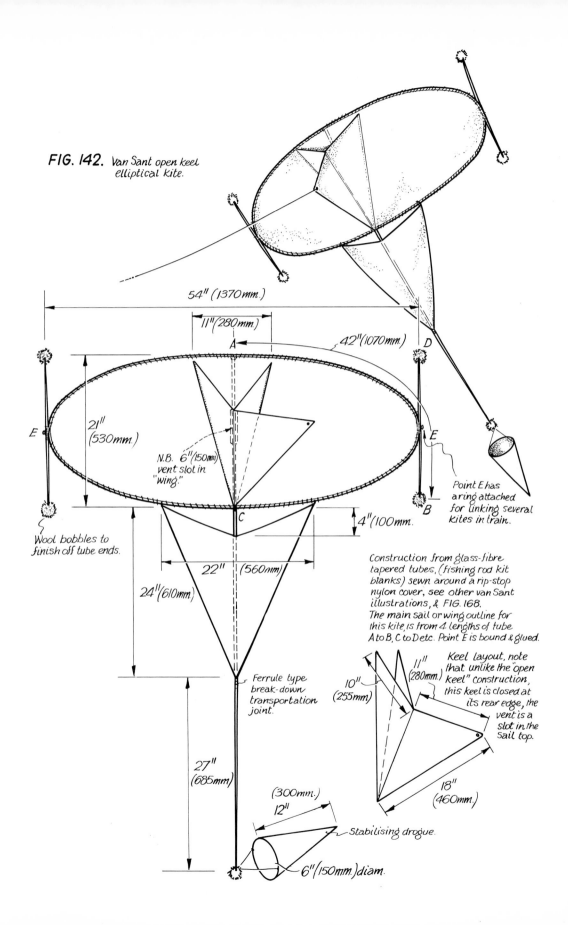

FIG. 142. *Van Sant open keel elliptical kite.*

54" (1370mm.)

11" (280mm.)

A

42" (1070mm.)

D

21" (530mm.)

E

E

N.B. 6" (150mm) vent slot in "wing."

Point E has a ring attached for linking several kites in train.

Wool bobbles to finish off tube ends.

4" (100mm.)

C

22" (560mm)

24" (610mm)

Construction from glass-fibre tapered tubes, (fishing rod kit blanks) sewn around a rip-stop nylon cover, see other van Sant illustrations, & FIG. 168.
The main sail or wing outline for this kite, is from 4 lengths of tube A to B, C to D etc. Point E is bound & glued.

Ferrule type break-down transportation joint.

10" (255mm)

11" (280mm.)

Keel layout, note that unlike the "open keel" construction, this keel is closed at its rear edge, the vent is a slot in the sail top.

18" (460mm.)

27" (685mm)

(300mm.)

12"

Stabilising drogue.

6" (150mm.) diam.

easier to transport than other Van Sants; but it does involve spending rather a lot on spar material.

CLOWN (Fig. 143)

So named because of its pierrot-style elements, this is the ultimate in the use of fishing rod blanks, if you can obtain (or afford) enough of them. Tom Van Sant had eight rod ends in his Clown, each linked and overlapped intricately as Fig. 143 illustrates. The sails cover the D-shaped areas, leaving most of the centre zones as open vents, and the whole is linked to a more rigid centre spar which also carries the single keel. This is one kite where size depends entirely on available material. The length of the rods determines the span. In Van Sant's case, the original was 10 ft (3 m) tall and 6 ft (2 m) at its widest.

FLEXIFOIL (Fig. 144)

In a way it is cheating to include this clever design in a 'making your own' section because it is difficult to describe how to start, or even finish, the intricate sewing that is involved. But the design as developed by Merry and Jones from Continental parachute experiments is worthy of close study. It is an air-filled kite where the open leading edge (curtain net strips) admits air into cells which are controlled by the rib-shaped walls. As the pressure builds up, the bag forms an aerofoil-sectioned wing. A spar of glass fibre allows the wing to curve under extreme loadings, and two lines attached to spar tips enable the flyer to perform aerobatics. Because this control-line kite has a better-than-average lift coefficient, it builds up considerable speed in manoeuvres and is most spectacular.

A simpler method of construction might be to use expanded foam for the rib shapes and cell walls with Solarfilm model covering to scale at the rear edge and ribs. This would not have the advantage of being able to be rolled

up as do the Flexifoil originals which collapse from 6 ft (2 m) to a small ball of nylon, with the spar jointed as two 3-ft (1-m) lengths. You are invited to display your inventiveness in devising easier ways of reproducing the aerobatic lilo!

CZECH DRACI (Fig. 145)

Traditionally east European, the winged box has a lot of construction in it but it is very rewarding in performance. This one has a span of approx. 50 ins (127 cm) and a length of 43 ins (110 cm), which can be scaled down if its one-piece assembly is difficult to carry about. The material required is $\frac{1}{4}$-in (7-mm) square spruce or round-section beech dowel, with strong tissue covering. Cloth never seems popular in Europe, but here is a case where the durability of nylon would improve the design and performance.

A basic triangular box kite of three spars and 11-in. (28-cm) spacers has a large open centre, with cord bracing. The top side of the forward box is converted with ribs to make a lifting section which is detachable. Then two sets of lateral spars are fixed to form the side sails or wings, and the kite is completed with a pair of vertical fins. Dependent on choice of covering – fabric or tissue – the sail attachment is sewn or glued in place with generous hems, especially on the unsupported edges of the wings. A two-part bridle is used for single-line flying. The kite is equally adaptable to control-line operation with two lines attached to duplicate bridles from the upper box spars instead of the lower.

STARBIRD (Fig. 146)

Like two Malay kites head-on to one another, and with pointed tails touching tips, the Starbird is surprisingly simple. Only three spars are needed, the two main diagonals 42 ins (107 cm) long and the lateral spar 48 ins (122 cm) long. Tied at the intersection, then

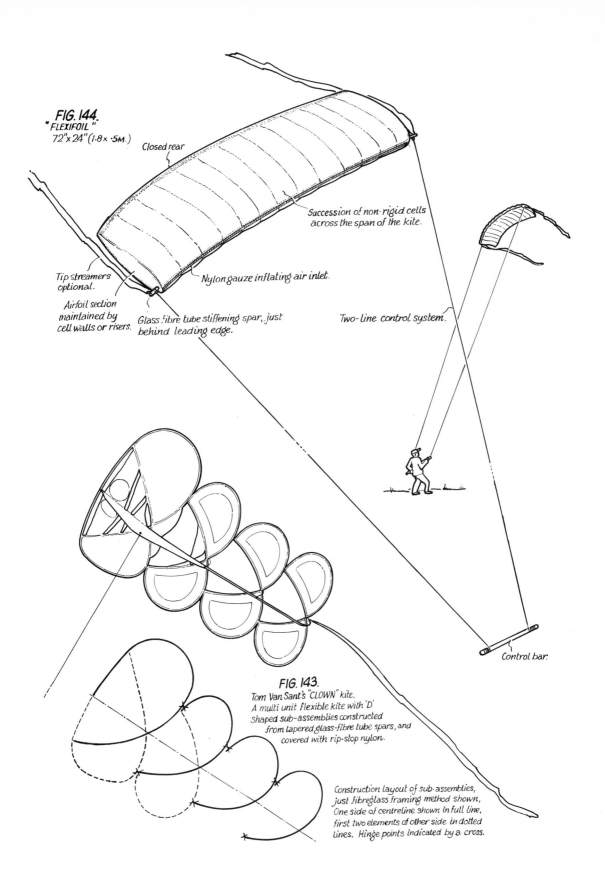

FIG. 144.
"FLEXIFOIL"
72"x24" (1·8 x ·5M.)

Closed rear

Succession of non-rigid cells across the span of the kite.

Tip streamers optional.

Nylon gauze inflating air inlet.

Airfoil section maintained by cell walls or risers.

Glass fibre tube stiffening spar, just behind leading edge.

Two-line control system.

Control bar.

FIG. 143.
Tom Van Sant's "CLOWN" kite.
A multi unit flexible kite with 'D' shaped sub-assemblies constructed from tapered glass-fibre tube spars, and covered with rip-stop nylon.

Construction layout of sub-assemblies, just fibreglass framing method shown. One side of centreline shown in full line, first two elements of other side in dotted lines. Hinge points indicated by a cross.

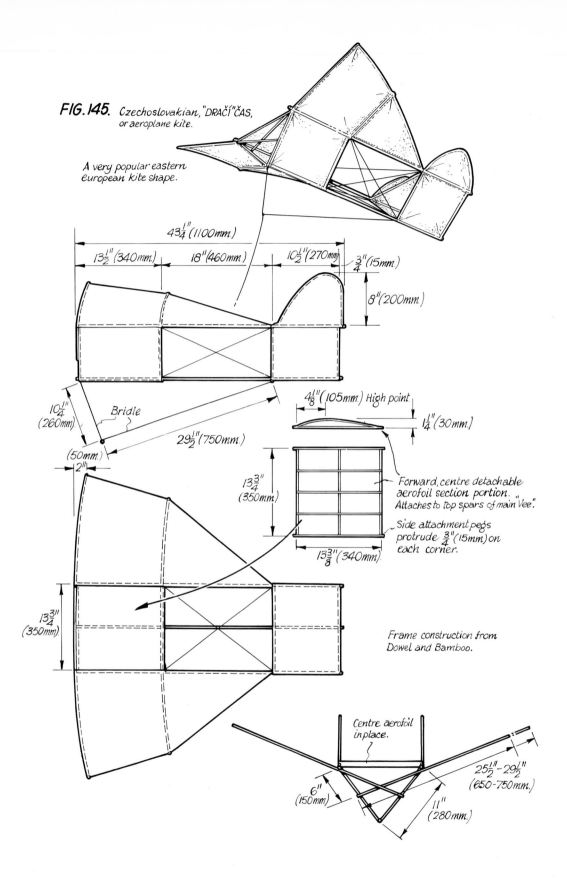

FIG.145. *Czechoslovakian, "DRAČÍ" ČAS,*
or aeroplane kite.

A very popular eastern
european kite shape.

$43\frac{1}{4}''$ (1100mm.)

$13\frac{1}{2}''$ (340mm.) 18" (460mm.) $10\frac{1}{2}''$ (270mm.) $\frac{3}{4}''$ (15mm.)

8" (200mm.)

$10\frac{1}{4}''$ (260mm.) *Bridle*

$29\frac{1}{2}''$ (750mm.)

(50mm.)
2"

$4\frac{1}{8}''$ (105mm.) High point

$1\frac{1}{4}''$ (30mm.)

$13\frac{3}{4}''$ (350mm)

Forward, centre detachable
aerofoil section portion.
Attaches to top spars of main "Vee".

Side attachment pegs
protrude $\frac{3}{4}''$ (15mm.) on
each corner.

$13\frac{3}{8}''$ (340mm.)

$13\frac{3}{4}''$ (350mm)

Frame construction from
Dowel and Bamboo.

Centre aerofoil
in place.

$25\frac{1}{2}'' - 29\frac{1}{2}''$
(650-750mm.)

6"
(150mm.)

11"
(280mm.)

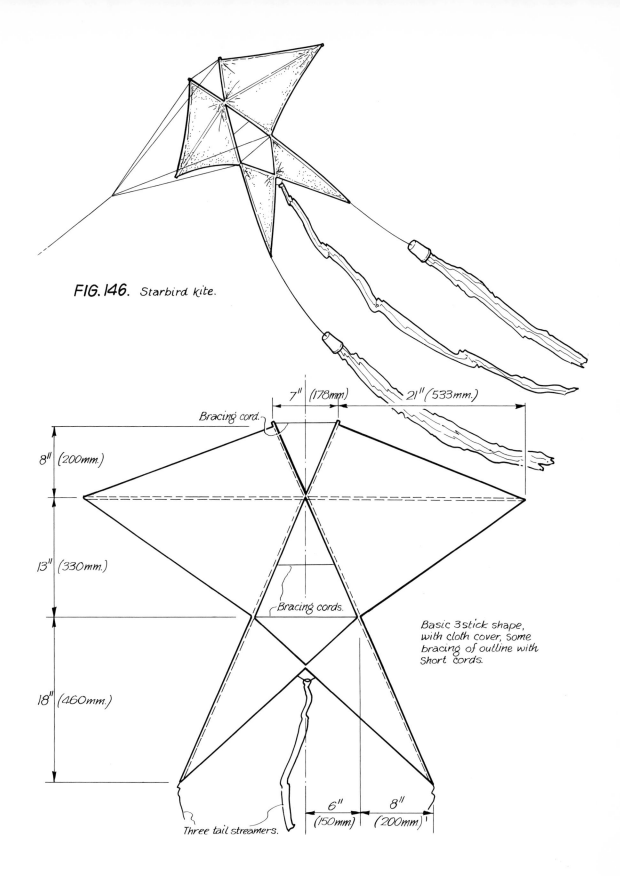

FIG. 146. Starbird kite.

7" (178mm)   21" (533mm.)

Bracing cord.

8" (200mm.)

13" (330mm.)

Bracing cords.

18" (460mm.)

Basic 3 stick shape,
with cloth cover, some
bracing of outline with
short cords.

Three tail streamers.

6"
(150mm)

8"
(200mm)

cord-braced to obtain the spacings and angles, the spars must be flexible enough to allow wind pressure to force a dihedral angle. The lateral spar can, of course, be bowed with a cord from tip to tip over the upper surface. The covering should be hemmed on all unsupported edges at least, and sewn or glued to the spars. The tail triangles link together with a sewn tape, and a streamer line can be fitted to this point. As shown in Fig. 146, the Starbird has plastic cups on the ends of its main streamer lines, an unusual application which might be developed further.

PEARSON ROLLER (Fig. 147)

Though kiting enthusiasm tends to surge and diminish, there are many groups of diehards who are aloof to such trends. One example is the experts who fly regularly in London's Kensington Gardens, close to the famous Round Pond. Alexander Pearson, a regular park flyer, devised this Roller – a name influenced by the German Rollo Drachen (Fig. 148). The kite is one large sail with generous dihedral and a large 'slot' or blank area separating it from a triangular rear sail. Alex Pearson's design breaks down and is rolled away in a neat tubular container for carriage. The stout dowels which form the main centre spar, the lateral for the mainsail, and leading edges for the rear sail are joined with aluminium tube (Fig. 167).

Made of nylon or proofed cotton, the sails have generously hemmed edges and are tensioned by a cord link which connects them at the slot. The beauty of this kite is in its simplicity and yet high performance. It soars rapidly, but depends on the fin and a rather long bridle for stability. The dimensions given in the sketch are for making a sail out of 36-in. (92-cm) wide material. Keep the same proportions if a larger or smaller Roller is made.

ROLLO DRACHEN (Fig. 148)

This is the traditional East German kite, similar in principle to the Roller in Fig. 147 but huge, complex and with a rear sail that is larger than the fore sail. Its advantage lies in the way it can be collapsed and rolled up for carriage, because the German kite flyers use dowels and aluminium tube joiners to link the components of the three spars. For anyone with patience in setting up seven-point bridle rigging, this is the kite to make. One cannot help thinking that a Pearson rear fin and a smaller rear sail would eliminate most of the complication.

HANDY CONSTRUCTION DETAIL

In making a kite, you have to apply considerable ingenuity. Apart from some US sets, there are no kits and you are left to obtain stock materials at hardware shops. These sketches are meant to inspire simplified assembly with the use of modern components.

Let's start with plastic tubing. Obtainable at car and motorcycle spares shops, thick-walled PVC tube has many applications, and its durability makes it ideal for joints. Fig. 149 shows how two similar pieces are bound to a cross shape after the centre spar has been slipped through half of each. The pressure of the PVC tube elements against each other forces them to make 90° bends which will act as sockets for a lateral spar. In Fig. 150, you can see how the PVC can be flattened and stretched to enter a keyhole slot in the front of a metal tube centre spar. Lower on the same spar, two sizes of tubing act as an anchor for a wire brace, as in a control-line kite.

At the tail of a plastic-sailed kite, PVC tube can be wrapped (Fig. 151) in the end extensions and secured to the main spar. Alternative uses of the tape for location of braces are seen in Figs 152 and 153. These have numerous applications on the kites described in this chapter.

A common difficulty is the provision of stout anchorages for lateral spars in tightly tensioned kites. It is always advisable to reinforce the sail material but to take the strain

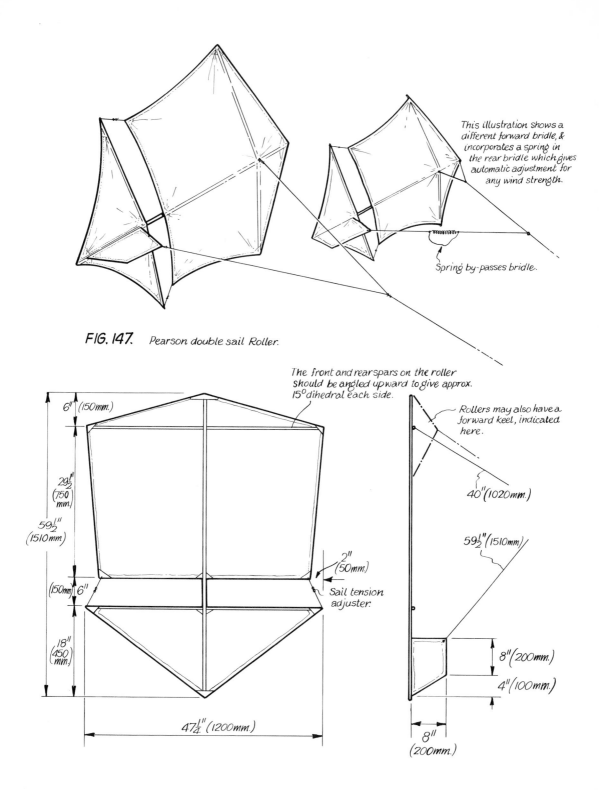

This illustration shows a different forward bridle, & incorporates a spring in the rear bridle which gives automatic adjustment for any wind strength.

Spring by-passes bridle.

FIG. 147. Pearson double sail Roller.

The front and rear spars on the roller should be angled upward to give approx. 15° dihedral each side.

Rollers may also have a forward keel, indicated here.

6" (150mm.)

29½" (750 mm.)

59½" (1510mm)

(150mm) 6"

18" (450 mm.)

2" (50mm.)

Sail tension adjuster.

47¼" (1200mm.)

40" (1020mm.)

59½" (1510mm.)

8" (200mm.)

4" (100mm.)

8" (200mm.)

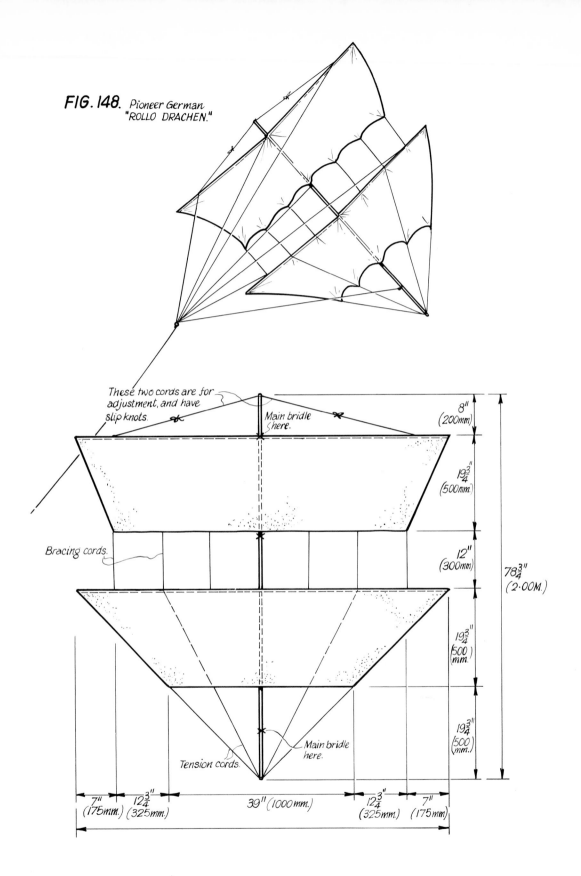

FIG. 148. Pioneer German "ROLLO DRACHEN."

These two cords are for adjustment, and have slip knots.

Main bridle here.

Bracing cords.

Tension cords.

Main bridle here.

8" (200mm.)

19¾" (500mm.)

12" (300mm.)

19¾" (500 mm.)

19¾" (500 mm.)

78¾" (2·00 M.)

7" (175mm.)

12¾" (325mm.)

39" (1000mm.)

12¾" (325mm.)

7" (175mm.)

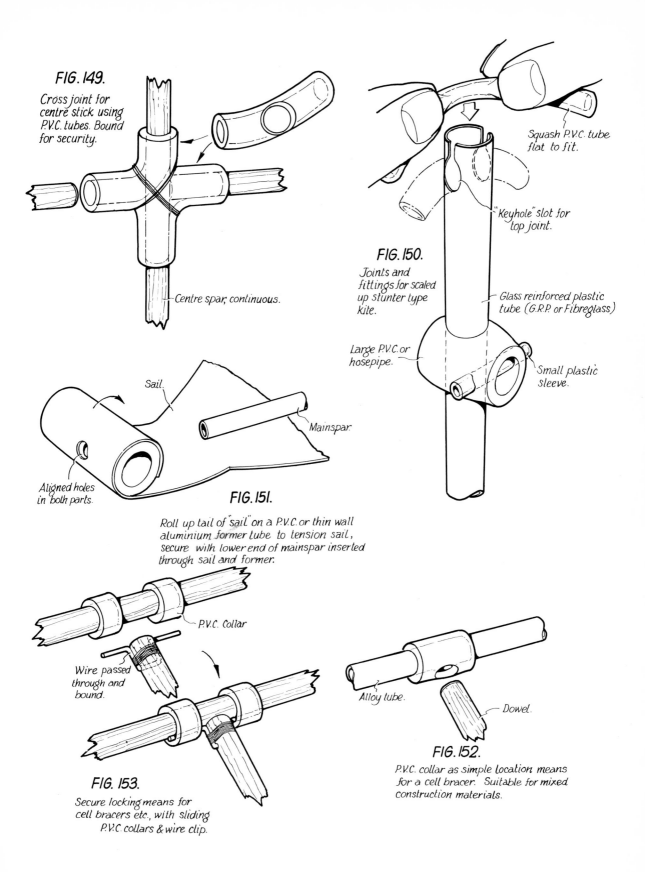

FIG. 149.

Cross joint for centre stick using P.V.C. tubes. Bound for security.

— Centre spar, continuous.

Squash P.V.C. tube flat to fit.

FIG. 150.

Joints and fittings for scaled up stunter type kite.

"Keyhole" slot for top joint.

Glass reinforced plastic tube (G.R.P. or Fibreglass).

Large P.V.C. or hosepipe.

Small plastic sleeve.

Sail.

Mainspar.

Aligned holes in both parts.

FIG. 151.

Roll up tail of "sail" on a P.V.C. or thin wall aluminium former tube to tension sail, secure with lower end of mainspar inserted through sail and former.

P.V.C. Collar

Wire passed through and bound.

Alloy tube.

Dowel.

FIG. 152.

P.V.C. collar as simple location means for a cell bracer. Suitable for mixed construction materials.

FIG. 153.

Secure locking means for cell bracers etc., with sliding P.V.C. collars & wire clip.

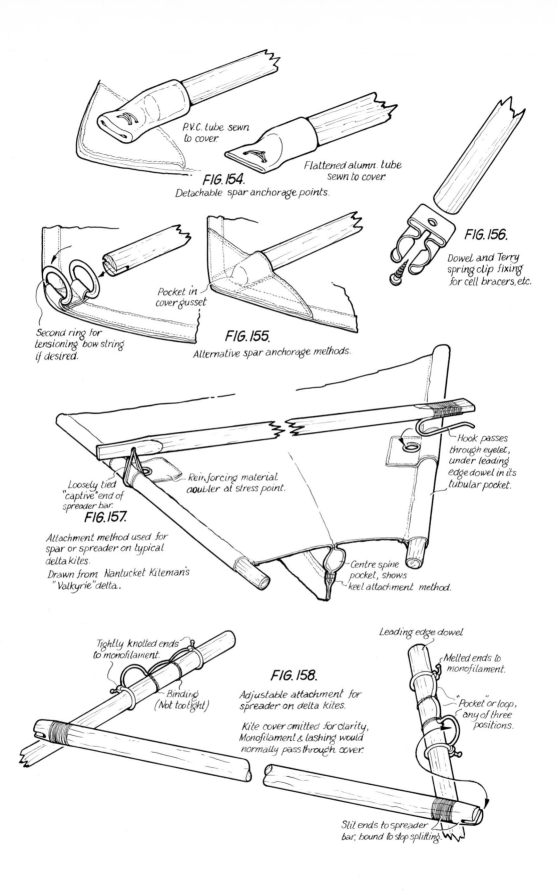

P.V.C. tube sewn to cover.

Flattened alumn. tube sewn to cover.

FIG. 154.
Detachable spar anchorage points.

FIG. 156.
Dowel and Terry spring clip fixing for cell bracers, etc.

Second ring for tensioning bow string if desired.

Pocket in cover gusset

FIG. 155.
Alternative spar anchorage methods.

Reinforcing material doubler at stress point.

Hook passes through eyelet, under leading edge dowel in its tubular pocket.

Loosely tied "captive" end of spreader bar.

FIG. 157.

Attachment method used for spar or spreader on typical delta kites.

Drawn from Nantucket Kiteman's "Valkyrie" delta.

Centre spine pocket, shows keel attachment method.

Tightly knotted ends to monofilament.

Binding (Not too tight)

FIG. 158.

Adjustable attachment for spreader on delta kites.

Kite cover omitted for clarity, Monofilament & lashing would normally pass through cover.

Leading edge dowel

Melted ends to monofilament.

"Pocket" or loop, any of three positions.

Slit ends to spreader bar, bound to stop splitting.

of a spar, plastic or aluminium tubing can be sewn (Fig. 154) on the tips. Another idea is to use a ring (Fig. 155) or a pocket sewn into the reinforcement patch.

The Terry clip in Fig. 156 can be fitted to box kite structures or any kite where a quickly detachable frame is desirable.

Delta kites have to be braced from leading edge to leading edge but the actual connection must be flexible. Fig. 157 is the popular Nantucket kite method (note also the detail of the centre spine pocket or sleeve) and Fig. 158 is another AKA idea which allows adjustment from loop to loop.

Joining the spars calls for making-up sockets, and here the fishing tackle shop can supply ferrules (Fig. 159). Never forget that the weakest part of any spar will be that point at which it suddenly changes section, so use binding at suspect points.

Control-line kites have a nose joint that brings three spars together. Tom Van Sant used 'body-putty' to form a permanent blob nose for his (Fig. 160), while the piano wire link in Fig. 161 appeared in the London-based Skite design. Bending this can be extremely frustrating.

How to connect bracing or other frame pieces to a leading edge or main spar? Easy – if you search out bag ties (Fig. 162), o rings as in Figs 163 and 164 – or if you patronise the fishing tackle shop to purchase rod rings as sketched in Fig. 165. Bind them neatly, and varnish over afterwards for protection.

Binding is also useful to scarf-join spars as in Fig. 166, or to make a cross link of aluminium tubes as in Fig. 167 which also shows the weakening use of a bolt through a drilled hole in the flattened part of the joiner.

When it comes to sail rigging and the flexible glass fibre fishing rod, the Van Sant system as shown in Fig. 168 is perfect. The only snag is the cost of the rods, even if they are so-called rejects.

Making a three-stick hexagonal or Bermuda-style kite calls for overlap and jointing of the sticks. Fig. 169 illustrates how flat sticks can be joined with soft wire, or more robust spars, half lap jointed. This carpentry may not appeal to everyone but frames for bird shapes (Fig. 170) or a Blériot-winged box kite of any large dimensions (Fig. 171), will benefit from such attention. One indispensable tool for cutting the joints is the razor saw, sold at model shops.

One joint that always seems to present difficulty in producing the desired result is the straightforward cross of two dowels. Binding must be symmetrical as in Fig. 172. Secure the cord by smearing with cellulose cement which not only waterproofs but also shrinks the binding to a secure tightness.

Eyelets are supposed to be finished by a special punch which is not very often part of the kitemaker's equipment. The solution is to use a ball bearing as in Fig. 173. Make sure that the eyelet is firm on the fabric or there is little point in having it there. Three eyelets in a keel are shown in Fig. 174 where they are intended for bridle adjustment. Note also the use of an eyeletted reinforcement to the upper edge of the keel and the sail sleeve for the centre spar. This allows a Delta design to have a laced keel which can be detached, adjusted etc.

Another useful adjustment is the use of a yacht bowsie in the bracing for tensioning a centre spar or spine of an Eddy design, or the lateral spar on a Malay. Fig. 175 illustrates how rings in the ends of the line can be used to fit slots cut into the spars.

Now some novelty details. Fig. 176 shows the buzzer or hummer. The secret of the 'zizz' is the very tight line. If a guitar string is used, there is little need for the stiff tissue. Don't expect the noise to carry far – in my experience 100 ft (30 m) is the audibility range.

Pendant banners, message strips or decorative trailers can be displayed best from a frame that gives a vertical (or horizontal) bar. Fig. 177 illustrates the simple L-shaped carrier which can be hitched quickly onto the kite line. The weight has to be just enough to

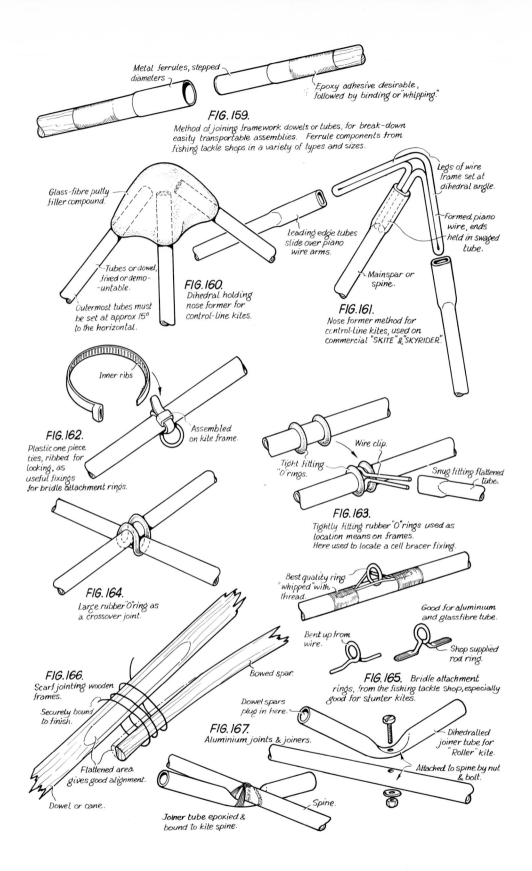

Metal ferrules, stepped diameters

Epoxy adhesive desirable, followed by binding or "whipping."

FIG. 159.
Method of joining framework dowels or tubes, for break-down easily transportable assemblies. Ferrule components from fishing tackle shops in a variety of types and sizes.

Glass-fibre putty filler compound.

Legs of wire frame set at dihedral angle.

leading edge tubes slide over piano wire arms.

Formed piano wire, ends held in swaged tube.

Tubes or dowel, fixed or demo-untable.

FIG. 160.
Dihedral holding nose former for control-line kites.

Outermost tubes must be set at approx 15° to the horizontal.

Mainspar or spine.

FIG. 161.
Nose former method for control-line kites, used on commercial "SKITE" & "SKYRIDER".

Inner ribs

Assembled on kite frame.

Tight fitting "O" rings.

Wire clip.

Snug fitting flattened tube.

FIG. 162.
Plastic one piece ties, ribbed for locking, as useful fixings for bridle attachment rings.

FIG. 163.
Tightly fitting rubber "O" rings used as location means on frames. Here used to locate a cell bracer fixing.

Best quality ring "whipped" with thread.

Good for aluminium and glassfibre tube.

Bent up from wire.

Shop supplied rod ring.

FIG. 164.
Large rubber "O" ring as a crossover joint.

Bowed spar.

FIG. 165. Bridle attachment rings, from the fishing tackle shop, especially good for stunter kites.

FIG. 166.
Scarf jointing wooden frames.

Securely bound to finish.

Dowel spars plug in here.

FIG. 167.
Aluminium joints & joiners.

Dihedralled joiner tube for "Roller" kite.

Attached to spine by nut & bolt.

Flattened area gives good alignment.

Spine.

Dowel or cane.

Joiner tube epoxied & bound to kite spine.

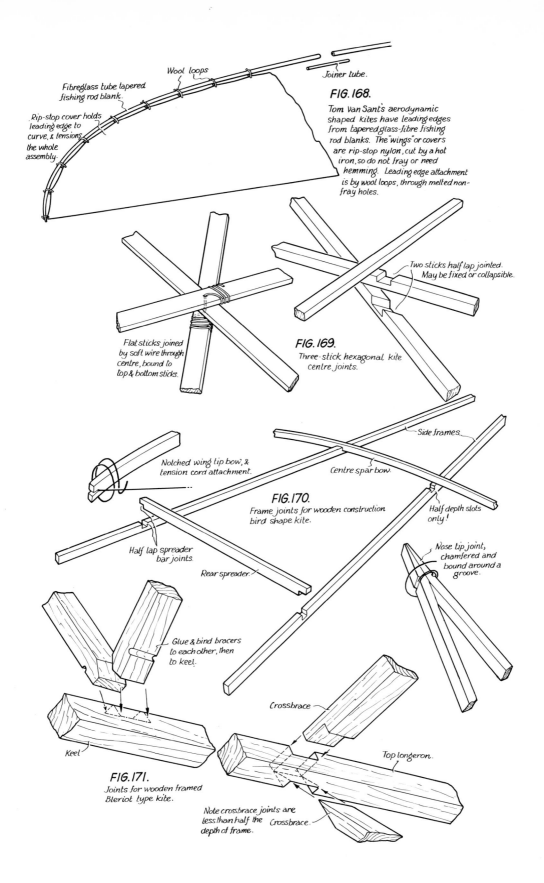

Wool loops

Fibreglass tube tapered fishing rod blank.

Joiner tube.

Rip-stop cover holds leading edge to curve, & tensions the whole assembly.

FIG. 168.

Tom Van Sant's aerodynamic shaped kites have leading edges from tapered glass-fibre fishing rod blanks. The "wings" or covers are rip-stop nylon, cut by a hot iron, so do not fray or need hemming. Leading edge attachment is by wool loops, through melted non-fray holes.

Two sticks half lap jointed. May be fixed or collapsible.

Flat sticks joined by soft wire through centre, bound to top & bottom sticks.

FIG. 169.

Three-stick hexagonal kite centre joints.

Side frames.

Notched wing tip bow, & tension cord attachment.

Centre spar bow.

FIG. 170.

Frame joints for wooden construction bird shape kite.

Half depth slots only!

Half lap spreader bar joints.

Rear spreader.

Nose tip joint, chamfered and bound around a groove.

Glue & bind bracers to each other, then to keel.

Crossbrace

Top longeron.

Keel

FIG. 171.

Joints for wooden framed Bleriot type kite.

Note crossbrace joints are less than half the depth of frame.

Crossbrace.

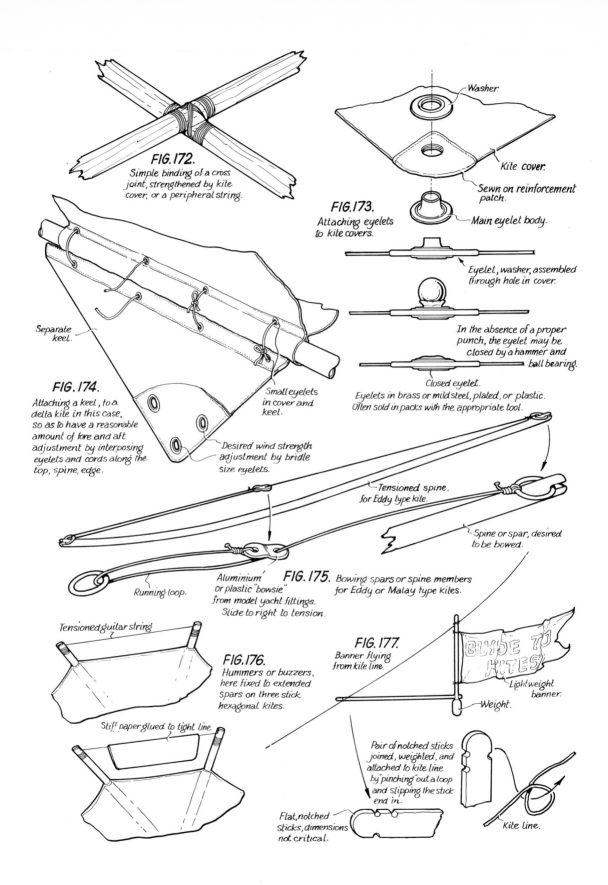

FIG. 172.
Simple binding of a cross joint, strengthened by kite cover, or a peripheral string.

FIG. 173.
Attaching eyelets to kite covers.

Washer.

Kite cover.

Sewn on reinforcement patch.

Main eyelet body.

Eyelet, washer, assembled through hole in cover.

In the absence of a proper punch, the eyelet may be closed by a hammer and ball bearing.

Closed eyelet.

Eyelets in brass or mild steel, plated, or plastic. Often sold in packs with the appropriate tool.

Separate keel.

FIG. 174.
Attaching a keel, to a delta kite in this case, so as to have a reasonable amount of fore and aft adjustment by interposing eyelets and cords along the top, spine, edge.

Small eyelets in cover and keel.

Desired wind strength adjustment by bridle size eyelets.

Tensioned spine, for Eddy type kite.

Spine or spar, desired to be bowed.

Running loop.

Aluminium or plastic "bowsie" from model yacht fittings. Slide to right to tension.

FIG. 175. Bowing spars or spine members for Eddy or Malay type kites.

Tensioned guitar string

FIG. 176.
Hummers or buzzers, here fixed to extended spars on three stick hexagonal kites.

Stiff paper glued to tight line.

FIG. 177.
Banner flying from kite line.

GUIDE TO KITES

Lightweight banner.

Weight.

Pair of notched sticks joined, weighted, and attached to kite line by pinching out a loop and slipping the stick end in.

Flat, notched sticks, dimensions not critical.

Kite line.

steady the hanging sticks. Messages can be changed, or a series of banners sent up on the line, provided the carrier kite is stable and a good 'lifter'.

The possibilities for kite making are end-less. This selection has been chosen to offer as wide a range of practical designs as possible. Try it for yourself – you'll have twice the fun if the kite is one you made with your own hands.

NINE

Important Patents

It is only natural that any inventor of a wholly original device should look to the protection of a patent in order to preserve his just and due rights. Kites have been the subject of innumerable patent applications, some so bizarre and unorthodox that they serve little purpose, and others which have become very important in the development of the commercial kite.

Reading a patent is not an easy business. The language is descriptive in a quaint way that tends to confuse the lay reader. Sketches are more easily understood and the key numbers refer to passages of text which tend to be repetitive in their intent to provide legal protection.

A selection of the more interesting patents is described in this chapter. The descriptions are not intended in any way to be other than a liberal interpretation. Those which have been chosen are not to be considered as recommended, nor are those which have been omitted considered less important. The significance of the selected designs is their originality. The dates quoted are mostly but not always the dates of application.

We open with the oldest and proceed in a chronological order, starting in 1890 with a revolving kite by Thomas Ansboro of Glasgow.

ANSBORO REVOLVING KITE (8492) 1890 (Fig. 178)

This early invention, which pre-dates many subsequent rotary kites, provides a collapsible hexagon which is pivoted in the centre and is mounted above a 'bellyband' and bridle strip. The kite has a peripheral cord, over which is spread a cloth sail. On alternate edges there are conical pockets so arranged that they catch the wind and cause the body to rotate on the spindle. The face of the kite is described as having a spiral painted on it in colours to give an optical illusion of wave-like motion. To collapse the revolving kite, two overlapping central spars were separated, and with the outline cord being arranged in two half sections, the halves of the kite could be folded as in a fan.

PANTCHEFF HEXAGON KITES (158,162) 1921, (158,502) 1921, (158,600) 1921, (198,051) 1923 (Figs 179 and 180)

This series of patents, the earliest of which was first applied for by Sophocles Xenophon Pantcheff in September 1919, deals with a method of making hexagonal kites with the covering stretched over the shape by tension of the peripheral cord. Several parts of covers might be used, and the drawings illustrate use of multiple colours on the tissue sail. They also show the tail made of thin ribbons attached to a central thread, secured in bunches, and the attachment of the three-line bridle for the tether line and the two-line bridle for the tail. This was, of course, the basis of the Atalanta range of kites.

FIG.178.

Fig.3.

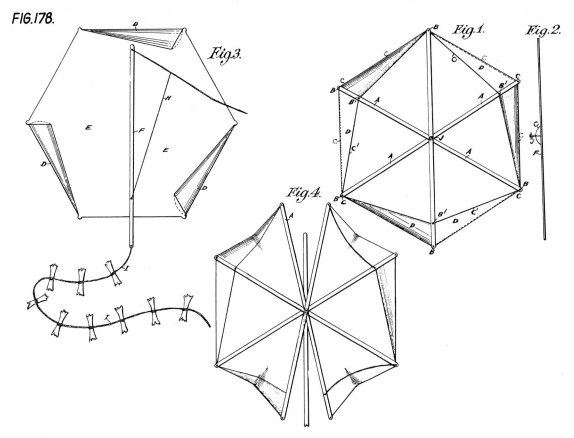

Fig.1.

Fig.2.

Fig.4.

FIG.179.

Fig.1.

Fig.2.

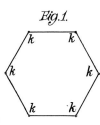

Fig.4.

Fig.5.

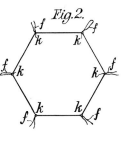

Fig.6.

Fig.3.

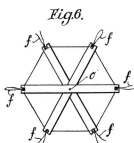

FIG.180

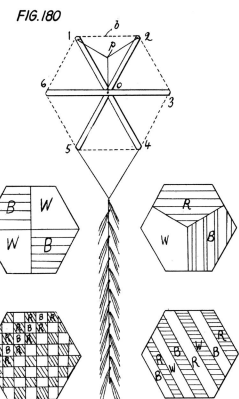

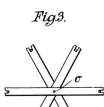

One interesting suggestion in the text is the passage dealing with the kite's purpose as a medical appliance whereby it would 'strengthen and cure eyes weakened by too constant use on near objects, a cure which would be greatly aided by the combination of colours on the translucent covering of the kite and the tail and the consequent transmission of different coloured rays of the spectrum.'

WALTER YOUNG PLANAR KITE (3,599,909) 1968 (Fig. 181)

This Malay-shaped kite provides a resiliently extendable third line (12) in the bridle with a spring (11) and an adjuster (13) which enables the kite to adjust itself to an optimum angle of attack for prevailing conditions. The kite is collapsible and can be aluminised for detection by radar, or carry a light, or be coloured for rescue purposes. This is the DY kite as used on the Himalayan climbing expeditions. The frame is of aluminium.

DUNFORD CONTROL-LINE AEROBATIC KITE (1,340,047) 1970 (Fig. 182)

Well known and most important for its specific description and sketches of the Donald Dunford kite and its control system, there are several interesting points in the text for this patent. It is stated that 'The sail of the kite has been found to be satisfactory when made of somewhat porous cloth', also, 'It has been found best . . . that the aperture in the kite . . . is about 16 per cent of the total sail area'. The difference in camber and relative incidence of the central v (5A and 5B) fore and aft sections, serves to stabilise the kite in pitch. The Dunford kite has been described in earlier chapters and is made precisely to the details in the original patent which is, incidentally, international.

We next move to a selection of American patents, not many of which have international acceptance.

DAHL SELF-BALANCING KITE (1,632,822) 1926 (Fig. 183)

Conrad Dahl of Springfield, Ohio, devised this use of separated flexible sails which were rigged to permit an automatic adjustment to the wind pressure upon them. In so doing he appears to have devised what has been called the 'Marconi' rig and suggested variations with up to three sets of foreplanes or 'head' sails. There is a difference of interpretation in that this Dahl Patent suggests that the head sails are held at their centres to the spar along the length of the root chord, whereas in the Marconi rig the sail is held only at the extreme front and tip points. Nevertheless the Dahl Patent, and its use of flexible covering, is very interesting for its date of origin and similarity of shape to the Marconi rig.

ASTLE BLOW-UP KITE (2,208,786) 1938 (Figs 184 and 185)

Percy Thomas Astle of Haven, Kansas, designed a range of inflatables where the kite was to have an inflatable tube round its edge and an inflatable core to the tail. The main surface was to be rubber sheet with the tube attached, and rigid brace members retained the shape. A variety of designs was suggested, but nothing is known of any manufacture. The kite could have advantages for use in fishing techniques, or for any over-water flying, but this was not mentioned in the application.

BACH FLYING WING KITE (2,463,135) 1947 (Fig. 186)

Primarily a device for either kiting or free-flying as a glider, the Flying Wing, by Robert F. Bach of Detroit, specified the use of tubing for spars, synthetic film for covering, the rear edge of the covering being billowed so that it adopted a conical camber in flight. Assembly of the three spars at the nose in a fitting which provided dihedral angle is another feature which pre-dates other kite assemblies. Had the

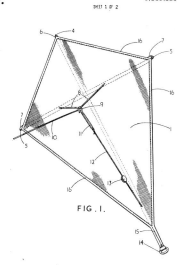

FIG. 181.

PATENTED AUG 17 1971

SHEET 1 OF 2

3,599,909

FIG. 1.

FIG. 182.

1340047

1 SHEET

COMPLETE SPECIFICATION

This drawing is a reproduction of the Original on a reduced scale

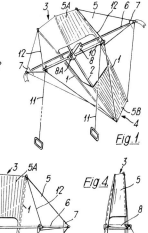

Fig. 5.

Fig.1.

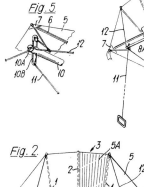

Fig. 2.

Fig.4.

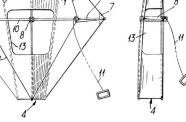

Fig. 3.

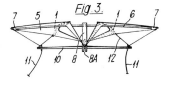

June 21, 1927.

FIG. 183.

C. DAHL

SELF-BALANCING KITE

Filed July 17, 1926

1,632,822

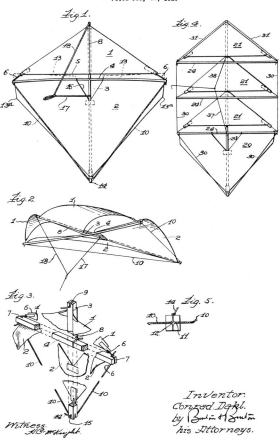

Fig.1.

Fig.4.

Fig.2.

Fig.3.

Fig.5.

Witness.
A.C. McKnight.

Inventor.
Conrad Dahl.
by
his Attorneys.

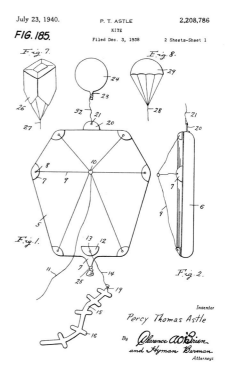

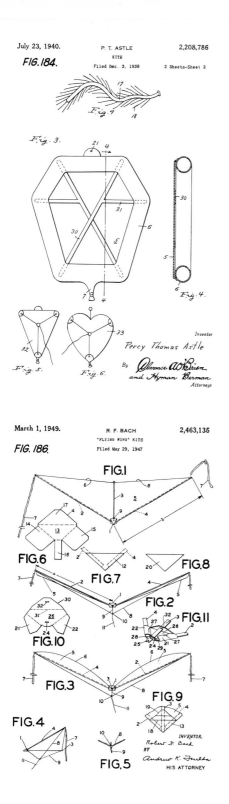

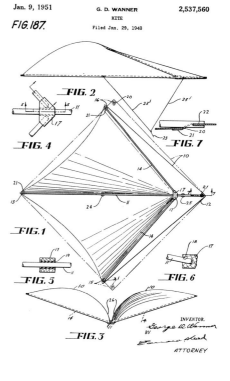

shape been of lower aspect ratio, this patent would have shown the first of what has since become an almost standard mode of assembly for flexible-wing kites. It would be very interesting to follow Robert Bach's design in a kite of modern construction to see the difference in performance between this wing shape and the diamond shape.

WANNER FLEXIBLE KITE (2,537,560) 1948 (Fig. 187)

George D. Wanner from the home of the Wright brothers, Dayton, Ohio, was granted this patent in 1951, and it is the first record I have found of the conical-cambered diamond-shape kite. A flexible square covering was fixed to the centre spar and two laterals were set at a swept-back and dihedral angle, to produce a conical camber on the covering at the trailing edge. The actual leading edge was unsupported, but it was under tension from the tips to the centre spar at the extreme nose.

'The kite is launched in the usual manner and when supported by the air, the upward pressure of the air on the cover moves the lateral portions thereof upwardly between the fore and the aft frame members and the respective lateral frame members to impart a dihedral form to the cover ... and the rear corner portions of the cover form a fixed rudder.'

That quotation describes all so-called Rogallo kites. It must be recognised that the two-line bridle, swept lateral spars and unsupported leading edge are features that are not seen on later designs, and for good reasons.

ROGALLO FLEXIBLE KITE (2,546,078) 1948 (Fig. 188)

Granted to Gertrude Sugden Rogallo and her husband Francis Melvin Rogallo, this patent for a kite that was fully flexible and eliminated the use of reinforcing members was one of the most significant applications granted.

The square sail was described as having seven bridle lines, so rigged as to hold the Rogallo shape against wind pressure. A double-line yoke to a long ribbon-like tail was included, and provision was made for multiple flexible kites to be linked together in train, each with a tail. Further sketches (Figs 5 and 6 in the patent) suggested how reinforcing spars could be used on the three lines of the leading edges and the centre line, as has since been used commercially.

There were several prophetic statements in the patent description. 'In order to enhance the attractiveness of our kite, we may construct it of transparent material such as cellophane ... and provide coloured pictures of birds, rockets, etc. ... We believe the principle may be applied to man-carrying devices such as airplanes, parachutes and gliders. ...'

Thirty years later it is a fact that tens of thousands of hang gliders using the Rogallo shape exist around the world.

EFFINGER AND STRUCK AIRCRAFT (3,153,877) 1962 (Fig. 189)

Bill Effinger and Henry Struck gave full credit to the Wanner patent and the Rogallo in their description of this powered flexible wing which was also a kite and a glider. An internal combustion engine driving a propeller made it a free-flight aircraft which glided back when the fuel ran out. Alternatively, a wire provided a bridle point for kiting. Made by the Gilbert Company, the aircraft flew as a Parawing but was not accepted sufficiently by the public to be rated successful. On the nose was a delta foreplane which acted as a stabiliser for free flight, and plastic parts were specially moulded to hold the engine. It is arguable that the design was ahead of its time, arriving before hang-glider shapes captured interest.

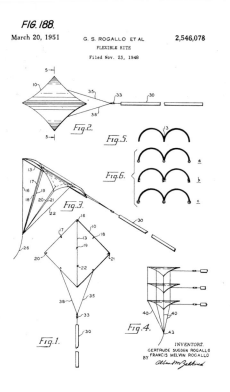
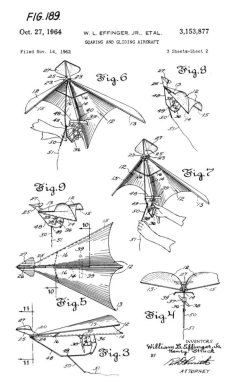
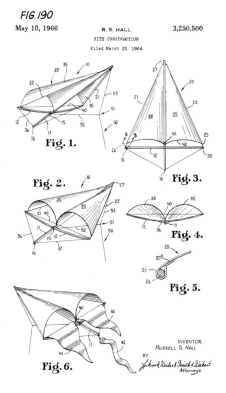
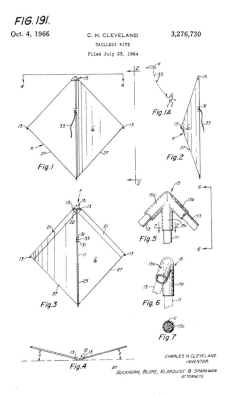

HALL FLEXIBLE KITE (3,250,500) 1964 (Fig. 190)

Russell S. Hall of Indianapolis produced this delta-plan-form, back-to-front Malay kite framework with two conical sails as a device which he claimed would have 'a greater tendency to fly straight-up or overhead of the place of mooring whereby advertising slogans and the like can be effectively displayed by the kite'. The pennants trailing from the lateral spar were to carry the advertising message. While no obvious development of the concept has appeared, the use of a rigid frame suggests that it was an original effort to keep away from the infringement of prior patents.

CLEVELAND TAILLESS KITE (3,276,730) 1964 (Fig. 191)

This is the famous North Pacific Products' Glite, as patented by Charles H. Cleveland of Bend, Oregon. Significant points in this simple use of the conical camber on a flexible sail are these:

'The covering can be of square form so as to result in a minimum of expense in forming kite coverings from rolls.'

'The connector [of spars] is of hollow one-piece tubular form which is preferably moulded of plastic.'

'The sticks are . . . of square cross-section with rounded corners and fit snugly with a compressed frictional fit within the leg and shank portions of the connector, which are of circular cross-section.'

'The axes of the connector are not in the same plane as the axes of the shank of the connector.'

'An important advantage . . . is that it is stable without requiring any critical adjustments.'

No one could argue with the claims for Cleveland's Glite. It must have achieved production runs exceeding millions since this patent described the first Kraft-paper-covered examples. Though dihedral is emphasised as

part of the design features, no mention is made of conical camber; in fact the Glite, and other kites used with control lines, have comparatively little bow in their covering.

HAWK KITES (British Patent 1,086,044) 1965 (Fig. 192)

This British patent for an un-named American is an extensive description of the Blackhawk type of kite designed by Ray Holland of Roswell, New Mexico. The specification describes how the use of a 'border string' around the tips of the bowed spars is tensioned to provide a rearward bow in the lateral spar and an upward bow in the longitudinal spar. The covering material is attached to the border string with a 'striking bird-like appearance' which is pronounced 'when wind pressure is on the wing cover material . . . the preferred embodiment of the invention having the appearance of a Hawk'.

Various shapes were sketched in the patent for aeroplane, delta or other plan forms and emphasis is placed on the fact that neither a tail nor a bridle is needed for this design. Reference is made to 'snow plough' stability with the analogy that 'the forward centre of gravity is like that of a snow plough pulled from a forward point'. The descriptions in the British patent are infinitely more involved than in others, and go to the extent of detailing the adhesives and tapes used for manufacture – even the flying of the kite is described through to trimming for aerobatics. To read the nine pages of text is to gain an education in kite concepts, manufacture and operation.

SLED (3,767,145) 1973 (Fig. 193)

This last patent was issued to Ray Holland of Roswell, New Mexico, and mentions the prior application 2,737,360 by Allison for flexible kites.

This version of the sled introduces curved spars which cause the kite to billow open in

FIG.192.

1086044 COMPLETE SPECIFICATION
3 SHEETS *This drawing is a reproduction of the Original on a reduced scale*
Sheet 1

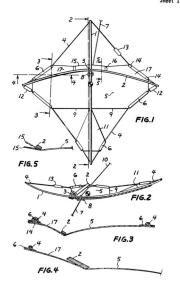

FIG.192.

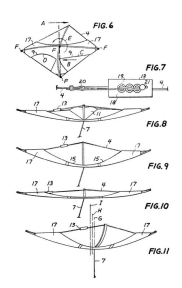

FIG.192.

1086044 COMPLETE SPECIFICATION
3 SHEETS *This drawing is a reproduction of the Original on a reduced scale*
Sheets 2 & 3

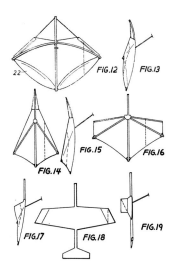

FIG.193.

Patented Oct. 23, 1973   3,767,145

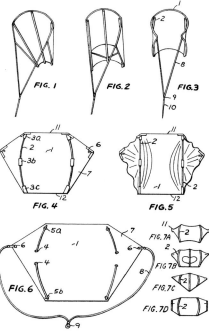

the wind regardless of the degree of gustiness or the size of the kite. The ribs, or spars, are so arranged as to be concave when the kite (not in flight) is stretched out flat laterally. When the kite is in flight the curved ribs cause the leading and trailing edges to be raised relative to the mid-section. The ribs tend to straighten when the wind drops, and this is claimed to billow the side 'lapels' out, so keeping the sled in shape, and reducing the tendency for it to collapse. These attributes certainly work in practice and help to make the sled a more stable kite that can operate in light winds or gusty conditions.

As time progresses, we shall see the addition of more patents to the list. The kite may well have been with us for centuries, but, as each succeeding year goes to prove, there are still many variations awaiting discovery to further our enjoyment of these fascinating riders of the wind.

Appendices

APPENDIX 1: EUROPEAN KITE MANUFACTURERS AND IMPORTING AGENTS

AEROBAT, PO Box 8, Stratford-upon-Avon, Warwicks, CV37 6LH, England.

AEROKITE, Unit 2, Pershore Industrial Estate, Pershore, Worcs, England.

AIRSPORT, 12a Lansdown Industrial Estate, Cheltenham, Glos, GL51 8PL, England.

ALBATROSS KITES, Hill End Farm Works, Tyttenhanger Green, St Albans, Herts, England.

AMPHIKITES, K. Stewart, 20 Cross Hays, Malmesbury, Wilts, England.

ARIEL KITES, Lewis Knight Co., LR Industries, North Circular Rd, London, E4 8QA, England.

BAKKER Peter, G.V. Aemstelstr. 24, Amsterdam, Netherlands.

BONNAVE & Co., 18/22 Rue de Bus, 59204 Tourcoing, France.

BROOKITE, Francis Terrace, Junction Rd, London N19, England.

C & L KITES, Ford Aerodrome, West Sussex, England.

CAMBRIDGE LEISURE, Rivermill House, St Ives, Huntingdon, Cambs, PE17 4BR, England.

COCHRANES of Oxford Ltd (Dunford Kites), Leafield, Oxon, OX8 5NT, England.

COLES ACTION TOYS, Ashwick, Chelmarsh, Bridgnorth, Shropshire, WV16 6BA, England.

CONACORD Werner Voigt, KG, 4780 Lippstadt 4, Seilerring 10, West Germany.

DAVIES W. R. (Sharon Lee Ltd), Fernbrook Ave, Southend-on-Sea, Essex, England.

DRAKO Ralf Dost KG, 2000 Hamburg 55, 52 Blankeneser, Bahnhofstr. 60, West Germany.

DUNFORD Sqdn Ldr D. W., 554 Banbury Rd, Oxford, OX2 8EQ, England.

DY KITES, The Stirling Clothing Co., Silver St, Oldham, Lancs, OCl 1HX, England.

FLEXIFOIL KITE CO., 52 Tottenham St, London, W1P 9PG, England.

FRISBEE (Skite), 16/18 Petersham Rd, Richmond, Surrey, England.

FRISCO's Cut-a-Kites, 3 Queen Caroline St, Hammersmith Broadway, London, W6, England.

GIRAUD-SAUVEUR Léon, 39300 Champagnole, France.

GLEN LEWIS, 51 Spurrell Avenue, Bexley, Kent, DA5 2EX, England.

GLOSTER Kites, Brookhouse Mills, Painswick, Stroud, Glos, England.

GREEN'S KITE CENTRE, 336 Coles Rd, Burnley, Lancs, England (shop).

GUNTHER, Paul, KG, 8330 Eggenfelden, Landshuterstr. 32, West Germany.

HALES, A. A., Ltd (North Pacific Kites and Pax), PO Box 33, Harrowbrook Rd, Hinckley, Leics, England.

JNT MODELS (Top Flite Kites), Long St, Easingwold, Yorkshire, England.

JONES (MODEL KITS), 13 Pen-y-Craig, Bethesda, N. Wales, U.K.

KEB Leisure Goods Ltd (Synestructics), Norfolk House, Norfolk St, Worksop, Notts, England.

KITE & BALLOON CO., 613 Garratt Lane, London, SW18, England (shop).

KITECRAFT, 38 Calvin Rd, Winton, Bournemouth, BH9 1LN, England (shop).

KITEMAKER, 82 Thornton Ave, London W4 1QQ, England.

KITE STORES LTD, Eric Gibson, 69 Neal St, London, WC2, England (shop)

KITES OF THE WORLD, 10 St Gregory's Alley, Norwich, Norfolk, N2R 1ER, England (shop).

KNOOP, 4190 Kleve, Rembrandstr. 16/Cargadoorweg 4, Nijmegen, Netherlands.

KOHNSTAM, R. (Gunther Kites), 13/15 High St, Hemel Hempstead, Herts, England.

LLOYD, A. (Zammo Kites), 114 Ladbroke Grove, London, W10, England.

MARKES & CO. (Dux), Spielwarenfabrik, 5880 Lüdenscheid, Wiesenstrasse 61, West Germany.

METTOY-PLAYCRAFT LTD (Wembley Kites), 14 Harlestone Rd, Northampton, NN5 7AF, England.

MULTIFLITE, Victoria Rd, South Shields, Tyne and Wear, England.

NIMBUS (C. W. Merriam), 3 Lipscombe, Capel Rd, Rusper, West Sussex, RH12 4PZ, England.

POWELL, Peter, PO Box 1000, Cheltenham, Glos, England.

QUERCETTI, Via Bardonecchia 77/16 Turin, Italy.

RF DEVELOPMENTS (Wepa-Kites), Priory Lane, St Neots, Huntingdon, Cambs, England.

SAFFERY Model Balloons, 93 Walcot St, Bath, BA1 5BW, England.

SAMPSON BROS (Toys) Ltd, Vanguard Way, Shoeburyness, Southend-on-Sea, Essex, England.

SAVAGE, Stephen and Anthea (Hammoco Designs Ltd), Ullenhall, Warwicks, England.

SCALE CRAFT LTD, 6 Shad Thames, London, SE1, England.

SCHMOHL KG (Pax), 7320 Göppingen, Heilbronnerstr. 12, West Germany.

SCHOFIELD Red Arrow Kites, Schofield Buildings, North St, Weston-super-Mare, Avon, England.

SEAMER Products Ltd (Tosta Kites), Eastbourne St, Hull, HU3 5EB, England.

SHAMA TRADERS (Indian Fighters), 50 Princess Mary Rd, Stoke Newington, London N16 8DG, England.

SHARON LEE LTD, Fernbrook Ave, Southend-on-Sea, Essex, England.

SKY CAT, Trenance Mill, St Austell, Cornwall, PL25 5AQ, England.

SKY SPORTS LTD (Sky Rider), Charterhouse, Eltringham St, London SW18, England.

STUNTFLYER KITES, PO Box 4, Bacup, Lancs, England.

THOMAS, Postfach 46, 5787 Olsberg 2, West Germany.

WAYLER REELS, 12 Weston Dene, Hazlemere, High Wycombe, Bucks, England.

WEPA-FLYER, Postfach 36, Zeyenaar, Holland.

WILLIAMS Allen Ltd, 112 Churchill Road, Bicester, Oxon, OX6 7XD, England.

WINDCRAFT, 36 Alma Vale Rd, Clifton, Bristol, BS8 2HS, England (shop).

YACHTMAIL, 7 Cornwall Crescent, London, W11 1PH, England (mail order).

APPENDIX 2: USA AND CANADIAN KITE MANUFACTURERS AND IMPORTING AGENTS

A N Reel Mfg, 176 Exchange St, Buffalo, New York 14203.

Above and Beyond, 1510 Walnut Sq., Berkeley, Ca. 94709.

Aerofoil Systems Inc., PO Box 834, Merritt Island, Fla. 32952.

Air Appliance Shop, 450 W. Fort St, Detroit, Mich. 48226.

Airforce Kite Works, 116 S. Jackson, Seattle, Washington 98104.

Airplane Kite Co., 1702 W. 3rd St, Roswell, New Mexico 88201.

Ben Franklin Kite Shoppe, 423 Whalley Avenue, PO Box 3088, New Haven, Conn. 06511, and Factory Square, Mystic, Conn. 06355.

Bennett Arnstein, 3049 W. 8th St, Los Angeles, Ca. 90005.

Cape Cod Kite Company, Shopper's Market Mini-Mall, High School Rd, Ext, Hyannis, Mass. 02601.

Come Fly A Kite, 154 Omni International, Atlanta, Ga. 30303.

Come Fly A Kite, 900 North Point, Ghirardelli Sq., San Francisco, Ca. 94109.

Come Fly A Kite, Carmel Plaza, Carmel, Ca. 93921.

Come Fly A Kite, Piccadilly Square, 817 Estate St, Santa Barbara, Ca. 93101.

Come Fly With Me, 3212 Highland, Manhattan Beach, Ca. 90266.

Condor Industries Ltd, 3914 St Peters Rd, Victoria, BC, Canada.

Creekmore Products (Reels), 2236 Lysander Avenue, Simi, Ca. 93065.

Delta Wing, 1011 Chester, SE, Grand Rapids, Mich. 49506.

Eastern Sea Inc., 717 Grant Avenue, San Francisco, Ca. 94108.

Eureka Paper Tiger, 12215 Colt Rd, Dallas, Texas 75251.

Explorers, 824 Chartres St, New Orleans, La. 70116.

Fish Creek Kite Co., RRI, Box 205, Hwy 42, Fish Creek, Wi. 54212.

Fly By Kite, 99w 10th St, Suite 120, Eugene, Oregon 97401.

Flying High, 36 Boylstan St, Cambridge, Mass. 02138.

Flying Tiger Associates, PO Box 49634, Los Angeles, Ca. 90048.

Full Circle, 112 King St, Alexandria, Va 22314.

Gayla Industries, Box 10800, Houston, Texas 77018.

Gentle Earth, 6723 Snider Plaza, Dallas, Texas 75205.

Go Fly A Kite Store Inc., 1434 3rd Ave, New York 10028.

Grandmaster Kites, 2825 N. Commercial Ave, Suite 11, Portland, Oregon 97227.

Heavenly Body Kites, Harbor House, 423 Front St, Key West, Fla. 33040.

Hi-Flier Mfg Co., 510 E Wabash Ave, Decatur, Illinois 62525.

High As A Kite, 691 Bridgeway, Sausalito, Ca. 94965.

High As A Kite, 131 Water St, Vancouver, BC, V6B 4M3, Canada.

Higher Than A Kite, 209 Osborne, Winnipeg, Manitoba, R3L 1Z4, Canada.

Hi-Roller Kite Spool, PO Box 73, Sausalito, Ca. 94965.

Horizons Ltd, 2224 Bandy Wood, Nashville, Tenn. 37215.

International Kite Co., PO Box 3248, 4051 University Ave, San Diego, Ca. 92103.

International Kites, 1891 Caspian Ave, Long Beach, Ca. 90810.

Jalbert Aerology Lab, 17 NW 20th St, Boca Raton, Fla. 33432.

Kathy's Kites, 3043 Grand Ave 209, Coconut Grove, Fla. 33133.

Kaleidoscope, 3295 Rochester Rd, Troy, Mich. 48084.

Keoki's Specialities Co., 433 Avery St, Elmhurst, Ill. 60126.

Kiddie Hawk Kite Corp., PO Box 398, Delray Beach, Fla. 33444.

Kite Cavalcade, 704 Route 35N, Cavallette, NJ 08735.

Kite City, 1201 Front St, Old Sacramento, Ca. 95814.

Kitecrafting, PO Box 86, Waverley Branch, Boston, Mass. 02719.

Kite Factory, PO Box 9081, Seattle, Washington 98109.

Kite Farm, 728 University Ave, Madison, Wis. 53715.

Kite Flier, 1350 Dixie Highway, Pampano Beach, Fla. 33060.

Kite and Gift, 333 Jefferson St, Suite 7, Fisherman's Wharf, San Francisco, Ca. 941333.

Kite Kompany Inc., 33 W Orange, Chagrin Falls, Ohio 44022.

Kite Line, Park Square Court, 400 Sibley Street, St Paul, Mn. 53701.

Kite Loft, 5 North Second St, Ocean City, Maryland 21842.

Kiteport Internationale, PO Box 5636, Daytona Beach, Fla. 32018.

Kite Ranch, Route 1, Box 890, Franktown, Col. 80116.

Kite Shop, General Delway, Cannon Beach, Oregon 97110.

Kite Shop Ltd, 1917 Kalakaua Ave, Honolulu, Hawaii 96815.

Kite Shop Ltd, 703 Front St, Lahaina, Maiu, Hawaii 86761.

Kite Shop, Jackson Sq., 542 St Peter's Street, New Orleans, La. 70116.

Kite Shop, 15 B St, Hampton Beach, NH 03842.

Kite Shop, 1313 S Country Club Drive, Mesa, Arizona 85208.

Kite Site, 1075 Wisconsin Ave, NW, Georgetown, DC 20007.

Kite Specialists Co., RR1, Box 157, Bloomington, Wisconsin 53805.

Kite Store, 848A Yonge St, Toronto, Ontario, M4W 2H1, Canada.

Kite Store, PO Box 27544 Philadelphia, Pa. 19118.

Kite Store, Carol Hamilton, 973 Grand Avenue, Pacific Beach, Ca. 92109.

Kite Store, 2 Boulder Ave, Gloucester, Mass. 01930.

Kite Store, 1430 Larimer St, Denver, Col. 80202.

Kites, 1209 N. Franklin Blvd, Pleasantville, NJ 08232.

Kites and Strings, 740 Ventura Place, San Diego, Ca. 92109.

Kites International, 1000 E Northwest Hwy, Mt. Prospect, Ill. 60056.

Kites Kites Kites, PO Box 845, Bowie, Md. 20715.

Kites Unlimited, 1206 Richmond Ave, Mt Pleasant, NJ 08270.

Kite Winder Inc., PO Box 370, Oneonta, New York 13820.

Kite World Inc., 540 De Haro, San Francisco, Ca. 94107.

Kiteworks, Beach Rd, Vineyard Haven, Martha's Vineyard Island, Mass. 02568.

Kitty Hawk Kites, PO Box 386, RH 158 at Jockey Ridge, NC 27959.

Kyte Specialists Co., 433 Avery St, Elmhurst, Ill. 60126.

Lees Custom Kites, 1327 13th St, PO Box 148, Clarkston, Washington DC 99403.

Let's Fly A Kite, 327 Buffalo St, Hamburg, NY 14075.

Let's Fly A Kite, 1168 Massachusetts Ave, Cambridge, Mass. 02139.

Let's Fly A Kite, 13763 Fiji Way, Fisherman's Village, Marina del Rey, Ca. 90291.

Let's Fly A Kite, 1432 N. Federal Highway, Dania, Fla. 33004.

Lucy in the Sky, 2203 Hermosa Ave, Hermosa Beach, Ca. 90254.

Lure of the Kite, The Lumber Yard, 384 Forest Ave, Laguna Beach, Ca. 92651.

Magic Kite Reel, McKinley Enterprises, 1543 W. Olympic Blvd, Los Angeles, Ca. 90015.

Marblehead Kite Co., 28 South St, Marblehead, Mass. 01945.

Mole Hole, 672 Notre Dame, Grove Point, Mi. 48236.

Morgan, Ron, Enterprise, 13107 Harbor Blvd, Garden Grove, Ca. 92643.

MW Management Ltd., PO Box 86670, North Vancouver, BC, V7L, Canada.

Mylar Star Kites, 3519 Caribeth, Encino, Ca. 91316.

Nantucket Kiteman, PO Box 1356, Nantucket, Mass. 02554.

New England Kitecrafting Co., PO Box 86, Waverley Branch, Boston, Mass. 02179.

North Pacific, Bend, Oregon 97701.

Outermost Kites, Box 1032, Union Sq., Provincetown, Mass. 02657.

Pear Tree, 1899 Park Ave, Costa Mesa, Ca. 92627.

Peter Powell Kites of America, 1914 Sands Drive, Annapolis, Maryland, 21401.

Pompanette, PO Box 276, Dania, Fla. 33004 (kite fishing).

Portland Kite Works, 209 NW Couch, Portland, Oregon, 97209.

Puget Sound Kite Works, Pier 70, Box 28, Seattle, Washington, 98121.

Quicksilver Kites, 701 Shrader St, San Francisco, Ca. 94117.

Rayco Reels, 7320 W. Lloyd St, Wauwatosa, Wisconsin 53213.

River City Kite Works, PO Box 26202, Sacramento, Ca. 95826.

Riverwind Kite Works, 612 N. Second St, Lacledes Landing, St Louis, Mo. 63102.

Rogallo Flexikites, Kitty Hawk, NC 27949.

Sale Shop, 13107 Harbor Blvd, Garden Grove, Ca. 92643.

San Francisco Kite Factory, 2231 Judah, San Francisco, Ca. 94322.

Shanti Kites, 210 Chatanooga St, San Francisco, Ca. 94114.

Sierra Kite Co., Box 1524, Sausalito, Ca. 94965.

Sierra Kite Co., 800 Anderson Drive, San Rafael, Ca. 94901.

Sky High Inc., 160 N Northwest Hwy, Palatine, Ill. 60067.

Stratton Air Engineering, 10859 Portal Drive, Los Alamitos, Ca. 90720.

Striegel, LG Mfg Co., 1223 Arcade Avenue, Louisville, Kentucky 40215.

Sunshine Kite Co., Redando Pier, Redando Beach, Ca. 90277.

Synestructics Inc., 9559 Irondale Ave, Chatsworth, Ca. 91311.

Time To Fly A Kite, 9667 Wilshire Blvd, Beverly Hills, Ca. 90212.

Tom Joe, International Acrobatic Kites, 1891 Caspina Ave, Long Beach, Ca. 90810.

Troyert Kite Supply, 4174 Kent Rd, Stow, Ohio 44224.

Ultrakite, 904 Century Building, Pittsburgh, Pa. 15222.

Unique Place, 344 Hamilton Row, Birmingham, Mich. 48011.

Vancouver Crafts and Kites, 2939 W 4th Ave, Vancouver, BC, V6K 1R2, Canada.

Weathers and Sons, 17707 SE Howard St, Milwaukee, Oregon 97222.

Whimsicalli Kites, 4113 Padre Blvd, PO Dwr. 488, Port Isabel, Texas 78578.

Wiggins and Reese Kite Co., General Delivery, Vineyard Haven, Mass. 02568.

Windiana Kite Works, 8660 Bazaar Drive, Indianapolis, Ind. 46240.

Windplane, Joe Butler, PO Box 123, Weatherford, Texas 76087.

Wind Shop, Old World Village Hall, 2751 E Grand River, East Lansing, Mich. 48823.

Windmill Kite Distributors Ltd., 3441 Kingsway, Vancouver 16, BC, Canada.

Windy City Kite Works, 1750 N Clark St, Chicago, Ill. 60614.

APPENDIX 3: KITE-FLYING ASSOCIATIONS

AUSTRALIA   *Australia Kite Club*
Tony Johnston, 3 Ross St, Kew 3101, Victoria.

BRITAIN   *British Kite Flying Association* (BKFA)
Ron Moulton, PO Box 35, Hemel Hempstead, Herts, HP1 1EE.
European Kitefliers Association (EKA)
Nick Laurie, Longstone Lodge, Aller, Langport, Somerset.

FRANCE   *Cerf Volant Club de France* (CVCF)
6 Rue de la Cossonnerie, 75001, Paris.

INDIA   *Kitefliers of India* (KFI)
3126 Lal Darwaza Bazaar, Sita Ram, Delhi 6.

JAPAN   *Japan Kite Association*
Shingo Modegi, 10-12-1 Chome Nihonbashi, Chuo-Ku, Tokyo.
Japan Kitefliers Association (JKA)
Tsutomu Hiroi, Taimaken 103, 1-12-1 Nihonbashi, Chuo-Ku, Tokyo.

NEW ZEALAND   *Waikato Kite Club*
C. P. Croft, 19 McCracken Avenue, Hamilton.

USA   *American Kitefliers Association* (AKA)
Valerie Govig, 7106 Campfield Rd, Baltimore, Maryland 21207.
Delaware Kite Society
Bill Beauchamp, Lewes Chamber of Commerce, PO Box 1, Lewes, Delaware 19958.
International Kitefliers Association (IKA)
Will Yolen, 321 E 48th St, New York, NY 10017.
Maryland Kite Society
R. F. Kinnaird, PO Box 10467, Baltimore, Maryland 21209.

APPENDIX 4: FURTHER READING

BARWELL and BAILEY, *How to Make and Fly Kites*, Studio Vista, London, 1974.

BRUMMITT, W., *Kites*, Golden Press, New York, 1971.

BURKHART, TIMOTHY, *Kitefolio*, Double Elephant, Berkeley and Wildwood House, London, 1974.

DUNFORD, DON, *Kite Cookery*, Cochranes, Oxford, England, 1977.

HART, CLIVE, *Your Book of Kites*, Faber & Faber, London, 1964.

HART, CLIVE, *Kites, An Historical Survey*, Faber & Faber, London, 1967.

HIROI, T., *Kites—Designs in the Sky*, Mainichi, Tokyo, 1974.

HUNT, LESLIE L., *Kite Making* (Getting Started Series), Bruce Publishing, USA and Collier Macmillan, London, 1971.

JUE, DAVID, *Chinese Kites*, Tuttle, Vermont and Tokyo, 1974.

LLOYD, MITCHELL and THOMAS, *Making and Flying Kites*, John Murray, London, 1975 and Beaver (pbk), 1977.

MAREE, PIET, *Make Your Own Kites*, Bancroft, Netherlands, 1974.

MOUVIER, J. P., *Kites*, Éditions Gallimard, Paris and William Collins, Glasgow, 1974.

NEWMAN, LEE SCOTT and JAY HARTLEY, *Kite Craft*, Crown Publishers, New York and Allen and Unwin, London, 1974.

PELHAM, DAVID, *Kites*, Penguin Books, London, 1976.

RIDGWAY, H., *Kite Making and Flying*, Arco Mayflower, 1962.

SAITO, HIGEO and MODEKI, *Kites – How to Make and Fly*, Tokuma Shotem, Japan, 1974.

STREETER, TAL, *The Art of the Japanese Kite*, Weatherhill, New York, 1974.

WHITE, BEN, *Kites* (Scimitar Series), E. J. Arnold, Leeds, 1977.

YOLEN, JANE, *World on a String*, World, U.S.A., 1973.

YOLEN, WILL, *Young Sportsman's Guide to Kite Flying*, Thomas Nelson, New York, 1972.

YOLEN, WILL, *Kites and Kite Flying*, Simon & Schuster, New York, 1976.

Index